MICHAEL FARADAY'S
MENTAL EXERCISES
AN ARTISAN ESSAY-CIRCLE
IN REGENCY LONDON

LIVERPOOL ENGLISH TEXTS AND STUDIES, 51

MICHAEL FARADAY'S MENTAL EXERCISES

AN ARTISAN ESSAY-CIRCLE IN REGENCY LONDON

EDITED BY
ALICE JENKINS

LIVERPOOL
UNIVERSITY PRESS

First published 2008 by
Liverpool University Press
4 Cambridge Street
Liverpool L69 7ZU

British Library Cataloguing-in-Publication data
A British Library CIP record is available

ISBN 978-1-84631-140-6 cased

Typeset in Garamond by
BBR Solutions Ltd, Chesterfield
Printed and bound by Biddles Ltd, King's Lynn

For Nicky

Contents

Part Two: Contexts

Faraday and Self-Education

The Improvement of the Mind

The Pleasures of the Imagination

Acknowledgements

It would be impossible to work on Faraday without incurring an enormous debt to Frank A. J. L. James. I am very grateful to him for supporting this project throughout, for giving me information on an extraordinary range of aspects of Faraday's life, and for making enormously helpful comments on drafts of this book.

The generosity of the Royal Institution of Great Britain in allowing me to edit the manuscript of the Mental Exercises has, of course, been crucial to this project. I am also grateful to the Royal Society for awarding me a grant to support the research for the book. Among the librarians and archivists who have helped me with materials, I particularly want to thank the staff of the Royal Institution archives, Asha Marvin at the Institution of Engineering and Technology, the staff of the Rare Books Room at the British Library and the staff of Glasgow University Library; and I am grateful to the National Portrait Gallery for allowing me to reproduce the cover image.

I owe special thanks to Anthony Cond at Liverpool University Press for his enthusiastic support for this book, and to three anonymous reviewers for their extremely helpful suggestions. I am delighted to thank Gillian Beer for directing me towards Faraday in the first place, Juliet John for good advice about the format of this book, and Sharon Ruston for her support for the project. In its earliest form, this edition was conceived as a collaborative venture with Fiona Tweedie, who contributed a great deal to the planning but was unable to work on the book as it now stands. Stella Pratt-Smith provided invaluable help by patiently and meticulously helping me check the transcription. George Biddlecombe, Norman Gray, Ronald Knox, Nigel Leask, Farah Mendlesohn, Sean Sollé, Catherine Steel and Susan Stuart supplied me with vital pieces of information and made excellent suggestions about where to find others. I am very grateful to Geoffrey Cantor and David M. Knight for their responses to parts of the book. Nicky Trott was the Head of the Department of English Literature in Glasgow while I was preparing this book and gave me endless support and guidance. Louise Pollock, with great good humour, solved all my IT problems.

I'm enormously grateful for the encouragement of my family and friends, and especially for many happy evenings spent with Susan Stuart and Norman Gray, Alec Yearling and Elizabeth Moignard, Susan Castillo and Vicky Gunn. My deepest debt is to Catherine Steel, ἣ δίδωσιν ἐμοὶ νήσους καὶ θεὰς καὶ πάντα τὰ κάλλιστα.

This book is dedicated to Nicky Trott, with love and gratitude.

Abbreviations

All Biblical quotations are from the King James Bible.

Cantor	Geoffrey Cantor, *Michael Faraday: Sandemanian and Scientist* (Houndmills: Macmillan, 1991).
Correspondence	Frank A. J. L. James (ed.), *The Correspondence of Michael Faraday*, 4 vols. (London: Institution of Electrical Engineers, 1991–99).
CPB	Faraday's Common Place Book, Institution of Engineering and Technology archive, Michael Faraday, MS Common Place Book, 2 vols.
CPS	City Philosophical Society.
GM	*The Gentleman's Magazine*, November 1819, p. 449.
Hamilton	James Hamilton, *Faraday: The Life* (London: HarperCollins, 2002).
Mental Exercises	Royal Institution archive, no. F13/A, 'A Class Book, for the Reception of Mental Exercises', 1818–19.
OED	*Oxford English Dictionary*.
RI	Royal Institution of Great Britain.
St Clair	William St Clair, *The Reading Nation in the Romantic Period* (Cambridge: Cambridge University Press, 2004).
Williams	L. Pearce Williams, *Michael Faraday: A Biography* (London: Chapman and Hall, 1965).

Introduction

Faraday and style

In the summer of 1818, Michael Faraday, then approaching his twenty-seventh birthday and employed as Chemical Assistant in the Royal Institution in London, persuaded four male friends to join him in forming a self-help writing group. The MS book of essays and poems that this group produced is held in the archives of the Royal Institution and is printed here for the first time, and in full. It offers a unique corpus of evidence about Michael Faraday's philosophical ideas and literary taste. The texts gathered in this edition rarely address scientific topics directly; but many of them develop ideas which were crucial in underpinning and enabling Faraday's ceaseless advocacy of and engagement in self-improvement, including scientific education. Further, they illuminate Faraday's relationship with the history, culture and manners of his own time. Perhaps even more importantly, these writings give new evidence about the ideas and taste of a social group which is underrepresented in histories of authorship in the early nineteenth century: highly aspirational, successful artisans whose purpose in writing was not the advancement of radical nor conservative politics, but to take their part as citizens in the polite culture of their time.

Michael Faraday was the third child of a Dissenting blacksmith and his wife who had moved to the capital from the rural north-west of England a few years before Michael's birth in 1791. The age of mass schooling had not yet begun, and the education provided by Sunday schools and other voluntary organizations tended to be linked to the Church of England and was therefore not available to the Faradays. Michael learned to read and write in a school near his home, but it was during the seven years of his apprenticeship to George Riebau, a bookbinder with premises in Blandford Street in London, that his literary education began, as Faraday read some of the texts which were brought in for binding. Later in life he particularly recalled enjoying the *Arabian Nights* in this way, and indeed he retained into his old age a strong taste for fiction.[1] But his reading during his years with Riebau contained a good deal of factual material as well as of imaginative literature: texts which biographers usually identify as having contributed particularly to his education include Jane Marcet's *Conversations in Chemistry*, Lavoisier's *Elements of Chemistry* and the *Encyclopaedia Britannica* article on electricity by the hack writer and balloonist James Tytler.

During his apprenticeship, then, Faraday gained a varied but unsystematic reading experience. From his late teens he supplemented this rather happenstance education by attending courses of lectures given by the London silversmith John Tatum at the City Philosophical Society, where he acquired a methodical grounding in contemporary science.[2] In supplementing his limited formal education with attendance at the CPS and other metropolitan scientific arenas, Faraday was engaging in a characteristic early nineteenth-century form of self-help. He and his contemporaries in the group represented, in a sense, the last generation of artisan self-educators for whom there was no large-scale network of provision. Opportunities for formal scientific education were limited for men like Faraday—and even more so, of course, for women of similar backgrounds. It was out of the question that someone of Faraday's social status, financial means and Dissenting religious beliefs should even think of Oxford or Cambridge, at that time the only universities in England; and in any case they did not offer dedicated science degrees until the mid-nineteenth century. Had Faraday been born a decade or so later, the Mechanics' Institutes would have been open to him, providing basic, intermediate and occasionally specialist scientific education for workers.[3] But the London Mechanics' Institute was not founded until 1823, by

1   E.g. Williams, p. 11; Hamilton, p. 9.
2   The most useful source of information on Faraday and the CPS is Frank A. J. L. James' article 'Michael Faraday, The City Philosophical Society and the Society of Arts', *Royal Society of Arts Journal*, 140 (1992), 192–99.
3   On the history of the Mechanics' Institutes, see for instance Harold Silver's classic study *The Concept of Popular Education: A Study of Ideas and Social Movements in the Early Nineteenth Century* (London: MacGibbon and Kee, 1965) and R. K. Webb's *The British Working Class Reader, 1790–1848: Literacy and Social Tension* (London: Allen & Unwin, 1955, repr. New York: Kelley, 1971); among more recent scholarship, Ian Inkster's 'The Social Context of an Educational Movement: A Revisionist Approach to the English Mechanics' Institutes, 1820–1850', in *Scientific Culture and Urbanisation*

which time Faraday was already a successful natural philosopher. The Literary and Philosophical Societies, which offered lectures and reading rooms in almost all large and many small towns, were older than the Mechanics' Institutes, some dating from the late eighteenth century, and were thus potentially available to men like Faraday in the 1810s; but these were often seen as rather middle-class institutions, and they rarely offered solid, substantial series of lectures on scientific topics.[4] The City Philosophical Society, on the other hand, was dedicated chiefly to science education, and though its membership appears to have been fairly diverse in age and politics, it had no pretensions to fashionability.[5]

As his apprenticeship drew to a close Faraday saw that, in addition to acquiring a scientific education, he needed to improve his English. Characteristically setting out to learn through practice, he formed a compact with his close friend and fellow classmate at the City Philosophical Society, Benjamin Abbott, to engage in a correspondence. Faraday's intention in initiating the correspondence was partly that he and Abbott should share scientific information, and partly that he might 'cure' himself of weaknesses in composition, clarity and grammar: 'Epistolary writing is one cure for these deficiencies,' he told Abbott, 'therefore, MF should practice Epistolary writing.'[6] Of the letters the two exchanged over the next decade or so, nearly 60 of Faraday's survive, though most of Abbott's are lost. Faraday's early letters are ebullient and often playful with language, but frequently omit punctuation, giving an impression of being

---

    in Industrialising Britain (Aldershot: Ashgate, 1997), pp. 277–307, is particularly helpful.

4   For a useful comparison of the role of Literary and Philosophical Societies with other emerging scientific societies, see J. B. Morrell, 'Bourgeois Scientific Societies and Industrial Innovation in Britain, 1780–1850', *Journal of European Economic History*, 24 (1995), 311–32. On the importance of lectures and debates in Literary and Philosophical Societies, see Michael D. Stephens and Gordon W. Roderick, 'Middle-class Non-Vocational Lecture and Debating Subjects in Nineteenth-Century England', *British Journal of Educational Studies*, 21 (1973), 192–201. Of the individual Societies, the Manchester Literary and Philosophical has probably received most attention from historians: see, for example, Arnold W. Thackray, 'Natural Knowledge in Cultural Context: The Manchester Model', *American Historical Review*, 79 (1974), 672–709.

5   For further discussion of Faraday, self-help and the CPS, see below, pp. 179–80; for texts of Faraday's lectures to the CPS, see below, pp. 180–86 and 188–98.

6   Letter to Abbott, 12 July 1812 (*Correspondence*, I, p. 4); see below, p. 176, for a longer extract. For an account of the relationship between Faraday and Abbott, see Frank A. J. L. James, 'The Tales of Benjamin Abbott: A Source for the Early Life of Michael Faraday', *British Journal for the History of Science*, 25 (1992), 229–40.

composed at high speed. His side of the correspondence, and presumably Abbott's too, contains a great deal of information on scientific topics, mainly chemistry, as well as introspective interludes which illustrate the affectionate and confidential nature of the relationship between the two men. The correspondence is laced with calls from Faraday for renewed dedication to the purposes of self-improvement, mingled with lamentations about how pressing demands on his time prevent him from writing as often as he ought: both of these concerns became frequent themes in Faraday's later literary and personal writing. But after a few years, though the correspondence continued in a very friendly tone, writing letters did not seem to Faraday to be solving his problems with style. A more rigorous effort was needed as well as a change from epistolary writing to a less private genre, since Faraday was by now working in a professional arena which demanded finely honed skills in writing and speaking for the public.

Towards the end of his apprenticeship, one of Riebau's customers gave Faraday tickets to attend four lectures at the Royal Institution by Sir Humphry Davy, the foremost experimental philosopher in Britain. Faraday made copious notes of Davy's lectures, wrote them up and bound them. On leaving Riebau in 1812 he drew himself to Davy's attention and showed him the volume of notes. Davy was sufficiently impressed with Faraday's competence and enthusiasm that when in 1813 a vacancy opened for a chemical assistant at the Royal Institution, he offered Faraday the post.

After some six months at the RI, Faraday was invited to join Davy's entourage on a scientific tour of Europe, and as Davy's servant and scientific assistant he had the extraordinary experience of travelling widely on the Continent during the final years of the Napoleonic Wars. During his 18 months abroad he was exposed to the culture of the great French, Italian and Swiss cities which had been all but inaccessible to most Englishmen for two decades. His concerns about his English were shelved while he concentrated on learning at least something of the languages of the cities he was visiting. Shortly after coming back to England in 1815 Faraday was resettled in his post at the Royal Institution and began a period of very arduous work, assisting with Davy's research, preparing equipment for the lecturers, editing the *Quarterly Journal of Science* and undertaking chemical analyses for clients. Despite his heavy workload, Faraday now returned seriously to the problem of his deficiencies as a writer of English. By this time it seemed likely to him that he would make a career in science; and he began to see the improvement of his literary style as part of a larger project to develop the skills that would be important in supporting and promoting his scientific work.

Since metropolitan scientific culture was at this time dominated by lecturing, Faraday began his new campaign to improve his English by concentrating mainly on public speaking. He attended Benjamin Smart's lectures on oratory at the Royal Institution and made his own debut as a lecturer at the City Philosophical Society.[7] These two venues—the RI and the CPS—illustrate the range of fora which existed in Regency London to cater to audiences of all classes and levels of interest in science. Founded to promote applicable, practical science, the Royal Institution was fashionable—all the more so because of Davy's celebrity— and attracted well-to-do audiences. The City Philosophical Society was different in almost all respects: it held its meetings in John Tatum's home at 53 Dorset Street; lectures were given by Tatum himself and by the membership, which was exclusively male and included artisans as well as professional men.[8] Working in the RI and attending lectures at the CPS, Faraday became very conscious of the kinds of oratory and rhetoric appropriate to different audiences and occasions.

Faraday had shown a keen interest in styles of writing and delivering lectures even before he left for the Continental tour with Davy. He developed his views on how to address a public audience in a series of letters to Abbott in the early summer of 1813, expounding on the details of the ideal lecture theatre, the use of experiments and diagrams, as well as the best methods of organizing and delivering arguments.[9] Faraday understood already that the reception of new research by the scientific world could be affected by the way in which it was presented by the researcher: thus, he gave great attention to the expression, style and presentation of lectures and was sensitive to the social and class aspects of speaking and writing. He emphasized to Abbott that different audiences

7   Faraday's notes on Smart's lectures are preserved in CPB (I, pp. 177–321). Smart published much of the substance of the lectures in his *Theory of Elocution, Exhibited in Connexion with a New and Philosophical Account of the Nature of Instituted Language* (London: printed for the author, 1819).

8   *Laws of the City Philosophical Society, Instituted January 1808* (London: printed by Ramshaw, 1812), p. 21. I am grateful to Frank James for pointing out that women appear to have been permitted to attend lectures at the CPS, though they were not allowed to be members.

9   *Correspondence*, I, pp. 55–65. This material was published as Michael Faraday, *Advice to A Lecturer* (London: Royal Institution, [1960]).

demand different qualities in lecturers. 'Polite Company,' he noted, with a little impatience, 'expect to be entertained not only by the subject of the Lecture but by the manner of the Lecturer, they look for respect, for language consonant to their dignity and ideas on a levell with their own.'[10] Even when his scientific reputation was well established, Faraday continued to be very alert to the power of good writing to smooth the way for the success of his scientific ideas, as his protracted efforts to give new discoveries rhetorically effective names illustrates.[11]

Faraday's aims for his public writing style never included self-expression in the sense of individuality, personality or distinctiveness. Rather, his goal was to let the truth of his subject speak for itself: he wanted his writing to be clear and powerful but not exaggerated, and to use a register and structure that were appropriate both to his audience and to the subject on which he was writing. When, on returning from the Continental tour, he returned to the problem of his English style, he seems to have been much less anxious about his grammar than he was when he initiated the correspondence with Abbott in 1812 (though his unpublished writing of this period is still often conspicuously lacking in punctuation; clauses run on as enthusiasm overcomes accuracy). Instead his anxiety now centred on a lack of naturalness and smoothness in his writing. The chief cause he identified was his workmanlike method of planning compositions, structuring his writing under a series of topic headings. This habit, he thought,

> introduces a dryness and stiffness into the style of the piece composed by it for the parts come together like bricks one flat on the other [...] I would if possible imitate a tree in its progression from roots to a trunk to branches twigs & leaves where every alteration is made with so much ease & yet effect that though the manner is constantly varied the effect is precise and determined.[12]

The difficulty was to find a way of achieving the greatest possible clarity while maintaining pleasing, flexible rhythms. Attending lectures and writing letters to Abbott were not enough to 'cure' the 'deficiencies' he now saw in his writing: in founding the essay-circle in 1818 he was

---

10   Letter to Abbott, 1 June 1813 (*Correspondence*, I, p. 57).
11   For discussion see Alice Jenkins, *Space and the 'March of Mind': Literature and the Physical Sciences in Britain, 1815–1850* (Oxford: Oxford University Press, 2007), pp. 125–38.
12   Letter to Abbott, 31 December 1816 (*Correspondence*, I, p. 149); see below, pp. 177–79, for a longer extract.

creating a fresh forum and spurring himself to dedicated effort. In his very first contribution to the essay-circle he looked forward optimistically to the rapid and marked success of his new venture:

> Persevere and our improvement is certain We shall trace with pleasure the visible alteration in the style and substance of our essays we shall be delighted with the ease with which we perform what at first appeared so formidable.[13]

The reader of the Mental Exercises must judge how far his optimism was borne out in practice.

Organizing the essay-circle

The fact that Faraday chose a self-improvement group as his method for tackling his stylistic problems was consonant both with his personal views on education and with the much larger context of the popular Enlightenment which had formed them. Self-help education was to be extolled and greatly extended later in the nineteenth century, first via the work of utilitarian-influenced bodies such as the Society for the Diffusion of Useful Knowledge and the Mechanics' Institutes, and later through emerging popular movements including trades unions and women's organizations. But though these large-scale national bodies promoting self-help education were not yet in operation in the 1810s, the Regency decade did nonetheless inherit a powerful tradition of self-improvement.

By the very early nineteenth century, this tradition took several forms, each offering highly publicized methods of self-improvement to those with aspirations towards auto-didacticism. These forms can be divided broadly into the collective and the individual. Collective or institutional forms offered social encouragement and material facilities for education; among these forms were the largely middle-class Literary and Philosophical Societies which were founded in many English industrial cities in the late 1700s. A very different but still collectivist ethos was that of the radical political groups, though these were under increasingly severe pressure from restrictive legislation during the years following the beginning of the war with France in 1793: as Alan Richardson points out, 'the political

---

13   Below, p. 55.

organization often functioned as a mutual improvement society as well.'[14] Yet a third kind of collectivist self-education enterprise existed in the much more informal groups of artisan naturalists and botanists which formed in some of the English industrial cities.[15]

As well as these fora, individual efforts towards self-improvement were a key element of the popular enlightenment. Methods for training the mental faculties were outlined in a considerable number of books published in the eighteenth and early nineteenth centuries, of which perhaps the most influential were Isaac Watts's *On the Improvement of the Mind* (1741) and Hester Chapone's *Letters on the Improvement of the Mind, Addressed to a Young Lady* (1773). Certainly Watts's book was among the most important influences on Faraday's self-education. Faraday acknowledged Watts's significance for him several times, including in his lecture on the means of obtaining knowledge, reproduced below, pp. 180–86.

In his scientific education, Faraday made full use of the institutional and public opportunities open to him, especially of course the lectures given at the RI; but his education as a writer mostly depended on private groupings. The 1818–19 essay-circle was the largest of these groupings, and the most highly organized. It seems to have been modelled, to some extent, on the egalitarian lines of the City Philosophical Society. The essay-circle was never given a name, but was referred to lightly and informally by its membership as a 'picknick class',[16] the record of its productions as a 'class book', and its members as 'brothers'.[17] It did, however, have a

---

14   Alan Richardson, *Literature, Education and Romanticism: Reading as Social Practice, 1780–1832* (Cambridge: Cambridge University Press, 1994), p. 237.

15   See for instance Anne Secord's influential article 'Science in the Pub: Artisan Naturalists in Early Nineteenth-Century Lancashire', *History of Science*, 32 (1994), 269–315 and her account of the interactions of class and moral values in a local knowledge economy, 'Elizabeth Gaskell and the Artisan Naturalists of Manchester', *The Gaskell Society Journal*, 19 (2005), 34–51; her discussion of cross-class interactions between naturalists in 'Corresponding Interests: Artisans and Gentlemen in Nineteenth-Century Natural History' (*British Journal for the History of Science*, 27 (1994), 383–408) is of particular interest in the context of Faraday and his efforts to write in a gentlemanly way.

16   Below, p. 118.

17   Below, p. 39 and p. 143. The term 'brothers' perhaps reflects the influence on the group of the Sandemanian church, a small Dissenting sect with its roots in Scottish Protestantism. Faraday was not at this time a Sandemanian, since he did not join the church formally by making his confession of faith until 1821; but as the son of a Sandemanian he was thoroughly familiar with the sect's practices and beliefs. Geoffrey Cantor notes the importance of brotherhood for Sandemanians, who 'consider

formal constitution, which seems to owe a debt to the 'Laws' of the CPS, though these, of course, were necessarily far more extensive than the eight rules that formed the essay-circle's equivalent. Both documents began with a statement of the maximum number of members, and went on to emphasize that the members were responsible for providing the content of the group's work.[18] This emphasis on equal duties and responsibilities among the membership was embodied in the strict rotation of the tasks of lecturing at the CPS and of copying the essay-circle's writings into the group's book.

Despite this principle of equality, there is evidence in the Mental Exercises that the essay-circle was very much Faraday's initiative. His is the first name in the list of members, and he took the first period of scribing. Beyond noting the dominance of Faraday's role in the group, little can be said confidently about the origins of the essay-circle. Clearly, it was a carefully planned venture rather than a spontaneous or haphazard grouping, but we have, for instance, no evidence to indicate how the members were selected, since they certainly do not include many of Faraday's habitual social circle at this time.[19] It is possible that the group may originally have been intended to have six members, though only five names appear on the register.[20] However, it is clear that the membership was cohesive in terms of sex and religion. All were male, and at least four of the five, including Faraday, were from families belonging to or connected by marriage with the Sandemanian church. Both the religious

themselves bound to practise brotherly love', and argues that Faraday extended this ideal to the scientific realm, noting that in Faraday's view, a 'striking similarity between true Christianity and idealized science is that each group of practitioners constitutes a brotherhood' (Cantor, p. 123).

18 *Laws of the City Philosophical Society*, pp. 11, 21.

19 Abbott was not a member of the essay-group, for instance, though in 1818 he was still living in Bermondsey. And several friends with whom Faraday enjoyed quasi-educational pursuits were also not part of the group. A note in CPB (I, p. 330) records a gathering of Faraday and four male friends on 1 May 1818: three of these (Nicol, Magrath and Newton) were not members of the essay-circle, though the fourth mentioned, Barnard, is likely to have been Edward Barnard, who was a member. Joseph Agassi describes the essay-circle as a 'select group of the City Philosophical Society that met for extra exercises' (*Faraday as a Natural Philosopher* (Chicago: University of Chicago Press, 1971), p. 28), but there is no evidence that any of the essay-circle other than Faraday was a member of the CPS (James, 'Michael Faraday, The City Philosophical Society and the Society of Arts').

20 The first article of its constitution restricts the membership to no more than six: see below, p. 40.

and gender aspects of the profile of the membership had implications for the subject matter of many of the contributions to the class book.

Besides Faraday, the members of the group were Edward Barnard, Edward Deeble, Thomas Deacon, and J. Corder. Barnard was 22 years old in 1818, one of nine children of a well-to-do London silversmith; Faraday was to marry his sister, Sarah, in 1821. Like the Faradays, the Barnards were a Sandemanian family and the practice of 'marrying-in' was common, though not obligatory, among Sandemanians in this period.[21] It seems likely that Deeble was the Edward Barnard Deeble listed in 1827 as filing a patent for a modular system for building jetties and, sadly, being sued for bankruptcy four years later; in that case, his middle name suggests a family connection with the silversmiths.[22] The Faraday biographer and scholar of Sandemanian London, Geoffrey Cantor, identifies Thomas Deacon as also belonging to a Sandemanian family.[23] The last member of the group, J. Corder, has not yet been traced, but must have been male: for one thing, it is inconceivable that a lone female would have been permitted to attend meetings with the four men.

As well as their similarities of sex and religion, the membership seems to have been fairly cohesive geographically. All the members whose addresses are known were Londoners: Faraday was by this time living in the Royal Institution in Albemarle Street in Piccadilly; Barnard was in the family business in Paternoster Square in the City, having just completed his apprenticeship under his father; and Deeble lived a couple of miles north, in Islington.[24] Though Corder's and Deacon's whereabouts are not

---

21   For a brief account of the Barnards, see Cantor, pp. 49–50, and pp. 296–98 for a family tree of the Faradays and Barnards.

22   New patents were widely reported. For Deeble's, see for instance Thomas Gill, *Gill's Technological Repository, or, Discoveries and Improvements in the Useful Arts*, I (1827), 127. The bankruptcy is listed in *The Law Advertiser*, 9 (1831), p. 22.

23   Cantor, p. 59. A Thomas Deacon married one of Edward Barnard's nieces, but as she was only born in 1816, her husband may not have been the Thomas Deacon of the essay group, though he may have been a next-generation relative. The ties between the Deacons and Barnards were presumably renewed when a Frances Deacon later married Edward Barnard's nephew David Reid (Cantor, p. 297). Large families and frequent intermarrying make tracing family connections between London Sandemanians very complicated.

24   On Barnard and the family silversmithing business, see Cantor, pp. 49–50. Addresses for Deebles, one without an initial, one a W. Deeble, appear in two lists in CPB (I, pp. 419, 445). A family of Barnard Deebles lived in Islington in the mid-nineteenth century, lending plausibility to the existence of a family connection between Edward Deeble and Edward Barnard.

known, they evidently lived or worked sufficiently near to the others to make it easy to meet regularly and to circulate the class book amongst the membership. Finally, it is probable that all the members belonged or could legitimately aspire to belong to the most prosperous and secure group among London working men: that is to say, master craftsmen, highly skilled artisans with their own premises and apprentices. Barnard, the son of the silversmith, came from what Dorothy Marshall has called 'the aristocrats of the working world'; Faraday's background was considerably humbler, but having been apprenticed in a good, forward-looking trade he could have expected to rise economically, and of course the move to the Royal Institution lifted him also into a different social group, though he was still, for stretches of his early years at the RI, working manually, commercially and under the direction of a 'master' in Humphry Davy.[25]

The agreement between the members (below, p. 40) makes plain the group's plan for conducting its operations. It was to adopt a two-month cycle. At the end of the first month, each member was to contribute a piece of writing. The scribe for that period would then have a month to copy all the contributions into the group's book. At the end of the two months, the group would meet to pass the book from one scribe to the next, and (presumably) to discuss the texts produced. The list indicating the order in which members will rotate the scribe's duties is on p. 39; the members appear to have stuck to the rota, though at one point a member complains that the book was not passed on to him at the start of his designated period.[26] The month listed beside each scribe's name is the first of the two covered by his period: i.e. for the first period, entries were to be submitted by the end of July 1818 and written into the book during August before a meeting at the end of that month.

Scribing was the only authorial role to which members put their names. No contribution was signed with the author's name. Most appeared anonymously; 13 were signed with a single letter, but the letters used (E, J, R, T and Y) are neither consistently first nor final letters of the members' Christian names or surnames. There is no key to indicate which letter denotes which member. The group's practice of anonymity was important for its internal organization, but of course it creates significant problems for scholars seeking to establish which contributions were Faraday's. I present some evidence towards authorial attributions in

25 Dorothy Marshall, *Eighteenth-Century England* (London: Longman, 1962), p. 36.
26 Below, p. 143.

Table 3 below. But the interest of the Mental Exercises is not dependent on Faraday's writings alone; and indeed efforts to identify contributions by one writer or another are to some extent out of keeping with the spirit of the group's enterprise. Part of their project was to enable each member to assume an unexceptionable, and to that degree an unidentifiable, public persona—to help the members learn to write in a way that blended in with what they saw as the best contemporary style, rather than to achieve a highly individualized or distinctive voice. In this respect their literary aspirations were, perhaps, classical rather than Romantic. But though the eighteenth-century periodical was a key influence on the group, the members did not adopt the model used by Addison, Steele and others, in which multiple writers contributed as a single, pseudonymous authorial persona such as 'Mr. Spectator'. The essay-circle members concealed their identities but retained their diversity.

In practice, the group's working did not run quite so smoothly as was planned. For one thing, members frequently contributed more than one piece of writing (during the first two-month period, July–August 1818, for example, six pieces were produced) and, less often, fewer. Members bent the rules about contributing their quota: one member, for instance, firmly took 'credit for *two papers*' at the end of the lengthy essay 'On Triflers' (p. 166); he may have been redeeming himself for having produced nothing during a previous period.

The tendency towards lateness or non-production of texts became a serious problem for the essay group. By the end of June 1819, almost a year into the group's life, Faraday was reproaching his fellow members for 'breaking our laws' by failing to submit compositions as agreed.[27] This piece, titled 'On Laws', complains about the slackness of the other members in not producing their compositions on time and exhorts the group collectively to greater efforts. Faraday had very high standards when it came to self-improvement; he was rather prone to disappointment in his fellow artisans' commitment, and not at all afraid to point out instances in which he and others had failed to live up to his expectations. The members of the CPS had already provoked him into criticism in a lecture published in 1817 and excerpted below, titled *Observations on the Means of Obtaining Knowledge*, in which he accused his fellow members of 'mere inertia of the mind' and of failing to make the most of the opportunities the CPS offered for self-improvement. Following this lecture he remained

27   Below, p. 143.

a member of the CPS, but evidently realized that it could not give him all the support he needed for self-education, since he founded the essay-circle the following year.

Despite Faraday's exhortations, by the autumn of 1819, the essay-circle was clearly losing momentum. Even Faraday's enthusiasm appears to have been fading—or perhaps he was simply finding it impossible to make time for original composition. Among the final half-dozen contributions, Faraday's is simply a transcription of part of an entry from the travel journal he wrote following a walking-tour he made in Wales in the summer of 1819 with his friend Edward Magrath.[28] The very last contribution in the book, however, is exceptional in the history of the essay-circle in that it crossed the boundary between private and public writing, appearing in print in a popular periodical. Thomas Deacon's comic anecdote in verse, 'At a Village on the Dunchurch Road' was printed in *The Gentleman's Magazine* in November 1819. It is poignant that the group folded immediately after Deacon succeeded in making the transfer from the club book to the public sphere. Did the members feel that Deacon's publication marked the success of their venture and the vicarious legitimacy of the others as authors, making the circle itself redundant? Or did they fear that Deacon's success set too high a standard for them to follow? Equally possible, however, is that the demise of the circle simply reflected Faraday's increasing absorption in scientific work, or the difficulty of maintaining such a cooperative enterprise over an extended period.

28   Below, pp. 160–61.

Table 1. The contents of the Mental Exercises, showing the periods of each scribe's work

Assuming that the group followed its rules so that each scribe wrote up the contributions for a two-month period, changes in the handwriting in the class book give evidence of the dates during which the compositions were copied into the book. This table shows that in only two of the eight two-month periods of the group's existence (March–April 1819 and May–June 1819) were the expected five contributions copied up. Two periods include fewer than five contributions, and four include more than five. November–December 1818 was the busiest period, with 10 pieces of writing contributed.

July–August 1818 (Faraday scribing)	On Study On Honour On Argument On Imagination and Judgement Hope On General Character
September–October 1818 (Deeble scribing)	On the Pleasures and Uses of the Imagination On Politeness Agis The Charms of Sleep Friendship & Charity An Ode to the PASS Garreteer's Epistle
November–December 1818 (Barnard scribing)	A Mathematical Love Letter On Seeing a Rose in the Possession of a Lady at the SMHPABNASL On Courage Irritus to the Manager Marriage is Honourable in All On Friendship On Mind and the Duty of Improving It A word for Page 73 On the Early Introduction of Females to Society Memoranda
January–February 1819 (Deacon scribing)	On prematurely Forming Opinion of Characters On the Death of the Princess Charlotte Affectation
March–April 1819 (Corder scribing)	On Conscious Approbation The Origin of a Critic Reflections on Death On Avarice On Tradesmen

May–June 1819 (Faraday scribing)	On Laws On the Changes of the mind On Marriage On Calumny Letter to the Secretary
July–August 1819 (Deeble scribing)	Enigma On Marriage Effeminacy & Luxury A Brother's Letter to Mr. Deeble Junius & Tullia A Ramble to Melincourt
September–October 1819 (Barnard scribing)	On Triflers 139th Psalm Infancy At a Village on the Dunchurch Road

Table 2. The contents of the Mental Exercises, showing dates given for the contributions

By no means all the contributions are dated. As with most of the group's practices, diligence in dating contributions decreased dramatically towards the end. In this table, contributions with explicit dates are listed immediately following the month in question; those copied into the book at around the same time, but without dates, appear afterwards, separated by a blank line.

A few pieces are dated very specifically ('On Conscious Approbation', April 5th 1819; 'On Laws', June 26 1819); most simply by the month and year. Listing the contributions in date order, as here, involves altering the order as it appears in the table of contents of the Mental Exercises, so that some contributions appear slightly out of sequence. This is because on a few occasions, pieces dated for a later month are copied into the book before those dated for an earlier month. However, the integrity of the two-month scribal periods is always preserved in the group's dating.

There is little consistency in the references of the dates. Some refer to the date of composition, as with 'On the Death of the Princess Charlotte', which is dated 1817, before the essay-circle began. Others are to the month during which they *ought* to have been written rather than to the month in which they were actually composed or copied up. For example, at the end of June 1819, eight weeks into his second two-month period as scribe, Faraday complained that he had received no contributions. Two contributions following this are dated 'For May 1819', though they were certainly not delivered during that month and very probably were not written until June or perhaps even July.

August 1818	On Study
	On Honour
	On Argument
	On Imagination and Judgement
	On General Character
	Hope
September 1818	On the Pleasures and Uses of the Imagination
October 1818	On Politeness
	Agis
	The Charms of Sleep
	Friendship & Charity
	An Ode to the PASS
	Garreteer's Epistle
November 1818	A Mathematical Love Letter
	On Courage

December 1818	On Seeing a Rose in the Possession of a Lady at the SMHPABNASL
	Irritus to the Manager
	Marriage is Honourable in All
	On Friendship
	On Mind and the Duty of Improving It
	A word for Page 73
	On the Early Introduction of Females to Society
	Memoranda
February 1819	On prematurely Forming Opinion of Characters
	On the Death of the Princess Charlotte
	Affectation
March 1819	The Origin of a Critic
April 1819	On Conscious Approbation
	Reflections on Death
	On Avarice
	On Tradesmen
May 1819	On Calumny
	On Marriage
June 1819	On Laws
	On the Changes of the mind
	Letter to the Secretary
July 1819	Enigma
	A Ramble to Melincourt
	On Marriage
	Effeminacy & Luxury
	A Brother's Letter to Mr. Deeble
	Junius & Tullia
	On Triflers
	139th Psalm
	Infancy
	At a Village on the Dunchurch Road

Writing the Mental Exercises

Despite some similarities with the City Philosophical Society, Faraday's essay-circle differed from it not only in scale but also, importantly, in its approach to authorial freedom. The CPS barred political and theological topics from its lectures and discussion evenings.[29] The essay group, on the other hand, formally granted its members 'entire liberty [...] in the choice of the subject, and the manner of treating it.'[30] In the context of Regency England, this statement of intellectual freedom was courageous. Repressive legislation, dating from the 1790s but greatly strengthened and extended in the late 1810s, attempted to suppress popular political movements, seditious publications and gatherings which might have subversive purposes.[31] Iain McCalman and other historians of radicalism have shown that there was often considerable overlap between London groups promoting instructive discussion and those 'disseminating radical and rational knowledge,' and that in practice debating rules designed to bar politics might be disregarded in favour of 'combative and dramatic' political polemic.[32] Though there can be little question of the CPS's members having engaged in such 'debates', the organization's explicit ban on politics did not prevent it from running into trouble with the reintroduced Seditious Meetings Act in 1817 when it was refused a licence

---

29   *Laws of the City Philosophical Society*, p. 18. Faraday took this prohibition seriously, partly perhaps because it chimed well with his reluctance to mix religious matters with other intellectual concerns. Others, however, attempted to bend the rules and were not reprimanded: Abbott recalled that the Dissenting clergyman Thomas Williams often used slightly veiled allusions to scriptural stories to illustrate his remarks (James, 'The Tales of Benjamin Abbott', p. 236).

30   Below, p. 40.

31   On the effects of this legislation on London print culture, see Ian Haywood, *The Revolution in Popular Literature: Print, Politics and the People, 1790–1860* (Cambridge: Cambridge University Press, 2004), esp. ch. 4. For a detailed account of the fragmented radical response to the legislation and other Establishment attempts at repression during the years of the essay-circle's existence, see J. Ann Hone, *For the Cause of Truth: Radicalism in London 1976–1821* (Oxford: Clarendon Press, 1982), pp. 271–305. E. P. Thompson's account of artisan resistance to the Combination Acts (*The Making of the English Working Class* (London: Gollancz, 1963; second edn Pelican, 1968; repr. Penguin, 1991), pp. 543–69) describes a 'moral culture' of 'solidarity, dedication, and intimidation' which is very far indeed from the enactment of civility and urbanity under way in the Mental Exercises group.

32   Iain McCalman, *Radical Underworld: Prophets, Revolutionaries and Pornographers in London, 1795–1840* (Cambridge: Cambridge University Press, 1988), pp. 116–17.

to hold meetings, though it was allowed to recommence its activities a couple of months later.[33] In the same year, the publisher and CPS member William Hone was prosecuted for blasphemy in a series of three infamous trials.[34] Faraday could not have been unaware of the possible dangers of founding a group dedicated to unfettered expression.

In fact, the writings produced by the essay-circle have conspicuously little to say about contemporary politics. A poem on the death of Princess Charlotte approaches as close to direct topical reference as the group was willing to go, and even that was entered into the class book over a year after the princess died.[35] Though several of the texts address questions of social justice, they often set their discussion in the context of the practices of much earlier, often ancient, societies. This distancing manoeuvre allows the authors to make severe though general criticisms of the contemporary world, as when one member wrote that 'whatever is great and noble in the Acts of Men may be found in the history of ancient times, and whatever is mean and despicable will be found among the moderns.'[36] But compared with contemporary writing by artisans such as Samuel Bamford or Christopher Thomson, the essay-circle's productions are almost wholly lacking in direct engagement with contemporary politics. No doubt this partly reflects the Sandemanian ethos. E. P. Thompson mentions the Sandemanians as among those contributing to the 'intellectual history of Dissent' within which lay 'the dormant seeds of political Radicalism'; nonetheless, Sandemanians offer a very strong instance of Thompson's warning that 'we should not assume that the "Old Dissenters" as a body were willing to take the popular side.'[37] Sandemanians were exhorted to avoid party politics, and to be very cautious about the usages of the world in general, instead focusing their attentions on moral and spiritual well-being.[38] For related reasons they were also 'exclusive', i.e. having nothing to do with

---

33   James, 'Michael Faraday, The City Philosophical Society and the Society of Arts', p. 195; Ian Inkster, 'London Science and the Seditious Meetings Act of 1817', *British Journal for the History of Science* 12.2 (1979), 192–96 (194).

34   J. Ann Hone identifies William Hone as one of just three 'major metropolitan radical publicists' following Cobbett's departure for America in early 1817 (p. 272). Joss Marsh's *Word Crimes: Blasphemy, Culture and Literature in Nineteenth-Century England* (Chicago: University of Chicago Press, 1998), pp. 24–39, gives a useful account of Hone's trials.

35   Below, p. 124.

36   Below, p. 121.

37   E. P. Thompson, *The Making of the English Working Class*, pp. 39, 57.

38   Cantor, p. 6.

the religious practices of other churches or their members. In practice, however, and especially in the charged climate of the late 1810s, an apolitical stance risked being difficult to distinguish from a conservative one.[39]

Only a few references to contemporary figures and events of national political significance occur in the Mental Exercises. One of the most intriguing is in the same contribution—a set of uncontextualized and unconnected apothegms—as the comparison of classical and modern morality: 'the Son of Napoleon is more legitimate on the throne of France than the present Dynasty on that of England.'[40] This sentence would have been likely to provoke serious consequences for its author and possibly for the scribe entering the contribution in the club book, had it come to the attention of the prosecuting authorities. But, though as it stands the sentence appears to be surprisingly subversive, it is not followed with explanation, a call to action or any information to clarify authorial intention, and it would be unwise to give it much weight as a reflection of the political attitudes of the individual author or the group as a whole. Its presence in the club book does, however, suggest that the essay-circle was not completely inhibited in its choice of topic or expression by fears about immediate political danger.

What, then, did the members of the essay-circle choose to write about, given their 'entire liberty' as to subject matter? Over the life span of the group, the topics altered considerably, and with them the tone and register of the writing. The manuscript opens with eight or so sturdy papers on abstract and high-minded topics of a moral or philosophical character, produced while the group was most respectful about its self-appointed task. The subjects of these papers are highly conventional, and the treatment is on the whole moralizing and impersonal. Later, however, the group relaxed somewhat and the members began to write about topics that touched them rather more personally. They also experimented in genre, sometimes contributing poems, letters or riddles instead of essays. Though references to contemporary events are still almost entirely absent,

---

39   I am grateful to Geoffrey Cantor for drawing my attention to Jean Hankins' article, 'A Different Kind of Loyalist: The Sandemanians of New England During the Revolutionary War', *New England Quarterly*, 60 (1987), 223–49, which examines the unhappy consequences for some American Sandemanians of a refusal to declare for either side in the American Revolution, resulting in their being assumed to be loyalists.

40   Below, p. 120.

a greater sense of the occasional emerges from these later and more varied contributions, as members engage with one another's writings (for example, in 'A word for Page 73', which pokes fun at the author of two earlier pieces and plays with the group's habit of anonymity).

Perhaps the most interesting strand in the later compositions is the substantial cluster of texts about what we might broadly and anachronistically call gender and sexuality. The topic is first broached in a poem titled 'Agis', which uses a popular pastoral ballad form to tell a very slight story urging people in love to enjoy the moment while it lasts. From here on, love, marriage and women generally are frequently discussed. Evidently there were personal reasons for the group's interest in these subjects: all were men in or about to be in their 20s, and two at least were shortly to marry—Faraday in 1821, and Edward Barnard in time for his eldest child to be born in 1823. Edward Barnard Deeble, if he was the essay-circle's Edward Deeble, married even earlier, in 1819. It may even be that the group members agreed with W. M. Enfield, who in 1818 recommended self-improvement to the Literary and Philosophical Society in Newcastle as—among other things—making men more attractive to women: 'he who exercises and improves his taste at the same time that he cultivates his understanding, will acquire an idea and feeling of propriety, grace, and elegance, which will […] recommend him to the attention of the more elegant and improved among his female acquaintance.'[41]

The contribution which addresses courtship and matrimony with the greatest personal reference is 'On Marriage', which appears late in the essay-group's life, split over two two-month periods. The piece opens by urging the importance of marrying within one's own station; love may cause one to diverge from this principle, but a man would be 'a base villain' who asked a wealthier girl to marry him without being able to provide 'those necessaries and comforts which from her superior station in life she has a right to expect' (p. 147). Having delivered itself of this conventional caveat, the essay rapidly reverses its perspective: instead of being concerned with the protection of the woman and her comforts, it becomes vehement about the vulnerability of the man proposing marriage: he risks suffering 'a state of misery bordering on frenzy' if rejected (p. 152). The writer expresses deep anxiety about social encounters with women: some women are in the habit of deluding men and making them 'victims

---

41 Rev. W. M. Enfield, *An Essay on the Cultivation of Taste, as a Proper Object of Attention in the Education of Youth* (Newcastle: I. S., 1818), p. 10.

to cruel & disappointed love', but other disasters spring from simple misunderstandings between the sexes, when men misread conventional female politeness for 'a particular & marked attention' (pp. 152–53). The seesawing between highlighting male and female peril continues, but the essay concludes abruptly by urging women to be 'guarded in all their actions' lest they inadvertently lead men on to misery that might end in suicide (p. 153). This piece has some of the characteristics of Faraday's writing, including the tendency to cease to punctuate at the more heated moments of composition; and the comic quatrain which appears at the end of the first section, noting that love can be avoided by will-power, appears also in CPB amid entries from the late 1810s. However, among the other contributions for this two-month period one is certainly, and another is possibly, by Faraday, which seems to suggest that 'On Marriage' cannot be his. Rather, the location of the quatrain on the page of the manuscript suggests rather that Faraday, as scribe, added the verse (possibly at a later date) as his own comment on the essay by another group member.[42]

Despite its deployment of standard sentimental and melodramatic tropes, 'On Marriage' suggests fairly profound social and sexual anxiety. A deep concern with moral behaviour, strongly identifying morality with prudence and self-protection, combined with an enthusiastic engagement in rhetoric and attitudes evidently influenced by fashionable literary and perhaps theatrical taste, gives a tonal unity to the group's writing about gender and sexuality, though that writing takes a variety of forms.

Sometimes these topics are raised in the context of discussions of social practice, as in the essay 'Marriage is Honourable in All', which takes up the question of whether it is better to marry very young or to wait until later in life. This debate, partly a way of discussing the competing merits of large and small families, was of wide interest in the early nineteenth century following the arguments surrounding Malthus's *Essay on Population* (1798). The author of 'Marriage is Honourable in All', however, addresses the subject chiefly from the moral point of view, largely avoiding discussing the political economy of marriage. The essay swings between sentimental raptures about female innocence ('what trials and difficulties will they not encounter for the man who has won their

---

42   In the MS, the first instalment of 'On Marriage' concludes with a short horizontal line; the quatrain appears after this line, in slightly smaller writing and on the left hand side of the page only (Mental Exercises, p. 169).

too susceptible hearts') and melodramatic warnings about male sexual depredations ('Ah! gentle fair ones pause ere ye assign over your dearest and most valuable rights' (p. 102, p. 105)). But it frames these excitable passages with discussions of parental and filial duty and the superiority of prudence to rashness in the choice of a wife; and of course the essayist ensures the propriety of his arguments by titling them with a text from the New Testament.

Other discussions of gender and sexuality abandon the moralizing essay format altogether, as in the fictional tale 'Junius & Tullia' which appears in the penultimate period of the Mental Exercises. Here, another classical setting provides a dramatic wartime backdrop for a Gothic story of a girl threatened with marriage to a deceitful priest while her brave lover fights for his city. Far less sensationally, the autobiographical piece following this describes a chance meeting between a Londoner (Faraday, in fact) on holiday in Wales and a very young Welsh girl who speaks no English. He gives her money, enjoys her pleasure in the gift and in her surroundings, and concludes 'I never felt more honorable in my own eyes (and I have plenty of vanity) than I did this evening whilst enjoying the display this artless girl made of her feelings' (p. 161). Both these examples fantasize gender relationships as highly dramatic encounters between active men and vulnerable, uncomprehending girls, and are much more confident about the stability of sexual relations and the dominance of male over female than is 'On Marriage'.

Some caution is requisite in judging this shift of emphasis in the topic matter of the essay-circle: it is not so simple as a change from conventional to confessional writing. The general subject of gender relations was, in its way, as much subject to literary convention as the high-minded themes of the first few essays. Indeed, the members' frequent and apparently delighted recourse to highly theatrical rhetoric when discussing these topics is a marker of the accretion of literary convention around the theme.

A broader sense of the conventionality or otherwise of the topics addressed in the Mental Exercises can be gained by comparing the essay-circle's subjects not only with those of the literary essayists they often emulated but also with those of other artisan self-education groups. The evidence about topics discussed by such groups is not abundant, but one suggestive comparison is afforded by an influential book written by Timothy Claxton, an artisan who became a leader in the movement for educating working men. Claxton was a very close contemporary of

Faraday's (he was born a year earlier than Faraday, in 1790), and was a member of the City Philosophical Society.[43] Though his *Hints for Mechanics on Self-Education and Mutual Instruction* was not published until 1839, it draws on Claxton's experience as an activist in the world of artisan self-improvement during the years of Faraday's essay-circle. As well as his experience in the CPS, Claxton was a founder of the short-lived London Mechanical Institution in 1817 before leaving for America where in the 1820s he helped to found the Lyceum movement, and his book gives many practical suggestions for individuals and groups involved in self-education.[44] Most helpfully for our purposes, it lists several categories of topics which could be used as the basis for a conversational evening among artisans. These begin with 'Questions on Morals', such as 'What would be the probable effects upon the Moral and Social Condition of Man from the general diffusion of Knowledge?', and conclude with a long list of 'Miscellaneous Questions', many of which are about women. This list suggests that gender relations may have been an expected topic for discussion in self-improvement groups, but on the whole Claxton's questions about women imply a much more radical outlook on gender than those expressed by the essay-circle.[45] Claxton recommends artisans to discuss, for instance, 'Are Females endowed by Nature with Intellectual Abilities equal to those of the other Sex?'. The essay-circle never discusses gender equality, and is not greatly interested in equality of any kind, except to try to establish hierarchies of meritoriousness among otherwise equal kinds of men. The group's attitude towards women is generally chivalrous (or we might call it paternalistic) rather than egalitarian, as for example in an essay deploring the 'Early Introduction of Females to Society':

> Independant of the destructive inroads late hours and a continued change of pleasures and amusements make on the too delicate constitution of these tender plants; it engenders an unsettled habit, a dissatisfaction of home, and of the

---

43 James, 'Michael Faraday, The City Philosophical Society and the Society of Arts', p. 194.

44 Richard D. Brown, 'The Idea of an Informed Citizenry in the Early Republic', in David Thomas Konig (ed.), *Devising Liberty: Preserving and Creating Freedom in the New American Republic* (Stanford: Stanford University Press, 1995), pp. 141–77 (p. 171).

45 A notable exception is Claxton's suggested question 'Are early Marriages generally advisable?', which is a very close match to the essay-circle contribution discussed above, 'Marriage is Honourable in All'.

solid comforts there only generally to be met with; they do not feel the value of their own innocent domestic circle (p. 119).

If we use its writing on gender and sexuality, then, as a sample of the essay-circle's social views, we find an interesting mixture of mild conservatism in its politics and conventional heightening in its rhetoric, but little of the personal or confessional in either. And this is not altogether surprising, since the goal of the essay-circle was not so much introspection as the achievement of stylistic acceptability. Conspicuousness in their arguments or in their register would not have served the members' purposes. It is entirely possible that the views they articulated in their contributions did not fully reflect their personal beliefs, rather as the conscious, public, imitative style they generally adopted in the Mental Exercises was probably not identical with the one they used for their private communications.

Table 3. Table of contents of the Mental Exercises, with internal evidence towards authorial attributions

Few Faraday scholars have attempted to distinguish Faraday's essays from those of the other members of the group. Williams, however, attributes 'On Imagination and Judgement' and its companion piece 'On the Pleasures and Uses of the Imagination' to Faraday, as well as 'On Mind and the Duty of Improving It'.[46] The first two of these essays are confessedly by the same author, and are marked with a 'Y' in the contents page of the Mental Exercises. Since Y appears in no other group member's name, it is reasonable to assume that it does indeed refer to Faraday. The attribution of 'On Imagination and Judgement' and 'On the Pleasures and Uses of the Imagination' to Faraday seems unproblematic, and Williams' reasons for attributing 'On Mind and the Duty of Improving It' to him likewise are sound.

Joseph Agassi has proposed that Faraday was the author of 'On Argument'.[47] It is true that an 'MF' monogram is written beside the title of this essay in the contents page of the Mental Exercises. The monogram, however, is not written in the ink used for the essay titles and clearly postdates the original document, though we cannot know by how long. Agassi does not mention the presence of the same monogram beside the title of 'A Mathematical Love Letter' in the contents page. There are good—though not conclusive—grounds for believing 'A Mathematical Love Letter' to be by Faraday, as I discuss in the footnotes to that contribution; and if so, it is not unreasonable to suppose that the 'MF' monogram gives reliable evidence regarding 'On Argument' also. However, only five essays were contributed during the first period of the essay-circle: if 'On Imagination and Judgement' is by Faraday, it would seem either that 'On Argument' is not, or that Faraday contributed two pieces while some other member contributed none; and it seems somewhat unlikely that the members of the essay-circle would have failed to follow their own rules so immediately after instituting them.

The table below, then, sets these external judgments about attribution to Faraday to one side, and presents only the evidence on authorship that is internal to the MS.

On Study	
On Honour	'E' noted in MS Table of Contents
On Argument	'MF' monogram added later beside title in MS
On Imagination and Judgement	'Y' noted in MS Table of Contents and at end of contribution
Hope	
On General Character	'E' noted in MS Table of Contents

---

46   Williams, p. 81, p. 93 n. 64.
47   Joseph Agassi, 'An Unpublished Paper of the Young Faraday', *Isis*, 52 (1961), 87–90.

On the Pleasures and Uses of the Imagination	'Y' noted in MS Table of Contents and at end of contribution Opening sentence explains that this is by the author of 'On Imagination and Judgement'
On Politeness	
Agis	
The Charms of Sleep	
Friendship & Charity	'J' noted in MS Table of Contents and at end of contribution
An Ode to the PASS	
Garreteer's Epistle	Identified in 'A word for Page 73' as being by the author of 'Agis' and an ode, presumably 'An Ode to the PASS'
A Mathematical Love Letter	'MF' monogram added later between title and first line in MS
On Seeing a Rose in the Possession of a Lady at the SMHPABNASL	'T' noted in MS Table of Contents and at end of contribution
On Courage	'R' noted in MS Table of Contents
Irritus to the Manager	
Marriage is Honourable in All	'T' noted in MS Table of Contents
On Friendship	'T' noted in MS Table of Contents and at end of contribution
On Mind and the Duty of Improving It	
A word for Page 73	
On the Early Introduction of Females to Society	'J' noted in MS Table of Contents
Memoranda	
On prematurely Forming Opinion of Characters	'Y' noted in MS Table of Contents and at end of contribution
On the Death of the Princess Charlotte	'T' noted in MS Table of Contents
Affectation	
On Conscious Approbation	
The Origin of a Critic	Marked 'Y' at end of contribution
Reflections on Death	
On Avarice	
On Tradesmen	

On Laws	By the scribe for May–June 1819: i.e. Faraday
On the Changes of the mind	
On Marriage	
On Calumny	
Letter to the Secretary	
Enigma	
On Marriage	
Effeminacy & Luxury	
A Brother's Letter to Mr. Deeble	
Junius & Tullia	
A Ramble to Melincourt	
On Triflers	
139th Psalm	
Infancy	
At a Village on the Dunchurch Road	

Reading in the Mental Exercises

The MS of the Mental Exercises gives a fascinating insight into the connection between artisan writing and engagement with the English literary canon in the Regency period. We cannot, as I argued above, be certain how far the views the members expressed in their essays matched their own real beliefs; but we can be sure that the texts they quote and cite were indeed part of their cultural repertoire, though of course it is very likely that they knew some at least of these texts in extracted rather than complete form, or at second hand via anthologies and other such sources. But this would not be untypical of many eighteenth- and early nineteenth-century readers' methods of accessing texts, whether the readers were prosperous and formally educated or not. Anthologies played a very important role in the development of mass cultural education, and in shaping the power relations between readers, writers and texts. As Barbara M. Benedict argues, literary anthologies up to the Regency 'sell cultural literacy' by 'representing social power to the reader as the mastery of current literary culture.' Most importantly for the essay-circle, anthologies taught their readers 'to participate, if only in imagination, in forging literary values.'[48] Benedict's account of anthology-reading as a means of encouraging readers into a kind of active conversation with canonical literature is a very good model for understanding the use that the essay-circle members made of the snippets—and more substantial extracts—they quoted from the English classics. The group members evidently sought to deploy their reading actively, not to adorn their work with decorative quotations nor to follow obediently the thoughts of other writers, but to use their knowledge of literature in an assured, even an urbane way. Developing an active relationship with the cultural canon was one of the advantages for which Regency advice manuals on education recommended essay composition: as one such manual explained in 1817, 'in composing, the pupil is thrown upon the resources of his own mind; and as these soon fail where they are not recruited, he is compelled to read, to observe, and to reflect; while the very act of writing his thoughts, insensibly teaches him to arrange them.'[49]

---

48   Barbara M. Benedict, *Making the Modern Reader; Cultural Mediation in Early Modern Literary Anthologies* (Princeton: Princeton University Press, 1996), p. 211.

49   William Jaques, *A Practical Essay on Intellectual Education [...]* (London: Hatchard, 1817), p. 72. Hatchard's bookshop in Piccadilly was and is only a few hundred yards from the Royal Institution in Albemarle Street: Hatchard's would have been Faraday's

The essay-circle members deploy their reading via intertextuality, using their knowledge of contemporary and earlier literature and history as—to adopt John Guillory's useful formulation—'*symbolic* capital, a kind of knowledge-capital whose possession can be displayed upon request and which thereby entitles its possessor to the cultural and material rewards of the well-educated person.'[50] This display of symbolic capital manifests itself in the Mental Exercises in three major types of intertextuality. The first is direct quotations, signalled as such, usually citing just the surname of the author and often using inverted commas to mark the quotation off from the essay group member's own words. This kind of quotation is used fairly often to begin or end a contribution, in which cases it acts as a bridge between the individual group member and the wider group. Such quotations link the knowledge of the lone writer to that of the readers in the essay-circle and the imagined public beyond the group. These are generally quotations from highly canonical literary figures. The canon in question, however, centres round eighteenth-century writers rather to the detriment of Renaissance ones: Pope and Johnson are more frequently quoted than Shakespeare or Milton.

The second degree of intertextuality in the Mental Exercises involves quotation that is not marked as such, either by naming the source or by using inverted commas or line breaks to separate the quoted material from the writer's own words. By far the most frequently quoted text of this kind is, not surprisingly, the Bible. The difference in the members' practices in quoting the Bible and English literature suggests that direct, signalled quotation involved a kind of ostentation or claim-staking which was unnecessary or even distasteful in the case of the Scriptures. Sandemanian practices of Biblical quotation seem likely to have had a considerable influence on the group's intertextual method in this case: congregations in Sandemanian churches would be accustomed to hearing exhortations in which sacred quotations were interspersed with the minimum of non-Biblical text in order to avoid straying from the undeniable word of God into fallible interpretations.

Most difficult to trace securely are the intertextual moments in which the essay-circle members seem to be adopting a ready-made trope or idiom which is not a quotation from a single source. In the footnotes

---

nearest large source of new books, and it is conceivable that he might have seen this book there.

50   John Guillory, *Cultural Capital: The Problem of Literary Canon Formation* (Chicago: University of Chicago Press, 1993), p. ix.

to the contributions I have tried to indicate locations where these tropes can be found in other, mainly early nineteenth-century, texts, but these comparisons must necessarily be speculative; and this is unsatisfactory, given the importance of this kind of intertextuality in establishing the strands of the connections the group members were making with their contemporary culture.

We do not know where most of the members of the essay-circle gained access to literary works. Faraday, of course, could have used the Royal Institution's library, which—although it belonged to a scientific organization—was well stocked with canonical English literature. Volumes not held by the Royal Institution during the late 1810s and referred to in the Mental Exercises include, most importantly, Watts's *Improvement of the Mind*, as well as Dodsley's *Oeconomy of Human Life* and Susanna Dobson's *Petrarch's View of Human Life*. The RI did, however, hold all 45 volumes of Chalmers' *British Essayists*, which collected several of the eighteenth-century periodicals including the *Tatler*, *Spectator* and *Idler* that were so influential for the essay-circle, another 14-volume collection of the *Spectator*, *Tatler* and *Guardian*, and a 12-volume edition of Johnson's *Works* that included *The Rambler*.[51] It also held all the major English poets cited in the Mental Exercises, including Collins, Cowper, Milton, Pope, Thomson and Young.[52] For most of the essay-circle, however, and perhaps for Faraday also, extensive library facilities would not have been necessary for composition. Around half the contributions in the Mental Exercises do not quote or refer to other writers at all. No contribution quotes or cites obscure or ephemeral sources (for example, articles in specialist periodicals).

---

51 W. Harris, *A Catalogue of the Library of the Royal Institution of Great Britain [...]* (London, 1809).

52 *Ibid.*

Table 4. Works cited in the Mental Exercises

The first column of figures counts only those works directly quoted or mentioned in the Mental Exercises; the second includes those which can be identified as sources or analogues of unacknowledged quotations.

It is not at all surprising that the Bible should be the most quoted text in writing by a group of Dissenters. Comparison of the two columns shows that the essay-circle members preferred to refer to the Bible without direct acknowledgement, including Biblical phrases in their sentences rather than separating them from their own discourse through use of inverted commas. The other most frequently quoted texts in the Mental Exercises are used quite differently: when the members quote Pope, Johnson, Thomson, Shakespeare or Cowper it is generally directly and with a formal citational signal such as inverted commas or the author's name. In introducing these canonical and fashionable authors into their writings, the essay-circle members are staking claims to cultural citizenship; it is therefore important for them that quotations be prominent. The exceptions are the few instances of hidden citation, such as the poem 'An Ode to the PASS' (pp. 82–88), which begins with a parodic rewriting of William Collins' 'An Ode for Music', but does not name Collins or his poem. Other than this 'Ode', the most striking instance of quotation not signalled as such is the direct borrowing of a long paragraph from Benjamin Franklin's *A Narrative of the Late Massacres in Lancaster County* in the essay 'On Honour' (p. 48).

	Direct quotations	Direct and indirect quotations
Aesop	1	1
Joseph Addison, *The Tatler*	1	1
Mark Akenside, *Pleasures of the Imagination*	1	1
Bible	4	12
New Testament	(2)	(4)
Old Testament	(1)	(7)
Apocrypha	(1)	(1)
Robert Burns, 'Despondency: An Ode'	1	1
William Collins	1	2
'Hassan: Or, the Camel-Driver'	(1)	(1)
'An Ode for Music'		(1)
William Cowper	2	2
'The Garden'	(1)	(1)
'The Progress of Error'	(1)	(1)
Sneyd Davies, 'Epistle XVII'	1	1
Robert Dodsley, *Oeconomy of Human Life*	1	1
Armand Jean du Plessis, Cardinal Richelieu	1	1

	Direct quotations	Direct and indirect quotations
Benjamin Franklin	2	2
A Narrative of the Late Massacres in	(1)	(1)
Lancaster County	(1)	(1)
Private Correspondence		
Horace, *Odes*	1	1
Samuel Johnson	5	7
The Rambler	(5)	(5)
Irene		(1)
Rasselas		(1)
John Locke	1	2
Essay Concerning Human Understanding		(2)
John Milton	2	2
'When I consider'	(1)	(1)
Paradise Lost	(1)	(1)
Charles Montague, Earl of Halifax, 'The Man of Honour'	1	1
Petrarch	1	2
Alexander Pope	6	6
'Essay on Criticism'	(4)	(4)
'Epistle to a Lady'	(1)	(1)
'Essay on Man'	(1)	(1)
William Shakespeare	3	4
As You Like It	(1)	(1)
Hamlet		(1)
Julius Caesar	(1)	(1)
Othello	(1)	(1)
James Thomson, *The Seasons*	3	4
Isaac Watts, *The Improvement of the Mind*	1	1
Edward Young, *Night Thoughts*	1	2

Table 5. Table of contents of the Mental Exercises, with texts quoted or borrowed

The table lists works and authors directly quoted or alluded to as well as those works from which we can be most confident that tacit borrowing took place. For evidence of this borrowing, see the footnotes relating to the relevant contribution. Nonetheless, the list given here must necessarily be to some extent partial and subjective. The texts are listed in the order in which they appear in the relevant contribution.

On Study	Watts Shakespeare, *Othello* Locke, *Essay Concerning Human Understanding*
On Honour	*The Tatler*, no. 251 Shakespeare, *Julius Caesar* Franklin, *A Narrative of the Late Massacres in Lancaster County* Montague, 'The Man of Honour'
On Argument	
On Imagination and Judgement	Pope, 'Essay on Criticism' *The Rambler*, no. 193 Exodus
Hope	
On General Character	*The Rambler*, no. 151 Franklin Johnson, *Rasselas* *The Rambler*, no. 82 Shakespeare, *As You Like It*
On the Pleasures and Uses of the Imagination	Addison, *The Spectator*, papers on 'The Pleasures of the Imagination' Milton, 'When I consider' Pope, 'Essay on Criticism' Milton, *Paradise Lost* *The Rambler*, no. 92
On Politeness	
Agis	
The Charms of Sleep	

Friendship & Charity	Shakespeare, *Macbeth* Sirach Thomson, 'Autumn' Richelieu Job John Jeremiah Horace Dobson/Petrarch Akenside, *Pleasures of the Imagination*
An Ode to the PASS	Collins, 'An Ode for Music'
Garreteer's Epistle	
A Mathematical Love Letter	
On Seeing a Rose in the Possession of a Lady at the SMHPABNASL	
On Courage	Deuteronomy New Testament
Irritus to the Manager	
Marriage is Honourable in All	Hebrews Thomson, 'Spring' Ovington, *Duties, Advantages, Pleasures* Dodsley, *Oeconomy* Pope 'Epistle to a Lady' Franklin
On Friendship	
On Mind and the Duty of Improving It	Johnson, 'Life of Cowley'
A word for Page 73	
On the Early Introduction of Females to Society	Cowper, *The Task* Pope, 'Essay on Man' Thomson, 'Autumn'; 'Summer'
Memoranda	Shakespeare, *Julius Caesar*
On prematurely Forming Opinion of Characters	Psalms
On the Death of the Princess Charlotte	
Affectation	
On Conscious Approbation	
The Origin of a Critic	Pope, 'Essay on Criticism'

Reflections on Death	Young, *Night Thoughts*
On Avarice	Collins, 'Hassan: Or, the Camel-Driver' Young, *Night Thoughts* Aesop
On Tradesmen	Philippians
On Laws	
On the Changes of the mind	Johnson, *Irene*
On Marriage	
On Calumny	Shakespeare, *Othello*; *Henry IV*, Part 2
Letter to the Secretary	Matthew
Enigma	
On Marriage	
Effeminacy & Luxury	Sneyd Davies, 'Epistle'
A Brother's Letter to Mr. Deeble	
Junius & Tullia	
A Ramble to Melincourt	
On Triflers	Cowper, 'The Progress of Error' Shakespeare, *Hamlet* Luke Matthew
139th Psalm	Psalms
Infancy	Burns, 'Despondency' Thomson, 'Spring'
At a Village on the Dunchurch Road	

Note on editorial policy

This book divides its material into two parts. The first prints the complete text of the 'Class Book, for the Reception of Mental Exercises' in which the essay-circle's work was copied up by the members. I have transcribed the manuscript, as far as possible, without making any editorial corrections: errors, including misspellings, absent or incorrect punctuation, repeated words, and so on, are preserved. I have not marked these errors with 'sic', because the repetition would become tiresome to the reader. The only excision I have made is to drop the original numbering of the contributions.

The transcription is annotated with footnotes of three kinds. One simply records manuscript corrections of scribal or (less frequently) authorial errors, such as the addition of a letter to correct a misspelling. In many cases it is impossible to determine who made these corrections: where the ink and handwriting differ from those used by the scribe, it is clear that the amendments were made after the original copying-up, but whether this was done at a meeting of the group, by the scribe during the following two-month period, or even by someone outside the group altogether, we cannot know. Fortunately, these later corrections are generally minor—usually the alteration of a spelling, the substitution of a singular for a plural, or vice versa.

The second kind of footnote provides information on sources or persons quoted or referred to in the contributions. Where these sources are canonical and easily locatable in multiple editions—such as quotations from Pope's major poems, or Shakespeare's plays—I have given only basic citations of line or act and scene number rather than page numbers in particular editions. However, where the essay-circle member's quotation diverges to any significant degree from the text in standard editions, I have included a contemporary edition's version of the original. The third kind of footnote is far more speculative: these attempt to give some context for usages, borrowings and clichés. Except where explicitly indicated, these contextual footnotes do not claim or even seek to identify the single source from which a usage may have been derived; rather they aim to give a sense of the general availability of that usage. In some instances the essay-circle member may not even have been conscious that the phrase he was using was well worn; at other times, a degree of playful rhetorical borrowing seems evident. The analogues I suggest in these footnotes should by no means be taken as comprehensive or even secure; in most cases, a wide variety of sources could have been suggested: I have chosen the ones that offered the closest comparison or that seemed the most likely to be easily available to early nineteenth-century readers without private libraries.

Part Two of this book extends this attempt to offer contexts for the contributions to the Mental Exercises into longer-scale extracts. Inevitably, given the evidence available, these centre round Faraday rather than the other members of the group. Thus, the first section reproduces Faraday's surviving writings of the 1810s on the subject of self-improvement, chiefly his lectures to the City Philosophical Society. The second gives extracts from a variety of sources by other writers on self-improvement: Watts and Johnson are represented because of their acknowledged influence on Faraday's views; then follow two Dissenting ministers' comments on the topic, included partly because they are closely contemporary with the essay-circle (one of the ministers, indeed, was a member of the City Philosophical Society). Related to these Dissenting comments, an extract from the radical periodical *The Black Dwarf* gives an flavour of contemporary writings in which the education of the working classes was heavily politicized, as a contrast to the way in which it is privatized and depoliticized in the Mental Exercises. The extracts from *Frankenstein*—published in the year the essay-circle was launched—show another very young writer exploring self-education in the context of both scientific and literary culture. And though Henry Brougham's *Practical Observations upon the Education of the People* postdates the essay-circle by several years, nonetheless it serves as a way of joining up eighteenth-century and emerging traditions of self-education. The final section of Part Two reprints two important eighteenth-century sources on the pleasures of the imagination—a theme addressed not only in the essay of that title, but also by the whole project of the Mental Exercises, which sought to enfranchise the group as members of a polite culture, with access to both the privileges and the pleasures which it could provide.

Part One: The 'Mental Exercises'

List of Members and Scribes' Rota

A
CLASS BOOK,
for the Reception of
Mental Exercises
Instituted
JULY, 1818[1]

1818[2]

Period		
	1 July	Mr. Faraday
	2 September	Mr. Deeble
	3 November	Mr. Barnard

1819

	4 January	Mr. Deacon
	5 March	Mr. Corder
	6 May	Mr. Faraday
	7 July	Mr. Deeble
	8 September	Mr. Barnard
	9 November	Mr. Deacon

1820

---

1   The MS on which this edition is based is held in the archives of the Royal Institution of Great Britain, no. F13/A. The MS gives a list of the contributions; this has been omitted here and included in the table of contents for this volume.

2   This list indicates which members will act as scribes during the periods noted. The work of the scribe is indicated in point 4 of the agreement which follows.

Members

M. Faraday

E. Deeble

E. Barnard

T. Deacon

J. Corder

Members' Agreement

It is agreed,

1. That the number of persons who join efforts to make this book useful, shall not exceed *Six*.[3]
2. That each person shall produce at certain periods, a paper, essay, a few observations, or some other production, which is to be considered as their lesson for that period.
3. That no other qualifications be required, than the production of the paper in due time, and a wish to improve.
4. That the Members do in rotation take charge of the book during the periods, and, receiving the written subscriptions, enter or cause them to be entered in an uniform manner.[4]
5. That each period consist of two months.
6. That the papers be ready for entrance in the book at the end of the first month.
7. That the Members do meet, as may be convenient, at the end of each period, for the regular transference of the book from one to another; and for the consideration of any other matters that may require it.
8. That as entire liberty is allowed in the choice of the subject, and the manner of treating it; so, also, none be considered as involved in the observations of another, or accountable except for his own productions.[5]

---

3   Cf. the *Laws of the City Philosophical Society, Instituted January 1808* (London: printed by Ramshaw, 1812), which open with a declaration that the membership shall not exceed 100 (p. 11).

4   Cf. the *Laws* of the CPS: the members are to lecture to the Society in rotation (p. 21).

5   Cp. the *Laws* of the CPS: 'That no topic of Theology or Politics shall be discussed in the society' (p. 18).

On Study

Of all the means which the mind possesses of obtaining knowledge, there is perhaps none more characteristic, more important, or of a more exalted nature, than Study.[6]

Study is a twofold act. It requires in the first place, the exercise of perceptive powers, & then the exercise of the judgement. Whenever the mind is studiously engaged on a subject, of whatever nature it may be, the first efforts are, to obtain a knowledge of the circumstances known concerning it: The mind is almost passive in this state; its exertions being, only to facilitate the reception of ideas through the organs of sense; and Contemplation is the mistress of the moment. Having received the ideas which represent the subject; the second operation of the mind, is, that of comparison or judgement. The various elementary parts of the subject are compared one with another, their accordance or dissimilitude noted, and a conclusion made respecting their general relation. This is a judgement: and it is the more correct in proportion as we have succeeded in gaining clear ideas in the first place, and accurately comparing them in the second.

The whole of this operation is what is implied in the word *Study*. It is, however, frequently performed in the various situations of life; without being dignified by that title. In conversation, particularly when of a controversial nature, judgements are frequently drawn during the discourse; though in general, it merely consists in the communication and reception of ideas, without any rigid observance of their relationship.— In consequence of these loose and desultory efforts of the mind, the term study is now generally confined to that state, when the mental powers are purposely directed with forced energy to the contemplation of an object, that a judgement as correct as possible may be drawn; and it is only in this way that it can be distinguished and separated from Reading, Observation, Instruction by Lectures, Conversation &c.[7]

Study is characteristic, because it is the most refined operation performed by the mind; it is important, for on it depends every

---

6 Compare Faraday's comments on study in *Observations on the Means of Obtaining Knowledge* (1815), below, pp. 185–86.

7 With 'study', these are the five 'methods of improving' identified by Isaac Watts in *The Improvement of the Mind: Or, A Supplement to the Art of Logic* (London: Edwards and Knibb, 1821), ch. 2.

improvement of civilised and social life; and it is exalted, even to the very head and front of all earthly power.[8]

It would be much to say, that, excepting man, the rest of animated nature has no power of comparing the result of their perceptions, or in simple terms of reasoning; the numerous and well authenticated cases of what the whole world concur in calling the sagacity of animals, seem to prove the contrary: But,[9] in whatever situation they may be placed in this respect, they certainly are very far below man; and can have no claims to the distinction attached to a studious being. It is here, indeed, that the separation between him and them is widest. The general organs of sensation and perception are similar in both, and in particular points, man is frequently surpassed by animals. But for reason he is constantly supereminent: to it he owes his mastery over them, and it is only when he loses that characteristic distinction by submission to his own base and degrading passions, that he approaches to their nature.[10]

Reason, Study, Judgement, for the words are almost synonimous, are not only characteristic of *man*, but of *men* also. The human being is as well distinguished from his fellows by it, as from beasts.[11] A man is important and superior, in proportion as his powers of mind excell those of theirs; and *powers of mind* is but another name for reason and judgement. Even the distinction which attaches to riches, though aided by all the gratifications and passions of an almost artificial human nature, is not sufficient to overcome the influence of mental power, but bows to the superior character of the wise man.

The *Importance* of study, is a point which no one will contest, when it receives the name of reason. Even Lock's man of a single syllogism will admit it,[12] for he is aware, that though lamentably deficient himself in the

---

8   *Othello*, I.3: 'true, I have married her: / The very head and front of my offending / Hath this extent, no more.' The phrase was applied in many other contexts in the late eighteenth and early nineteenth century.

9   'But': originally 'but', the capital written over the lower case 'b'.

10   Cp. Faraday's comparison of animals' inability to improve themselves or leave evidence of their existence behind them with man's ability in these areas in 'Observations on the Inertia of the Mind', below, p. 189.

11   Cp. Thomas Williams, *The Moral Tendencies of Knowledge: A Lecture, Delivered before the City Philosophical Society [...]* (London: printed for the author, n.d. [1815]), p. 24: 'Literature and Science form the broad line which distinguishes man from the animal world around him.'

12   In book IV, ch. 17 of his *Essay Concerning Human Understanding* (1690), John Locke challenges the importance of syllogisms in reasoning (RI 1809, 1821).

powers comprehended in this term, it was the exertion of those belonging to others, that raised the world, and him with it, into its present convenient, comfortable, happy state.[13] Though he may not be able to comprehend each advance made by man from the savage to the civilised being; yet, he can perceive obscurely the whole effect, and blesses the influence, though almost unknown to him, which produced it. To the man of mind it is infinitely more important. He not only sees clearly what the world owes to this precious gift of heaven, but he perceives that his own happiness here is dependant on it. 'Tis in the exertions of mind only, that the mind can take pleasure; and the result of its exertions is an irresistable advance towards an improved state.[14] Every good feeling too, as far as good feelings can be influenced by earthly motives, is fostered by it. Take two beings with equal reasoning powers; the one shall from circumstances find pleasure in things unworthy of him, habits shall have caused him to seek enjoyment in eating, drinking, or disgraceful conversation; his powers of reason must then be a continual reproach to him, and he will never feel content but when he has gotten rid of them. The other shall employ his time in objects worthy his attention, and in feelings worthy his heart, and all his pleasures shall be doubly heightened by the approval of his reason and his conscience. Thus is morality improved and life rendered worth possession, and thus is established the *importance* of reason to mankind.

The *exalted character* of Study cannot be unknown to him who has contemplated though but in the slightest manner human nature. The last and noblest effort of the mind in all her operations is judgement, for in that she concentrates whatever else was before received. In that, incloses the highest good that can result from her perceptions. Judgement, is the fulcrum on which all our actions turn, & by means of which they produce their effects. Every other effort of the mind is preparatory to it, every action of the body is in consequence of it. It may be compared to the focus in which are received the rays that are coming *to action*, from which emanate those that are going *to perform*.[15] Whatever our

---

13   The essayist's complacent view of the contemporary state of the world perhaps reflects what Cantor describes as the Sandemanian tendency towards a 'non-factional form of conservatism' (p. 95).

14   Cp. Isaac Taylor, *Self-Cultivation Recommended: Or, Hints to a Youth Leaving School* (London: Rest Fenner, 1817), p. 119: 'What wonders have been produced by the exertions of mind! Had all men of talent been [...] unproductive, our world had never risen to knowledge, refinement, comfort, or general happiness.'

15   'Focus' and 'rays' were part of the technical terminology of optics.

perceptions, thoughts, or ideas; or however they pass through the mind, they are useless, unless judgement receives and guides them. Look at the day dreams of this man; the idle pleasures of that man; how completely they waste the time, how sure their annihilation. And why? judgement has not stamped them; they have not been embodied, and cannot remain in existence:—but, had she purified them, would they not have given rise to something good or useful?; to somewhat applicable either to the being himself or to his fellow creatures?—In fine, Mind though possessing many powers, without the power of judging would be void. It is that which completes and elevates it to the highest rank in created nature.

Such then is the value of reason or study, or in more distinct terms, of the power of comparing things and drawing a judgement of their relation. Of the propriety therefore, or rather of the imperious duty which is incumbent on us of improving it as far as we are able,[16] there can be no doubt; and any means which may be suggested for this purpose deserve a favourable consideration

The powers of the mind, as well as those of the body, become more energetic and competent to great things in proportion to the use that is made of them.[17] The eye that is used to discriminate small shades of difference, or distinguish minute objects, soon gains facilities which are the results only of practice. The ear that has been formed by application, will readily distinguish the smallest error in musical expression or in harmony, though quite inappreciable to those that are untutored.—And the mind will from exercise gain a facility and correctness of judgement, which the idle must ever despair of attaining. What is called knowledge of the world, is in fact nothing more than an extension by practice in one direction, of the powers of reason and judgement; and it is somewhat singular, that the practice which has been found so useful in a particular part of human knowledge, should not have been applied more generally.

---

16   'Imperious duties' were a frequent part of the rhetoric of early nineteenth-century progressive writers, from Hazlitt to Cobbett, and especially of Protestant and Dissenting missionary writing. Hazlitt, indeed, mocked the phrase in his discussion of British foreign policy in his 1813 'Illustrations of Vetus' (*Political Essays* (London: Hone, 1819), pp. 34–50 (pp. 41–42)).

17   Cp. Hugh Blair, 'Sermon IX. On Idleness', in *Sermons*, 5 vols. (London: Cadell and Davies *et al.*, 1818, new edition), III, pp. 161–85 (p. 171): 'If we consult either the improvement of the mind, or the health of the body, it is well known that exercise is the great instrument of promoting both.' And cp. Williams, *The Moral Tendencies of Knowledge*: 'The mind can no more enjoy health than the body, without a certain degree of exercise' (p. 28).

But it appears that to generalise correctly is difficult, 'though the induction seems distinct.[18]—Half the world may be observed busy in the pursuit of riches: and neglecting for them the comforts and pleasures of life; though the only use of wealth, is the purchase of those very things: and in the same way, every one commends the knowledge of the world, but forgets that general knowledge includes it

As their are no discrepancies in the natural state of things,[19] a mind which can judge aright of generals will be accurate in particular cases; and therefore, the general improvement of the mind should be preferred to a partial instruction of it. The devotion of some portion of time to the formation of a habit of reasoning, seems to be an excellent method of improving the mind; and this can perhaps be done in no way so well, as by purposely considering a single subject over, and by giving body and form to the ideas in writing. In this case, the thoughts all tend to one object and become methodised; and by giving them expression, they become clear and distinct; and are brought out from the misty, confused state, in which they so frequently pass before the mind.—The result of the first effort of this kind, is, either the formation of distinct and connected ideas on the subject; or the expulsion of confused and incorrect ones. The second, third, and future efforts, not only add to this stock of corrected ideas; but they expand the thoughts, they connect particular and subordinate positions by general relations, and enabling man to throw off his confined opinion of things, present him with a view of nature & society, on the great and inclusive scale in which they really exist.

Now it is the humble endeavour of a few individuals, to secure to themselves a portion of the good that belongs to a well regulated and disciplined mind; and to expand their views, and render them distinct, by urging themselves into an active and delicate perception of things. It is believed, that by practising the mind in attention, and progression; a habit of industry and improvement will be formed.—The rules, or regulations, which preceed these remarks, are supposed to be sufficient to ensure the advantages resulting from method, without in any way confining exertions; and whatever opinion may be formed of the plan,

---

18 Picking up from the reference to Locke's attack on syllogisms, 'induction' here continues the theme of methods of reasoning.

19 The uniformity of nature was a widely held tenet of early nineteenth-century science.

still we may without vanity say that it merits praise, since it has humility for its character and improvement for its object.[20]

August 1818

On Honour

"There is nothing honourable that is not innocent and nothing mean but what has guilt in it"[21]

Honor is a virtue that should inherit the breasts of all men, and is in the opinion of some innate with our nature. It is a virtue, which in the strict sense of the word will be found (in the ordinary occurrences of life) to be all that is requisite to make men happy, from it we may deduce every other virtue, and on this basis rests every degree of social order. But the manner in which it is treated in modern times must be a matter of severe reflection on the degenerate state of mankind, and will point us out as beings born but to view a happy state, which from the stubbornness of our nature, we must not inherit. Among the various works of Antiquity, all seem to have their admirers, whether Painting, History, or Poetry; and *their* will be found in every age,[22] or nation, that degree of veneration, which seems to hold them as sacred, and gives them at least a superiority over all things modern, yet after this it must be a matter of serious regret, that so much of the principle of moral philosophy, should not be selected as seems to have been the chief ornament of every state, and the most potent staff of every individual. If we look back into the remote pages of History, we find that honor was the foundation of every social virtue. Honor raised kingdoms and protected thrones, Honor united Friends and conquered enemies, and indeed Honor was but another name for virtue's self. Shakespeare seems to have treated it well in the form of Honesty in the quarrel of Brutus and Cassius. He places the impetuous Cassius in

---

20 Cp. Williams, *The Moral Tendencies of Knowledge*: 'The first genuine tendency of true knowledge is *humility*' (p. 22).

21 *The Tatler*, no. 251 (16 November 1710): 'there is nothing honourable which is not accompanied with innocence; nothing mean, but what has guilt in it.' In the form quoted, however, the maxim was included in several collections of extracts, including Thomas Tomkins' *Rays of Genius Collected to Enlighten the Rising Generation* (London: Longman, Hurst, Reese and Orme, 1806), p. 156.

22 '*Their*': underlined to indicate the error in spelling.

an ungovernable rage, with his drawn dagger, threatening the life of his colleague; when Brutus replies with all the coolness of the noble Roman,

"O Cassius, there is no terror in your threats;
"For I am arm'd so strong in Honesty,
"That they pass me as the idle wind,
"Which I respect not.[23]

And yet there is so little stability in the glories of the moderns, that it has been the labour of ages to find how to give validity to promise, or security to common intercourse.

A more concise manner of remarking the fallen state of mankind, cannot be resorted to than by a simple comparison in the leading features of society in a remote age, and those of the present. Everyone must be capable (even from the most early stages of life) of observing the various intricacies of the law, and perhaps with all their provision and multiplicity of clauses, they are but a small portion of what is yet to come, that innumerable volumes must yet be written, and every succeeding generation must still find them insufficient, how few the transactions in civil intercourse without the binding security of the law, that even between brothers, that even between Parents and Children, and more than all between Friends, their is no validity even in the most simple affairs without the watchful barrier of the law.

It will not be an object consistent with the present view to complain of the unaptness of the law, nor to dwell long on the unequal dispensation of justice; but how few the laws that governed larger and wiser states must (in comparison with our own) shew that little of that superior disposition which inherited the breasts of the antients has descended to us, and though a noble Ancestry be the boast of kings, they are but the weak and distant shallows from a nobler Fount.

The greatest display of this virtue may always be seen in each state, when at the highest condition of prosperity, so we may naturally infer that honor was consistent with the happiness of individuals and the general prosperity of kingdoms. Among the Heraclidae, the Scythians, Greeks, Parthians and Romans it shone with more than ordinary brightness.[24] It seemed to inspire Courage, Generosity, and a Reverence for the Deities

---

23 Shakespeare, *Julius Caesar*, IV.3.
24 Heraclidae: the descendents of Heracles.

in every nation, while the History of each, supplies us with a boundless number of examples, of Heroism, and virtuous conflicts.

The Spanish Historians relate a memorable instance of Honor, and regard to truth. A Spanish Cavalier in a sudden quarrel slew a Moorish Gentleman, and fled. His pursuers soon lost sight of him, for he had unperceived thrown himself over a garden wall. The owner, a Moor, happening to be in the Garden, was addressed by the Spaniard on his knees, who acquainted him with his case, and implored concealment. "Eat this" said the Moor (giving him half an apple) "you now know that you may confide in my protection" He then locked him up in his Garden apartment, telling him as soon as it was night, he would provide for his escape to a place of greater safety. The Moor then went into his house, where he had just seated himself, when a great crowd with loud cries and lamentations, came to his gate, bringing in the corpse of his Son, who had just been killed by a Spaniard. When the first shock of surprise was a little over, he learnt from the description given, that the fatal deed was done by the very person in his power. He mentioned this to no one; but as soon as it was dark retired to his Garden, as if to grieve alone, giving orders that none should follow him. Then accosting the Spaniard, he said "Christian, the person you have killed is my Son, his body is now in my house. You ought to suffer; but you have eaten with me; and I have given you my faith, which must not be broken" He then led the astonished Spaniard to his stables, and mounting him on one of his fleetest horses, said, "Fly far, while the night can cover you; you will be safe in the morning. You are indeed guilty of my Son's blood: but God is just and good, and I thank him I am innocent of your's, and that my faith given is preserved"[25]

The various Stories of Camillus the Roman Dictator (his generous triumph over the Falisci) or of Brutus or Fabricius, Crassus or Demosthenes[26] would all serve to illustrate the Dignity of Virtue and will prove as the Poet say's

---

25   This entire story (from 'A Spanish Cavalier' to 'my faith given is preserved') is plagiarized from Benjamin Franklin, *A Narrative of the Late Massacres in Lancaster County* (1764).

26   Classical instances of honourable behaviour. Camillus (c. 446–365 BC), laying siege to the city of Falerii, refused to accept the hostages brought to him by a Faliscan traitor. Gaius Fabricius Luscinus was (according to Plutarch) unbribable. In Shakespeare's *Julius Caesar*, Brutus is frequently (and sometimes ironically) described in terms of his honour.

"The richest treasure of a generous breast,
That gives the stamp and standard of the rest;
Wit, Strength, and Courage are wild dangerous force,
Unless this soften and direct the course.[27]

August. 1818. E.

On Argument MF.[28]

Many a time have I been present, when in consequence of singular, but inadvertent associations, two persons have been engaged in an argument, or rather perhaps were approaching towards it, without being at all aware of the circumstance. And, I have often observed at those times, that one, or perhaps both, instead of answering directly to what has been advanced, start off from the fair open path of the conversation, and break it up, or conclude it, by attributing foolish or improper opinions to the opponent; which are unwarrantably asserted, either by word or manner, to be not worth answering.

Now though we may expect of persons, who let their conversation run so irregularly as to get into an argument before they are aware of it, that they would treat it in a somewhat loose and immethodical manner, I know of no right, nor can I conceive of any, by which a person is entitled to call that foolish, false, or improper, which he cannot answer. It is easy to say *Yes*, and *No*, particularly when the speaker will assign no reasons to support his monosyllables; and it is easy to assume an appearance of sagacity and experience, and give unjust censure the dress which belongs only to correct criticism. It is also easy for a man to imagine that his own views of things, however partial and imperfect they may be, are right; but these facilities do not by any means make such modes and feelings just, nor is a man's wisdom increased in proportion to the good opinion he has of himself.

---

27   Charles Montague, Earl of Halifax, 'The Man of Honour' (from *The Poetical Works* (1716)), ll. 33–36.

28   Faraday's monogram is written in a different ink; it is impossible to say when the monogram was added. Joseph Agassi identifies this paper as by Faraday ('An Unpublished Paper of the Young Faraday', *Isis*, 52 (1961), 87–90), though he points out that L. Pearce Williams, the Faraday scholar and biographer, disagreed over the attribution and showed Agassi that the initials following the title of the essay 'are not Faraday's usual initials' (p. 90).

That *every* one has a right to enjoy his own opinion is allowed; but that *any* one may condemn the opinion of another is denied. Why should I borrow the reason of another, or place my own in subjection to it? Why should I go elsewhere for what nature has planted in my own breast?—I should be the very meanest of all beings, so to degrade my nature—but I should also be the most tyrannical of the human race, if I wished, and endeavoured, to make my opinion govern all others. For I am not entitled, 'though I have a mind within myself, to make other men, who also are supplied within, of my mind too.—I am made, as to reason, independant; each other man is also independant, and therefore the opinion of one is worth just as much as that of another; and if it should happen to be unanswerable, it certainly ought not to be contemned.—I claim no privilege for individuals, except that of Liberty; no exemption, but from impertinence: but I would have that elevation destroyed which some are pleased to assume to themselves—An elevation, which though in the fancy of the possesser, it has an imposing dignity, in reality only serves to lift him up to contemptuous observation.

If those who are so ready to condemn an opinion before they have heard the arguments for it, were capable of viewing the whole subject at once; they would soon become concious[29] of the many blunders they make about persons and things, by their hasty and irregular manner. By the very act of condemning unheard, they assume that they themselves know every thing, the person before them nothing: it is, therefore, not much afterwards to give the offender any character that may be convenient, and they are always ready to say with the Inquisition "Gallileo was a heretic and deserved to be burnt because he said the earth moved round the Sun."[30]

It is also an injustice to an argument, to quote contrary opinions without supporting them; or to compare the opposite opinions of the *same* person. Nothing of this kind proves, that what has last been said, is either right or wrong. It only shews that other persons, or perhaps the same person, thought differently at other times.—Because I said yesterday, that St Paul's church was larger than St. Peter's, and to day that St. Peter's is the largest of the two,[31] no one can advance the contradiction as a proof

---

29   'Concious': not crossed through, but 'scious' inserted above the line in different ink.
30   Cp. below, pp. 121–23, 'On prematurely Forming Opinion of Characters'.
31   There is a discussion of the relative merits of St Paul's in London and St Peter's in Rome in a review of Thomas Malton's 'Picturesque Tour through the Cities of London and Westminster', *Monthly Review*, 41 (1803), 295–305, esp. 300, 304. Faraday had

that *neither* is largest: the only thing is, that it diminishes confidence, but does not affect argument.

Neither can a person's own discrepancies in actions with his principles, be urged against those principles: as is very often absurdly done. If the tradesman who commends Honesty, enters into all the knavish tricks and customs, which though dishonest, have escaped the law, and are legal; nay, even thoug he should offend outright against his own lax and convenient opinions, still, his secession would not compromise honesty, or make it a jot the more unworthy. Nor are the principles of the Christian Religion at all injured, by that entire want in many of its professors of what is sincere, honest, and virtuous.—Indeed every argument must depend upon itself for support; or, must be destroyed by argument fairly opposed to it.

To conclude man *is* independant of others for his opinions, and *ought* to be so. Every man has a right to form his own judgement; and, if he chooses, to decline hearing the judgement of others. But, no man has a right to force his judgement on others, nor even a title to have it heard, unless he can support it by argument.—Conviction frequently attends upon falsehood; Truth is often accompanied by scepticism; and, as no one can assert of others, that their conviction is well founded, each should be suspicious of that he has harboured in his own breast.

August. 1818.

On Imagination and Judgement

> "In every work regard the writers end
> "Since none can compass more than they intend.[32]

It is a common sentiment applied to a state of doubt or hesitation that *to make a beginning* is often more than half accomplishing an undertaking,

---

visited Rome in 1814 and commented to his mother in a letter of 14 April 1814 that he had seen 'St Peter's [...] and a vast variety of things far too numerous to enumerate' (*Correspondence*, I, p. 72). But the comparison may refer to two churches in London or to two in Rome.

32 Alexander Pope, 'Essay on Criticism' (1711), ll. 257–58. Like Isaac Watts, who suggested that no English poet 'has a richer and happier talent of painting to the life, or has ever discovered such a large and inexhausted variety of description' as Pope (Watts, *The Improvement of the Mind*, 'Of the Sciences and their Use', sect. 36), Faraday was an admirer of this poet and of his *Essays* in particular. He copied out 'Man never is, but always to be blessed' from the *Essay on Man* in CPB (I, p. 136).

in conformity to this maxim it will give me pleasure if I can prove that it has some foundation.[33] I shall endeavour to find out the cause of my own hesitation in the present case which if accomplished may in part do away with the difficulty in future.

Altho' we may be convinced that "resolutions will not execute themselves"[34] and although we may have every inclination necessary to commence the pursuit of a laudable object yet there is a much greater difficulty in following up an idea which reason teaches us is for our benefit, than that which is spontaneously dictated by the imagination.

The imagination is continually supplied by means of our senses either at the time or by recollection of what has passed through them[35] I suppose the ideas are merely formed from the simple appearance of things which the imagination delights in transforming or exchanging however devoid of truth, to endless variety—But Judgement by ratiocination will endeavour to find out the cause by the effects centre its exertions and allow of no deviation from its object except that which it feels is necessary for its accomplishment. Suppose for instance I watch the flitting of the summer clouds their fantastic forms and beautiful variety I may continue to gaze with secret satisfaction in a state nearly allied to thoughtlessness or I may by Fancy led wander in the realms of Fairy land and see shepherds with their flocks, woods castles mountains of snow and as great a variety as there are changes in the scene.[36]

This I consider the province of Imagination It requires no exertion of the mind but naturally produces a considerable degree of sensitive pleasure Now I think if we endeavour to trace the feeling which is connected with

---

33   E.g. John Ray, *A Compleat Collection of English Proverbs [...]*, (London: Allman *et al.*, 1817), p. 54: 'Well begun is half done'.

34   Johnson, *The Rambler*, no. 193 (21 January 1752).

35   This is an important principle of late eighteenth- and early nineteenth-century aesthetic theory: see for example Edmund Burke, 'Introduction: On Taste', in *A Philosophical Inquiry into the Origins of our Ideas of the Beautiful and the Sublime* (1757): 'the imagination [...] can only vary the disposition of those ideas which it has received from the senses.' Perhaps the most important sources of this view come from Locke's *Essay*, II, ch. 2, §: 'it is not in the power of the most exalted wit, or enlarged understanding, by any quickness or variety of thought, to INVENT or FRAME one new simple idea in the mind, not taken in by [sensation or reflection].'

36   Faraday was interested in clouds and had in the past been a cloud-spotter: cp. his letter to Abbott, 20 July 1812: 'from thence I went home Sky-gazing and earnestly looking out for every Cirrus, Cumulus, Stratus, Cirro-Cumuli, Cirro-Strata and Nimbus that came above the Horizon' (*Correspondence*, I, p. 8).

judgement we shall find a very considerable difference. Suppose while I am contemplating the clouds I wish to know the nature of their formation my mind would (provided it was capable) immediately have recourse to first principles simple substances gaseous bodies and exhalations their separate natures combinations and appearances with the effects of light &c.[37] Thus I should by Induction endeavour to ascertain what the clouds are and why they have such a appearance—This operation of the mind produces no pleasure of sense but on the contrary a degree of pain owing to the necessary concentration of the mental powers to one object for a lenghten'd time. It is by this we overcome apathy and impart a motion to our mental inertia[38] 'Tis upon this position that I imagine ratiocination is so irksome and in opposition to the *almost* universal inclination that pervades mankind that they would rather though convinced the contrary is for their good, follow the airy whims of Imagination

Still I consider that Imagination owes as much to judgement as judgement does to imagination When a decision is made Imagination immediately enlists it under its banner to enrich and increase the extent of its operations. Altho' the feeling arising from judgement is not a sensitive pleasure it is of a nobler kind 'Tis an extension of our powers apparently by our own exertions an exaltation of our nature which produces self complacency—Judgement is united to learning its employment is the finding differences and truth is its offspring while imagination is busy in tracing likeness and wit is the result[39]—It would be too much perhaps to say which produces the greatest satisfaction but certainly that resulting

---

37 A paper by the chemist and meteorologist Luke Howard on 'The Natural History of Clouds', reprinted from the *Philosophical Magazine* and the *New Cyclopaedia*, appeared in William Nicholson's *Journal of Natural Philosophy, Chemistry, and the Arts*, 30 (1812), 35–62.

38 Cp. Faraday's essay 'Observations on the Inertia of the Mind', below, pp. 187–98.

39 Cp. Hugh Blair, 'A Critical Dissertation on the Poems of Ossian', in James Macpherson (trans.), *The Poems of Ossian*, 3 vols. (London: Miller, 1812), I, pp. 79–243 (p. 198): 'the judgement is principally exercised in distinguishing objects, and remarking the differences among those which seem like; so the highest amusement of the imagination is to trace likenesses and agreements among those which seem different.' CPB (I, p. 385) notes the location of a passage in George Harvey's *Ossian's Fingal: An Ancient Epic Poem* (London, 1814). Another source which CPB indicates that Faraday was at least acquainted with, George Campbell's *Philosophy of Rhetoric* (2 vols. (Edinburgh: Constable *et al.*, 1816)), comments similarly in distinguishing between 'ratiocination' and imagination: 'what gives the principal delight to the imagination is the exhibition of a strong likeness, which escapes the notice of the generality of people' (I, pp. 166–67).

from judgement is the noblest and that of imagination the most enticing but where a union of the two takes place in a strong degree there there will always be a great cause for our admiration. The fairest fruits are the highest hung and few there are who can reach them.—It is a wise dispensation of the Deity that as for the health of the body exercise is made absolutely necessary so it is for the mind; to drive away ignorance and superstition and to keep in proper bounds the delusive vapours of Imagination.[40]

Having endeavoured to prove that an undertaking like ours requires some compulsion or exertion to *those* who *have not* habituated themselves to reason upon one subject we may perhaps find other causes which increase the difficulty—In the present case it may be that the mind has conceived a plan which of itself is of so general and extensive a nature (its own improvement) that it requires still to be divided and subdivided before it can decide where to settle therefore it is not the want but the superabundance of subjects which present themselves that are the cause of difficulty. The mind wanders about as if lost in the extent of country to which it has been so lately admitted strange to every thing around it has only the inclination to become acquainted without the power to decide where to commence its system of research[41] It is misled with the extended view in the distance it wanders through the mazy valleys of knowledge and is thunderstruck at the towering hills of science.

Here many are lost their spirits fail them they believe it is only for birds of stronger wing to attempt the boundless flight.[42] But we must return[43] back to the door which admitted us and commence our Journey with

---

40   Cp. below, p. 129, 'On Conscious Approbation', 'vapours and phantoms of his imagination.'

41   Cp. Faraday's description of the sublimity of astronomy in a letter to Abbott, 11 June 1813: 'the subject is so immense that the mind is lost in the contemplation of it [...] A mind engaged for too great a length of time amongst such illustrations and on such matter would become lost & confused and unable to follow rightly the path of reasoning that the subject requires' (*Correspondence*, I, p. 62).

42   This sentence and the final one of the previous paragraph suggest an adaptation or perhaps an echo of James Beattie's poem, 'Elegy' (written in 1758), frequently excerpted and anthologized through the first decades of the nineteenth century: 'Reason's meteor-rays [...] / Disclosing dubious to th'affrighted eye / O'erwhelming mountains tottering from on high, / [...] / And weary ways in wildering labyrinths lost. / O happy stroke, that burst the bonds of clay, / [...] / And wings the soul with boundless flight to soar' (in Beattie, *The Minstrel, or, The Progress of Genius, with Other Poems* (London: Rivington *et al.*, 1811), pp. 26–29 (p. 29). Beattie, unlike Faraday, is offering an optimistic vision of death.

43   Return: 're' struck through.

a different and a shorter view with modest but persevering exertions[44] Careful that we are not led astray by the flowers of the imagination which are more fascinating than the useful herbs of reason It is easier to flutter from blossom to blossom inhaling the sweets and delighting the sense with the odours of Fancy than to settle upon and find out by experience the intrinsic value of the more useful though not so obtrusive qualities of the herbs of reason These though bitter at first to the taste only require time to relish them and will soon prove tonics and invigorators of the mind.[45]

Again the difficulty of commencing this plan of improvement may arise from finding one'self in some measure confined to method. We feel it necessary that our first essay should be in the style of a preface and therefore not having the choice of a subject the mind is compell'd to enter though unwillingly into the first attempt while the very circumstances which should be the spur to our exertions are the means which retard the accomplishment of so easy a task.[46] The conciousness of our inability to perform with elegance or even accuracy that which we never before attempted, the want of words to express the few and shallow notions we may have of a subject and the want of practice in arranging them at this time become very officious they are the enemies we have to conquer 'tis their last expiring effort for we are resorting to the very means which will liberate us from their paralysing influence for ever.

Persevere and our improvement is certain We shall trace with pleasure the visible alteration in the style and substance of our essays we shall be delighted with the ease with which we perform what at first appeared so formidable.—I expect to read this paper at no distant period with a triumphant pleasure at my success well convinced that these means will give me clearer views of subjects with which mankind are by nature so much interested.

Y. August. 1818.

---

44   Cp. Johnson, The Rambler, no. 137: 'the widest excursions of the mind are made by short flights frequently repeated' (see below, p. 217).

45   Bitter herbs: Exodus 12.8.

46   Cp. the first number of Johnson's Rambler (20 March 1749): 'The difficulty of the first address on any new occasion, is felt by every man in his transactions with the world, and confessed by the settled and regular forms of salutation which necessity has introduced into all languages. [...] Perhaps few authors have presented themselves before the publick, without wishing that such ceremonial modes of entrance had been anciently established, as might have freed them from those dangers which the desire of pleasing is certain to produce, and precluded the vain expedients of softening censure by apologies, or rousing attention by abruptness.'

Hope[47]

In those ages of the world, when man was young in the witcheries, and arts, of Society; and when he existed in the state in which the Gods had placed him; Hope reigned over all his thoughts and wishes, with undisputed and uninterrupted power: and, also, with an infallibility, which the beings of later ages know not. The celestial powers had made man a little below themselves; but they had given him hope, who supplied what was wanting, and made him equal to the deities. No deception, no disappointment attended her. Wherever she came, she made happiness; for wherever she came she promised better things, and her promises never came short of performance.

At first Man was contented. He found a world for him full of good things, and enjoyed them. But, his nature was formed to be progressive. His state was intended to be changeable, and each moment was to improve him. Though contented with the present, he felt an impulse urging him on to an improved future; and Hope sanctioned the feeling. Gifted with powers far surpassing those of any other created thing, Idleness would have been a crime: Already raised to such eminence by the powers above him, what else had he not reason to expect from them: The results therefore of his own exertions, and the favours of the Gods, lay before him; and only required time to make them his.

The constant employment of Hope, was, to show man those things which were to reward his exertions. She presented him with a view of futurity; which being always subordinate to existing means, had, in the distance, a prototype, the sure termination of a regular chain of causes and effects. She cheered Man, by bringing almost into his possession, the object, to the attainment of which his exertions were directed; and she only removed it to replace it by the reality. Constantly hovering before him, her glass made the distant thing seem near; the object before confused, and irregular, distinct, and defined. Man saw his path more clearly; he trod in it with more alacrity; and rested in success.

---

47   'The Rev. Simon Olive-branch' (the pseudonym of William Roberts) published derisive comments on the fashion for literary beginners to write about hope in his periodical *The Looker-On* (25 January 1794): 'An *Address to Hope—Lines to Hope—Sonnet on Hope*—or an *Acrostic on Hope*, form the usual first attempts of the rhyming tribe. In truth, we have sung the praises of Hope, until it has become a duty, whatever we may *feel*, to join in the chorus' (reprinted in Alexander Chalmers (ed.), *The British Essayists* (London: Johnson *et al.*, 1808), vol. 44, pp. 189–99 (pp. 189–90).

But Hope was no pander to hasty, improper, unfounded wishes. Extravagant desires disappeared before her; Imaginary objects vanished in her presence. Every thing, seen through her glass, had a real existence; for visions, and fancies, could not exist beyond it.—She constantly cheered and encouraged, but she sometimes corrected and moderated.

In addition to the admirable powers and sensations, with which man had been furnished, for the support of his existence, his prosperity, and his nature; other influences and feelings, had been added, to elevate the character of his pleasures: and, to render him, at the same time, more susceptible of exalted enjoyment, and more abundant in its sources.— Sensibility rendered him more delicate of perception; Courage, more independant; Confidence placed him more at ease; Freedom was given him, that he might exult in its exhilarating influence; and Conscience, though no barrier to its extension, was a Monitor against its abuse.

Whilst man retained his true claim to that title, by acting in accordance with his gifted nature, all these influences and impulses ranged themselves with hope; and each, in their several way, aided her exertions. Sensibility called Man's attention to her promises; Courage, and Confidence, secured their fulfilment; Freedom, Conscience, and the other powers, were active in directing him rapidly and rightly; in varying the views of hope; and in contributing to the final end of improvement, enjoyment, and happiness.

In union with the Liberty which man enjoyed, was the Will. This was formed with an implied subjection to the Reason; and, was the power which commanded what that directed. In the excess of Liberty, however, which it enjoyed, it could depart from the dictates of reason; but it then always tended to injure either one part or another of the system of humanity, and produced a certain effect of deterioration.

It may be observed, that, the will was essential to the well-being of man; inasmuch, as it not only had a powerful influence in retarding, or stimulating, all mental sensations; but, was the important agent, by which the mind operated on the corporeal parts of the system. It could produce nothing but good when every influence possessed its due power; because the welfare, the improvement, and the happiness, were inseparably linked together.

But, unfortunately, the will was not always guided in its commands by attention to every necessary influence; and it at times directed acts, which, though they accorded with the Sensations considered, opposed others which were left unnoticed. It was generally, more inclined to favour present and sentient influences, than those which regarded distant and spiritual relations; and, it at times gave way to the immediate gratification of a particular passion, though it thereby ensured a certain diminution of the happiness of a future time.

Still more unfortunately, Habits, which had insensibly been placed on man to preserve him as he was made, perfect and happy, gave their passive influences to these departures from rectitude; and rendered them more and more frequent, until at last, even the Mental powers themselves, being subordinate to them, were changed in their nature, and became mere monsters. A sort of degenerated race, unlike what they were, though somewhat resembling their past images in form and appearance.—They were now constantly changing; sometimes powerful, sometimes weak; sometimes governing others, sometimes being governed; and, instead of commanding, and causing, circumstances, and things; they seemed subordinate to, and dependant on them. Sensibility, at times made man mad; at others, it disappeared, and humanity, pity, affection, and numberless other good influences, withdrew with it. Courage, became mere Rashness; and exerted itself indifferently to obtain both good and bad ends. Freedom, was of the will alone; for it had resigned some powers to the shackles of prejudice, others to the gyves of habit; and Reason itself walked heavily laden with chains and fetters. Emulation, became Ambition; Independance, Tyranny; Ease, Idleness; Cautiousness, Cowardice; Respect, Servility; Pity, Contempt; Self knowledge, Egotism; Carefulness, Avarice; Enjoyment, Sensuality; and every influence was in some way altered, and debased.

Hope beheld the ruins of human nature with regret. She feared that her power with man was utterly destroyed, or useless: but willing to inspire him to better things, held her glass before him. The passions resumed their wonted office; but it was no longer assistance they brought, but interference; and Man, looking through their medium, saw all things distorted and changed. For a cottage, he beheld a Palace: for sufficiency, profusion. He saw joys awaiting him, where there were none: and what contained abundant pleasure, appeared to him, a vacant, blank, space.— Hope held before him the respect and good opinion of his fellows; what *were* Emulation and Independance, offered their means, but Ambition and Tyranny only gained for him, censure, and hatred. Hope offered him pleasures; but Sensuality disappointed him.

Since that time, Hope has been constantly charged with the disappointments which man incurs, from the misguiding influence of his passions. She has been called Fickle, Uncertain, Evasive; and made the constant companion of deception. But, thus degraded in character, and opposed by the united powers of her rebellious, natural allies; she is still the being that cheer's man's existence, and makes life supportable. She, of what the Gods gave, has only had her powers diminished: the rest have been altered either in part, or entirely. She is constantly active in elevating the results of rectitude, and urging man to reform; but the rest are the slaves of circumstances.

After this fatal revolution in the Mental powers of life, she called in Experience to her aid; and he, actively engaged in the combat with them, continually exposes their fallacies, and imperfections; and dispels their illusions. Man, weak Man,[48] placed under the influence of both, is sometimes the devotee of one side, sometimes the slave of the other: but, even in his most degraded state, he carries with him the conviction, (though at times almost rendered latent,) that, experience is an infallible guide, and that Hope never disappoints, when introduced by Reason, and Virtue.

Aug. 1818.

On General Character

There is such a degree of pleasure in the perusal of the various works of eminent authors, that whenever we return to them, it seems like the revival of an old acquaintance, or the meeting a friend who has long been absent. We sometimes know of what they are about to treat, but find out their peculiar excellence by the search of diligence, or a sort of conversation with them, and deduce their merits or demerits according to our own judgements. We find in some much that we admire; in others part that we doubt: and in many that we would wish to dispute with them, were they alive, or present, but for the want of this opportunity, we are content to argue in our own minds their truth, or fallacy and seek partisans and advocates among our contemporaries

There is an Essay by Johnson, which from its peculiar tenets, can never be forgotten by any of those who have read that Author; it is that which

---

48 'Man, weak Man': this phrase appears in a variety of eighteenth-century poems, including John Gay's 'Fable VI: The Miser and Plutus', in Gay, *Fables* (London: Rivington *et al.*, 1816), pp. 18–20 (p. 19): (addressing gold) 'O bane of good! seducing cheat! / Can man, weak man, thy pow'r defeat?'

treats of the various turns or Characterics of the mind, from infancy to decrepitude.[49] In it our author, with a great deal of ability and argument, endeavours to point out the various passions, and their general influence or time of empire in the Soul, and places them in such a happy order of Succession, that if it were universal it would secure us from every effect of chance, and make us go on like a piece of machinery from stage to stage, till the wearing of wheels or some other consequent defection would put an end to our work. He gives it as his opinion that this succession of passions, or changes of the mind is general and remote.[50] If it were general it certainly must be very remote: it were happy for mankind if it were general, but I think it is so far from being the case that we continually see characters in the great Theatre of the world, who enter, pass through the whole course of action, and make their exit, without leaving any proof, of the inheritance of any second passion whatever, though there may be a little worldly policy that has dictated some deviation in them.[51] It is true, that particular passions are frequently or almost universally predominant in man at one age or other, yet there is little of that rotation obvious in ordinary life which our author endeavours to point out not even to the "eye of the vigilant spectator"[52]

If this rotation were universal, men would treat each other according to their ages, or according to the discipline necessarily attendant on that period of life; and opinions would be current as the coin of the realm, and would rise, or fall, in each topic; by the supposed influence of the then reigning passion. Johnson is well known to have had a very just conception of this matter, but I must confess that it is too remote for my observance, or else he has not been sufficiently explicit on that subject.

It is the great Misfortune of our nature, that we inherit some particular passion more or less to the end of our lives, and that so few have the charity to consider it an infirmity to which themselves are subject in other shapes. In some it is a self approbation which in many instances

---

49   *The Rambler*, no. 151 (27 August 1751).

50   'Yet, amidst all the disorder and inequality which variety of discipline, example, conversation, and employment, produce in the intellectual advances of different men, there is still discovered, by a vigilant spectator, such a general and remote similitude, as may be expected in the same common nature affected by external circumstances indefinitely varied' (*The Rambler*, no. 151).

51   Perhaps cp. Shakespeare, *As You Like It*, II.7 ('All the world's a stage') (see below, n. 61).

52   See above, n. 49.

is carried to such extreme points, that we are obliged by our feelings to have a contempt for those we would wish to respect, merely from the rooted foundation of prejudice. As one might advance in opposition to all received opinions, that the earth stands still and the sun performs its revolutionary task because in the early part of the scriptures there is some mention of it.[53] Others will condemn all the research of the Natural Philosopher, and treat the ascension in balloons,[54] and the search into the electric fluid of the clouds,[55] as acts not to be countenanced by any moral christians, and will view them as unpardonable impieties; these are instances when found among those with whom we are immediately acquainted, if we would not feel anger we must have pity.

There is a powerful degree of obstinacy to be observed through the whole tenor of the actions of some men, which Johnson places as a passion attending on the decline of life, and though it may be common to some in all times of life, it is certainly more prevalent at that period.[56] In the 82nd Rambler he has but too much caricatured the stubborn state in which the mind is sometimes fettered, though in many cases it would be found equally difficult to convince men, that the notions and principles imbibed by them were erroneous, with the Virtuoso who would prefer the antiquity of Maps and Charts totally incorrect, to all the Geographical discoveries since the flood[57]

Among all the Candidates for public esteem there are few if any who have past their lives without having performed something worthy the admiration of their fellow creatures, yet there seems such a universal competition for the palm of fame, that each must reduce all others to a state of useless pastime, in order to give consequence to his own pursuits;

---

53 For example, Genesis 19.23: 'The sun was risen upon the earth when Lot entered into Zoar.'

54 The first manned balloon flight was made in Paris in 1783 in a balloon designed by the Montgolfier brothers.

55 Cp. Benjamin Franklin, letter of September 1753 on the electricity of clouds, in e.g. *The Complete Works*, 3 vols. (London: Johnson *et al.*, 1806), I, 269–84.

56 *The Rambler*, no. 151, on old age: 'the opinions are settled, and the avenues of apprehension shut against any new intellligence'. And cp. Johnson, *Rasselas* (ch. 29): 'When the desultory levity of youth has settled into regularity, it is soon succeeded by pride, ashamed to yield, or obstinacy delighting to contend.'

57 *The Rambler*, no. 82 (29 December 1750) is an imaginary letter from an obsessive scientific collector, who describes himself as 'the most laborious and zealous Virtuoso.' Among other things, he has collected 'the maps drawn in the rude and barbarous times, before any regular surveys, or just observations.'

as the Man of science vies with the man of literature and those of the various branches of science vie with each other, 'til[58] what was once called the republic of letters and science, has become a revolting democracy.

Sometimes there is such an eagerness shewn in the pursuits of some men, that they cannot for a moment allow any utility in those of another; as the Historian in following the various Heroes of antiquity through their great achievements watching their hazards, their perils, and their conquests, would say at the foot of Mount Athos "here have I traced the greatest the most magnimous of monarchs"; and if I should behold a Xerxes cutting a Promontary in two to transport his Millions of souls,[59] or if this mountain were cut into the statue of an Alexander, with his cities rising in his hands what does it signify to me if it were composed of granite of freestone or of marble?[60] There is no war in this Element, nor was it in the wisdom of clay or stone, that conquered Persia, or placed the noble crown on the head of Ptolemy.

As this world is (in the words of Shakespear) but a stage,[61] it is necessary that there should be men of all characters, to make the play complete; yet it cannot be imagined that Envy can add dignity to any but must render the breast in which it finds inheritance truly despicable.

E. Aug. 1818.

On the Pleasures and Uses of the Imagination

In my first essay, I endeavoured to shew the difference, existing between the execution of a work of the Imagination, and one of the reasoning powers of Judgement.[62] I intend now, to make a few observations on the pleasures which are derived from the Imagination, and on the use which the cultivation of those powers, may be of to us; particularly in the study of language, and in the increase of our enjoyments from those arts or sciences, that are directly under the protection of the muses.

---

58   'Til': originally 'till', second 'l' crossed through.
59   The Persian king Xerxes cut a canal through the Athos promontory in order to avoid having to sail around it to invade Greece.
60   The Greek architect Dinocrates, who designed Alexandria, proposed to cut Mount Athos into an immense statue of Alexander the Great, holding a city in one hand. 'Freestone': sandstone or limestone that can be cut easily (OED).
61   Shakespeare, *As You Like It*, II.7.
62   'On Imagination and Judgement', above, pp. 51–55.

I mentioned, that the effect of judgement on the mind was not a sensitive pleasure; but, that of the Imagination was; now, I think we shall find upon further consideration, the pleasures of the Imagination to be of a much superior and more refined class than sensual pleasures; and still differing from those of the judgement.[63]

Our sight is the parent of the greater part of the ideas belonging to the Imagination; and so wonderfully comprehensive and powerful in supplying us with them, owing to its extensive range, and rapid conveyance to the mind, that it appears to be the most perfect of our senses; and most admirably adapted to this particular province.[64] Although the sense of feeling would give us ideas of the bulk and form of objects, yet how limited would be its extent, and how confined the pleasure from that source, even though aided by the other senses of Hearing, Taste, and Smell.[65]—I consider, these last must greatly assist; although the ideas we have by memory of a fine odour, a ravishing harmony, or a delicious flavour, are not always combined with an image; and which I do not think is absolutely essential to those pleasures: The finest composition of an eminent Musician was written after a dream, in which his fancy had conjured up the devil playing a most delightful piece; his own although very fine, he acknowledged had but a slight resemblance to this

---

63　This essay is strongly influenced by Addison's famous *Spectator* papers (411–21) 'On the Pleasures of the Imagination', which were originally published in June 1712. Peter Mack is among the historians who have highlighted the importance of Addison's *Spectator* papers as stylistic models for eighteenth- and early nineteenth-century students of literary writing ('Addison's Essays as Models for Composition in School Anthologies and Textbooks of the Eighteenth and Nineteenth Centuries', *Paradigm*, 13 (1994), pp. 42–52). The first paper in this sequence, on which Faraday modelled his own essay most closely, argues that the pleasures of the imagination 'are not so gross as those of sense, nor so refined as those of the understanding.' This sentence is used as an example in Benjamin Smart's course on rhetoric which Faraday attended, and at which he took extremely full notes (CPB, I, pp. 177–321) in January 1818 (Smart, *The Theory of Elocution, Exhibited in Connexion with a New and Philosophical Account of the Nature of Instituted Language* (London: printed for the author, 1819), p. 93.

64　Like Addison, Faraday begins with a discussion of sight. In this first sentence, Faraday repeats Addison's praise for sight's ability to cover large distances and his description of sight as 'the most perfect [of] our senses' (Addison, paper 411).

65　Cp. Addison: 'The sense of feeling can indeed give us a notion of extension, shape, and all other ideas that enter at the eye, except colours; but at the same time it is very much strained, and confined in its operations, to the number, bulk, and distance of its particular objects' (paper 411).

harmonious product of his Imagination.[66] In this case it is likely, he did combine an image or cause of the music; no doubt the devil and his own favourite instrument; but, there are times, and it is then that the Imagination is most delighted, and exercised, as in the tales of fiction or of magic, where we often find these senses pleased, without being able to form ideas of the cause, or to combine any image with the gratification. The taste, as it appears to me to be a grosser sense, and more connected with matter, is not so easy to separate; but with the other two, we may certainly be in raptures without an idea of the cause. However, when they have been once combined with images received by the sight, they are so in future at will; as it is, in language we often use the cause instead of the effect; and it is possible to find in one descriptive piece of poetry, that the senses have formed an union to raise the finest images, and most delightful feelings of the imagination.—It is evident after all, that it is to the sight we must ascribe the greatest honor, owing to its extensive powers, as mentioned in the beginning.

A sensitive mind will always acknowledge the pleasures it receives, from a luxuriant prospect of nature; the beautiful mingling and gradations of colour, the delicate perspective, the ravishing effect of light and shade, and the fascinating variety and grace of the outline, must be seen to be felt; for expression can never convey the extatic joy they give to the imagination, or the benevolent feeling they create in the mind: There is no boundary, there is no restraint 'till reason draws the rein, and then imagination retires into its recesses, and delivers herself up to the guidance of that superior power.—Milton has beautifully lamented his loss of sight, which deprived him of those reviving pleasures; but it did not prevent him from enjoying them by recollection; and it cannot be doubted, that his descriptions were enriched and enhanced by the privation.[67] His works remain a masterpiece of Imagination.

Thus those images which we have once received, we can resuscitate and vary to our own fancy however luxuriant; the power never forsakes us, we can indulge ourselves with it either in the field or in the closet; in the light of day or in the darkness of night; but those times I think produce the finest ideas, when they are entirely from memory, and when all the senses

---

66   Probably a reference to Giuseppe Tartini's violin sonata in G minor (the 'Devil's Trill Sonata'), said to have been the composer's attempt to record the music he heard the devil playing for him in a dream.

67   Probably a reference to Milton's sonnet, 'When I consider how my light is spent' (publ. 1673).

are at rest.—What a field for the Imagination, (as well as the Reason,) is exposed by the powers of the microscope, the telescope, and the discoveries in natural philosophy. How it wanders in the infinite divisibility of matter, or in the immensity of space; how can we restrain it in the contemplation of the heavenly bodies, as other systems; as other worlds. To describe it in all its operations would be impossible, but it is necessary to say, that the Imagination has an equal facility in forming ideas of the sublime, as well as of the beautiful; of the terrific, as well as the pleasing. But we are not considering the various degrees of effect which objects produce on the Imagination, although it is nearly connected with the subject; that would be entering into the cause of beauty, which at present we shall avoid: It is the effects and not the cause of these ideas which now occupy our attention. We are not considering, why certain objects produce peculiar effects; but knowing that they do so, our study is to find out, how to convey at pleasure these delightful emotions to the mind, and these pleasing images to the imagination.

As the situation in which a large proportion of mankind is placed, deprives them of a great source of these enjoyments; the scenes of nature; and as we are but seldom present when occurrences take place of extraordinary moment to us, as individuals, or to the world; we must have recourse to other means to create these pleasures. Sensibility is necessary to give the greatest zest for them, and a person must be born with it to enjoy them naturally; but as there is as great a variety and gradations of sensibility, as there is variety in our countenances, we must object to the monopoly of it by a few, and endeavour to cultivate that portion we inherit to our greatest advantage. The refinement of the mind is the cultivation of the imagination. Language is the first and most efficient agent we can employ, and I believe we may call it, the natural way of conveying to those who have been absent, circumstances that have taken place; and the nearer we can raise in their Imagination, ideas and feelings, corresponding, or superior to those that they would have entertained had they been present, to the greater perfection have we brought this means.— This is description; it is this which interests us every day; it is the business of the historian, and peculiarly the province of the Poet.

Men having never been found without possessing this means of intercourse, has induced me to call it natural; but it certainly is artificial; even in the present day, we are obliged to agree upon terms and names for things which are new to us, before we can understand each other; therefore being artificial, I conceive it will admit of the greatest improvement from art. If we suppose two men placed in an island by themselves, totally ignorant of each other's language, or of any language; would not their first endeavours be to agree upon names for substantives? we find it so with babes and foreigners: then I suppose, names for action or verbs; and so on; 'till they would soon be able to convey information to each other. Thus we find from the beginning, words are made use of to raise images or ideas in the Imagination. Therefore to use such words, a suitable style, and those figures in our language which are most likely to convey the ideas, and influence the passions we wish, should be our greatest care; especially in ornamental or poetical composition: and this is done, only by feeling the effect of our epithets, and the truth of our metaphors, comparisons, and other figures.

As I am only illustrating the pleasures of Imagination, it is not necessary for us to enter more minutely into this subject; except to give an example or two, where sound is also combined in producing a desired effect. Although Johnson seems rather to doubt the effect of words, except from the ideas or images which the mind connects with them, yet there are many who have had naturally a feeling for harmony inseparable from the poet who have thought and wrote otherwise.

Pope appears to have thought it essential, and has given examples of it in his Essay on criticism.[68]

> 'Tis not enough no harshness gives offence,
> The sound must seem an echo to the sense.
> Soft is the strain, when Zephyr gently blows;
> And the smooth stream in smoother numbers flows.
> But when loud surges lash the sounding shore,
> The *hoarse rough verse* should like the torrent roar.
> When Ajax strives some rocks *vast weight* to throw,
> The line too labours, and the words move slow.
> Not so when swift Camilla scours the plain,
> Flies oer th'unbending corn, and skims along the main.[69]

———

> On a sudden open fly
> With impetuous *recoil* and *jarring* sound

---

68   The 'Essay on Criticism' is also cited above, p. 52, as the epigraph to 'On Imagination and Judgment', and below, p. 129, as the epigraph to 'The Origin of a Critic'.
69   Pope, 'Essay on Criticism', ll. 366–75.

> Th'infernal doors; and on their hinges *grate*
> *Harsh* thunder;[70]

Johnson cannot conceive an idea of swiftness in the last line of the above quotation from Pope,[71] but if we observe, we shall find that the words have a liquid tendency, and an exceeding easy union; nor are we obliged materially to alter the position of our organs of speech in commencing each word, as we are in the example above it; as "*Rocks vast weight*"—; this produces undoubtedly a sensation of difficulty.

By paying attention to this food for the imagination we shall be able to receive, as well as impart, more pleasure in conversation, reading, &c and wherever language is concerned.

It would be an endless task to enumerate all the advantages of a polite or cultivated imagination. But a person possessing one has resources of enjoyment which the vulgar cannot conceive; he imbibes the feelings of the poet, he is present with characters and situations described, and is warmly interested in the catastrophe. He is the same with the statuary, or the painter;[72] in viewing a landscape he will penetrate into the recesses of a wood, bathe in the waters, explore the ruins of old castles, or disappear behind some heath clad hill, no doubt in quest of something that appears but faintly described in the distance: he will continue in chace of some meteor of the fancy, 'till he is found wandering by reason; who will be sure to bring him safe back, well pleased with his flight; or perhaps some friend by a slap on the back, will wake him from his reverie, at the same

---

70 Milton, *Paradise Lost*, II, 879–82. Faraday picks up on his earlier reference to Milton and perhaps on Addison's praise for Milton in *The Spectator*, no. 417.

71 Johnson, *The Rambler*, no. 92 (2 February 1751): 'The swiftness of Camilla is rather contrasted than exemplified; why the verse should be lengthened to express speed, will not easily be discovered.'

72 Cp. Addison, *The Spectator*, no. 411: 'A man of polite imagination is let into a great many pleasures, that the vulgar are not capable of receiving. He can converse with a picture, and find an agreeable companion in a statue. He meets with a secret refreshment in a description, and often feels a greater satisfaction in the prospect of fields and meadows, than another does in the possession.' In a letter written from Geneva in 1814, Faraday commented to Abbott: 'You know Ben my turn is not architectural nor though I can admire a beautiful picture do I pretend to judge of it' (*Correspondence*, I, p. 76). 'A man of a polite imagination can converse with a picture, and find an agreeable companion in a statue' is used as an example in Smart's *Theory of Elocution* (p. 111).

time, informing him, that there are things of more importance at that time to claim his attention, in the common business of life.[73]

Y. Sept. 1818.

On Politeness

C. Civility and Politeness are[74] due to every one; and you have done wrong in thus violently transgressing their bounds.[75]

A. I deny that I have transgressed. I know well enough what civility is due to others, and in this instance at least I have given it.

C. Do you really conceive that you behaved politely, when you told him, in three or four words, that he was mean?—that he grasped so hard and hastily in dealing with his friend, as well as the world as to evince a mean disposition?—Was this a polite remonstrance or was it politely dressed?—

A. I do not know what your sense of politeness is; I told him nothing but the truth; and I was urged on to it by the circumstances of the moment. Did he not merit it? Was he not at the very time, sanctioning the lowest opinion I had of his meanness?—Did he not even appeal to me; and in what therefore am I to blame?—

C. Not in your thoughts, but in your words, I allow your opinion of him to be quite right; but I cannot admit that expression of it which you claim.—It interferes with the general good will which should connect all persons together; It breaks the charm, which renders every member of society, a friend to every other Member It destroys intercourse, or makes it difficult: It creates enemies and separates friends; and it converts the pleasant and smooth surface of life which politeness produces, into a stormy and tempestuous ocean.

A. It is not worth while spending more time on the affair—I do not see that I am wrong; so let it pass.

---

73 Cp. Addison, *The Spectator*, no. 413, on the pleasures of the imagination: 'our souls are at present delightfully lost and bewildered in a pleasing delusion and we walk about like the enchanted hero of a romance who sees beautiful castles, woods, and meadows, and at the same time hears the warbling of birds and the purling of streams; but upon the finishing of some secret spell the fantastic scene breaks up, and the disconsolate knight finds himself on a barren heath or in a solitary desert.'

74 'Are': written over the original 'is'.

75 'Their': written over the original 'its'.

C. Yes but it is worthwhile, and the time would not be mispent, which would be effectually occupied, in persuading you to take a different view of intercourse; and to lay aside that harsh habit of expression, in which you now constantly appear in Society. You *oblige me* to assume a tone similar to your own; but I do it, only that you may comprehend the spirit in which I *wish* you, for your own advantage, to be more polite.

A. If you *will* keep this subject alive, you must give me reasons, and not mere assertions, I am not to be bound and fettered in my comprehension of things, by the fashionable and nonsensical opinion of the day.

C. I am ready to give you reasons; and in addition to those I have urged against your manner, could adv—

A. They are specious; and in my manner,[76] as you call it, I would advise you to substantiate one thing, before you build another on it.

C. Then, what I have said is not true! And roughness, is just as good an introduction to the polished world, as civility and attention!

A. You go either too fast or too superficially. I did not say, it was untrue; but true or not, it is not directly applicable. If you mean to vindicate modern politeness,[77] or oppose my views of intercourse, you must do it on first principles, and not by giving general assertions, which dropping here and there, seem to embrace the whole object, whilst they in fact, only conceal it. If you assert the inconvenient results from my mode of behavior; you must also prove them extensive, and unbalanced[78] by any advantages. If you praise the polished surface of polite life;[79] you must shew me, that the mass of that life is good internally; otherwise, you can hardly hope to convince any thinking being, that he will do well to resign his Sincerity for Dissimulation.

---

76 'My' inserted in different ink (perhaps the original author's correction to a scribal error).

77 'Modern politeness' was a topic of considerable debate during the first two decades of the nineteenth century. David Hume's distinction between 'modern politeness, which is naturally so ornamental, [and] runs often into affectation and foppery' and 'ancient simplicity, which is naturally so amiable and affecting, [but] often degenerates into rusticity and abuse, scurrility and obscenity' was influential in the debate ('Of the Rise and Progress of the Arts and Sciences' (1742), in *Essays and Treatises on Several Subjects*, 2 vols. (Edinburgh: Cadell and Davies *et al.*, 1809), I, pp. 115–42 (p. 135).

78 Originally 'unballanced'; second 'l' crossed through.

79 Cp. Thomas Clarkson, *A Portraiture of Quakerism [...]*, 3 vols. (New York: Stansbury, 1806), I, p. 336: 'Their manners, though they have not the polished surface of those which are usually attached to fashionable life, are agreeable, when known.'

C. Well then, I will begin at first principles; since you choose[80] to be so logical: though you well know, that in many concerns and points of life, and eminently on this particular one, expediency is our only guide; and that then we cannot direct ourselves by rules so strictly mathematical, as you desire.

A. Oh, I want no advantage. I know my subject well enough to be confident of its strength, and power of resistance to attack. I by no means wish you to resign, any argument or circumstance that will help you;—but go on.

C. Well then,—As a general intercourse between the individuals upon the earths surface is required; and as in populous places that intercourse, is with every individual, almost unintermitted, except during sleep; it must be an important object with those who carry it on to approach it in its nature, as much as possible to pleasure; so that the employment which is exerted for the well being should at the same time be a source of enjoyment too.

A. Well.

C. This being the case, it is the business of every one, and advantage too, to adopt that manner in action, and that mode in expression, which will be agreeable to others. he should judge from what pleases him, of what will please others; and he should constantly offer that, that he may receive the same in return. He should first adopt a general habit of agreeableness, and then he should assiduously bend it to the particular manners, and characters of the persons which whom he comes in contact.

A. Go on.

C. In pursuance of this object, he should respect the peculiarities of the persons before him. He should avoid unpleasant subjects, and as[81] if by accident introduce those which he knows to be agreeable. When he cannot assent, or dissent with the person, he had better say nothing. He should yield to the habits of those around him. He should avoid fastidiousness, and put the best construction on what passes before him. He must at times be blind, deaf and dumb. He should respect, though he may use the weak side of the character of his companion in conversation; and should be attentive to the weaknesses and foibles he may meet with. He may if he chooses think freely, but he must not say all he thinks. Even policy directs him to keep his secret information for his own use and

---

80 'Choose' inserted above the line instead of original 'chose'.
81 'As' inserted above the line in the ink and hand of the scribe.

advantage. And finally, when the strict rules of right and wrong do not forbid him, he should be any thing to any body, that he may gain their favour and make himself friends: and in this way, he will effectually give the world pleasure, and forward his own interest.

A. _____ _____ _____ _____ ____[82] And this is what I ought to be?—

C. I think so.

A. And what you wish to make yourself?—

C. Yes.

A. But you are not so to me just now?—

C. You oblige[83] me on the score of Friendship, not to be so. You have forced me to tell you disagreeable things.

A. Oh never mind that. _____ But you are honest just now?—

C. What do you mean?—

A. You have told me sincerely, of what you think *my* faults, and have laid open to me the secrets of the polite man?

C. I have endeavoured to do so.

A. Then you are honest?

C. I have been sincere and open?—

A. And what am I to deduce from this?—

C. What you please.

A. But what will not please you. _____ That honesty and politeness, are *incompatible*.

C. I do not understand you?—

A. Possibly not:—but that will not alter things.

C. Well, but explain.

A. What?—I speak so plainly, that I surely cannot be misunderstood, it is for the polite man, who has twenty meanings at once in his expression, to twist his words and give a convenient sense to them. I who use words only in one sense, have nothing to explain.

C. Then do you mean to assert, that the polite man moves in the same dignified sphere, with the thief and the robber.?—

A. It is of no use C. for you and I to discuss in this short terse way, if we will use different languages—In answer to your last question, I should say *Yes* but my meaning would not be yours. By the Polite man I should

---

82 These lines reproduce greatly extended dashes in the MS. Similar lines also appear in 'On Triflers', below, pp. 165–66.

83 Originally 'You will oblige me', the 'will' crossed through.

not mean the really polished person; for he cannot be mean, or do wrong, without losing his title; but I should mean the man *you* have described, the insect of modern times, the person who has no objection to oscillate and waver about the strict line of probity and honor, bending it to his own convenience, that by flattering and humouring the passions and weaknesses of his fellows, he may forward his own interest, & meanly stoop to the habits of artificial life—By the dishonest person, I mean one who would secure to himself, things at the expence of truth and right; No matter what the things are, whether property, or character, or reception, or good will, or favour; nor what the departure from rectitude which is to give them, whether in deed, word, or thought:—the spirit is the same; and though speaking in modern language, I may say *it is refined*, yet it is not changed; and the modern Gentleman is a knave, just as much as the Man of Honor is a Murderer.

C. Very handsomely, and politely Expressed. but _____

A. Stop: Let me have my turn—What I said last, was only in answer to your question; and would if pursued, lead us off from the main point of our conversation. Now, you have already given your opinion of universal intercourse, from which you derive the necessity of politeness; and it is but fair, that I have the advantage of putting my construction on the matter: Will you give me leave?—

C. I wonder you ask it?—

A. I should not, unless I had been sincere in wishing to have it.

C. Well you have it.

A. Don't be offended.—You ought not to expect fashionable politeness from me, till you have proved its propriety; a point, which is at some distance as yet. But to proceed; you say, that as a general and almost uninterrupted intercourse is necessary between the individuals in the world; it ought to be made as much as possible a source of pleasure. This is granted; but the approach of a necessary occupation to pleasure is just as requisite in every part of our life; and is in fact only a convenient and agreeable circumstance, that hangs incidentally on to the main business and purpose. The pleasure of communication, is like the pleasure of any thing else necessary to human existence, a blessing attached to, and superadded to the duties, which when performed preserve our existence; and which makes them agreeable to us, as well as necessary. Take for example, food; It is necessary that we should eat, that we may live; and the pleasures of taste are added to what we eat to heighten the enjoyment of life, In the same way communication is necessary, and kind communication is pleasure.

But abuse the means of enjoyment and you disgrace even the necessary act. Make the taste a superior consideration to the appetite, and you invert the order of nature. Gluttonize and you do worse than starve. So if you lose sight of the use of communication, and talk instead of informing, you make the pleasure replace the purpose; if you deceive instead of instruct, you had better be dumb. The made dishes[84] of a Gourmand,[85] may be compared to the *White lies* of the Modern Gentleman; and disease results from the use of both. In the first case it is only of the body, in the latter it is of the Mind.[86] The nasty habits of the Glutton, keep the clean man at a distance; and the practices of the Man of Politeness, are just as contaminating to the mind of thought and integrity.

C. Yes, Yes; but you run away with yourself. You are fastidious. It is not necessary that you should plunge into such sad offences as you would imply, to be polite. Criminality and agreeableness are by no means linked together;[87] nor can I imagine you so absurd as to suppose so.

A. I have not said so.—I must tell you *again*; that I cannot follow you in such general language; and if you choose to wander about, you must wander alone—I spoke of the politeness you described to me. I spoke of that which varnishes the world at present, and gives it so deceptive an appearance. I know, very well, that there is a mode of behaviour to which the word politeness was formerly applied, which has every propriety possible belonging to it, but you cannot identify that with the manners of the modern mental Dandy; and it is of no use endeavouring to vindicate the latter, by referring to the former for evidence: They never can coalesce, and have nothing to do with each other. I have, in my mind, a model of politeness, which I am sure even you would not find fault with; and it would, if practised, occasion more pleasure by far, than the modern method. With every necessary, with every kind attention, it combines sincerity; It would have an object in each act, but the object should never appear out of the bounds of virtue. You may sometimes see it adopted amongst the members of a kind and affectionate family; where the interest which each one feels in another, induces sincerity, and the love

---

84 'Made dish': a fancy dish of various ingredients (OED).

85 'A' inserted above the line.

86 Cp. Faraday's close comparison of gluttony and lying in 'Observations on the Inertia of the Mind', below, pp. 195–96; and cp. his definition of the gourmand as 'a being, in which mind exists in union with matter in the lowest state of degradation' in 'On Mind and the Duty of Improving It', below, p. 113.

87 'Linked' is an insertion in a different hand.

causes attention; evinced in useful aid given and not in necessary acts;—I am as far removed from true politeness as any one, but on a different side to the fashionable world. They have overshot the mark, and are so far beyond the point where sincerity and attention are in greatest force,[88] and where true politeness resides, that they have lost sight of sincerity altogether. I have not yet reached the desired spot; but I have the satisfaction of knowing that I am sincere if not attentive; and that therefore as far as regards the essential duties of a human being, (and these are the points about which we ought to move) I am not so distantly removed, and have not so many influences between me and it as they have; and though appearances are against me, realities are not necessarily so.

C. I have been polite enough to suffer you to talk thus far without interruption, and I think polite even in your way. But though I commend your principles, I do not see that they at all interfere in the strange way which you imagine. It is not depreciating to any one, even in mental character, to prepossess by his appearance and _____

October 1818.

Agis

Young Agis one day at the foot of a Hill,
  Where a streamlet ran murmur'ing along,
With inward joy mused on each trickling Rill,
  Till it fain would have tempted his Song.

When high on the hazel, that hung o'er the stream,
  A soft twitt'ring Bird did alight;
It sang so melodious, it anxious did seem,
  To add to his pensive delight.

And straight to the spray that o'ershadow'd his Ear
  The songster in transport then flew;
But when he would place to his bosom more near,
  Sweet Robin then quickly withdrew.[89]

---

88 'Are' inserted above the line.

89 'Sweet robin' appears not infrequently in Romantic-period popular pastoral, including Elizabeth Hands' 'A Pastoral: As Thirsis and Daphne' (1789), which is written in the same catalectic amphibrachic metre as this verse, and in the much better known lyric

Then the Echo that waits in the green woodland Vale,
　　To mock the lost joys of the swain;
So listen'd to all the sad moan in his Tale,
　　And told it o'er each distant Plain.

The wing'ed God of Love, on his Pinions appeared
　　To ease the fond Youth of his care:
And told this fair moral, which when he had heard,
　　Might teach him of Ills to beware.

"When the bliss of fond love shall awake up thy fire,
　　And Delia shall tender her Heart,
Ne'er let thy true Friendship in Coldness expire,
　　But hasten the Joy to impart.

For soon shall the flow'ret its beauty withdraw,
　　And thorns must succeed every Rose,
While Nature shall stamp o'er the World this fair Law
　　The lilly is sweet while it blows."

　　　　　　　　　　　　　　　　October 1818.

The Charms of Sleep

Of all the Arts the human breast can know,
That prompt ambitious hope, with fiery glow;
That reek the heart in anger'd fretful care,
And mock with shades, or all our joys ensnare;
In every path a Casuist is found
To urge adventure o'er some doubtful ground.
But I, O muse, can ne'er contest the Palm,
Nor busy Science e'er my Spirits warm:
But in the shades of night O be my Theme,
And playful Fancy tell the varied Dream
Of Hero's, Poets, or the hoary Sage
That crept through life or graced each happy Age

'Proud Maisie' from Walter Scott's novel *The Heart of Midlothian*, which was published
in 1818, the same year as 'Agis' appeared in the Mental Exercises.

Of Fete, or Wonder, Fashion or of Fame,
Or graced an Annal with a mighty name.
In this sure bourne the soul shall find a Rest,
And in soft sleep the happy shall be blest.[90]
Oh sleep from which all happiness can spring
And chequer'd Fate, can hang on fancy's wing.
O gentler Death, in whose reposing Arm
Both Prince and Slave, shall find thy soothing charm.
Whence is the source that mocks thy brothers power?—
That hides our cares and all our griefs devour.
Now steals thy balm o'er the sad captives brow,
And happier dreams avert his inmost Woe.
A World wide opens to his soaring Soul
Where life and liberty knows no Controul;
The fettering Steel from off his limbs shall shake
And Dungeon cares his memory forsake.
Like poor Gergona, Misery's sad Child
Whose guileless bosom ever soft and mild,
From Europes milder states, a Captive torn,
And o'er Guergelas sandy desert borne:
To grace the triumph of a brutal band
That knew not human laws nor heavens command.
In slavery he past the joyless hour,
Nor murmur'd 'gainst the horrid Chieftains Power;
Hope told his heart that soon the sable Night
Would come, and with its balmy joys invite:
But long he toil'd, nor long his eyelids close,
His wakeful moments watchful as his woes.
At last with more than common care oppress'd
Found in the hateful Cell a peaceful Rest;
Then playful fancy, with her wonted Art
Awoke those Joys, that dreams alone impart;
At once he knows, he sees his native home,
And o'er each fancied bliss his heart does roam,
His dear Companions, and his kindred all,
His lisping brother on his name does call,

---

90   Possibly cp. Shakespeare, *Hamlet*, III.1 ('To be or not to be').

But still no lasting joys can hold him here,
To part they meet, to part, ah too severe,
His favor'd love breaths rapture in his soul,
But soon that rapture owns a sad controul.
His fair Almena, still for ever true,
Hangs on his breast, and breaths the sad adiew.
He starts! he wakes! he stares on all around,
And sinks in sorrow on the dewy ground.
Oh heaven! he cried if this must be thy Will,
Teach me in silence yet to bear it still;
But grant my soul may leave this Tyrants power,
And shield me in such dreams an happy hour;
To heaven again he turns his tearful eyes,
Breaths the last moan, in silence, droops, and dies.

October 1818.

Friendship & Charity

Alas! my dear Albert, how rare is true and sincere friendship; this observation will frequently occur to you, in journeying through the varied scenes of this bustling world; may you my friend enjoy its purest blessings. I have endeavoured in the following short sketch, which I beg your acceptance of, to depicture the true character of a man worthy the name of a real friend.[91] Octavius was born of respectable, tho' not wealthy parents: having in them the brightest examples, and being naturally of a kind and obedient disposition, could not fail of imbibing those good precepts, they were ever anxious to instill into his youthful bosom: his assiduity in business, and prompt attentions to the Duties of his Office, soon advanced him far above even a medium station in the world.[92] Octavious was one of those favoured few; possessed of a considerable share of the milk of human kindness:[93] and which indeed flowed so liberally within his youthful breast; that in him the friendless and unfortunate

---

91 'Depicture' in this sense dates only from 1798 (OED).

92 The writer is following the model of Johnson, Addison and other essayists who frequently used character descriptions of individuals (called by a single, allegorical or otherwise pseudonymous name) to illustrate larger moral points.

93 'The milk of human kindness': Shakespeare, *Macbeth*, I.5.

was[94] sure to find a sympathising heart: a comforter in sorrow and affliction. Unrequited friendship had often involved his feeling heart into the most bitter and poignant grief; for what can be more distressing than to observe in beings who have shared our comforts when in sorrow; and accepted freely of our profered services; than that unpardonable crime ingratitude; yet how many of its votaries do we constantly find, floating up and down the world, forgetful of benefits conferred.

It was truly observed that friendship is a medicine for misfortune, but ingratitude dries up the fountain of all goodness.[95]

Octavious's just and feeling arguments, are such as cannot but be greatly admired and must forcibly strike the attention of every observant reader, it would be well if they were securely treasured up in our hearts, that when we see a fellow creature in sorrow and distress, instead of witholding our hands from acts of generosity, and fondly acquiring within ourselves the *probability* of the unworthiness of the man we might say with Octavious, for what end are we born, why is the power of doing good placed within our reach, are we individually more worthy of this worlds good than those who implore our assistance: or those still more lowly who hover round us like the fowls of heaven, and ask their humble dole?[96]—Oh! no he continues, do not let us one moment indulge the false, the delusive idea; but rather imagine, of what little importance the giver of all things would seem to attach to riches; in as much as it pleaseth him to confer them on the most unworthy unthankful creatures: ought we not then rather to consider them as held in trust, to be used and not abused, to be distributed as opportunity suits, and as worthy objects of compassion presents themselves to our notice. Ingratitude had not closed the path to the feeling heart of Octavious; for he observes, why should I refuse assistance to my fellow creatures, should I shut up my bowels of compassion because of ingratitude in *a few*?[97]—banish the thought. Thus it appears, he has taken up just opinions of genuine and sincere friendship; as well as extensive ideas of true charity: his house is the sure refuge for the destitute; he feels happy in contributing to the comforts of

---

94   'Was': 'were' added in a different hand above the line.

95   Cp. Sirach 6.16: 'A faithful friend is the medicine of life.' 'Ingratitude dries up the fountain of all goodness': a saying attributed sometimes to Cardinal Richelieu and sometimes to St Bernard.

96   Thomson, 'Autumn', ll. 171–74, describing the poor: 'unhappy partners of your kind / Wide-hover round you, like the fowls of heaven, / And ask their humble dole.'

97   'Bowels of compassion': 1 John 3.17.

others; and as it were considers it an obligation conferred on himself.—
no cheerless appliant unfolds to him his tale of woe in vain, he kindly
sympathises with the unfortunate, pleads the cause of the fatherless, and
makes the widows heart leap for joy, happy, thrice happy Octavious, to
be the favoured child of fortune.[98] When we consider how few there are
who are justly intitled to the appellation of a true friend; how eminently
should we then prize those deserving the name. it was justly said, a true
friend, is not born every day, and again, a sure friend is best known in
adversity, we know not whom we trust till after trial, there are some that
will keep us company while it is clear and fair; which will be gone when
the clouds gather. We may cast our eyes around and observe many in
society whose acquaintance we would willingly court; and in whom we
may observe pleasing, and engaging manners, but when we approach
nearer and become more familiarized, find a total absence of those softer
feelings of social friendship; that at once disgusts and astonishes us, a race
who seem to be born for themselves alone; divested of common feeling
for their fellow creatures, let us turn aside in disgust, the very idea is too
painful to dwell on. Man without society would drag on a miserable
existence: formed by nature for the enjoyments thereof, and impelled
continually towards it, by a multitude of powerful and invincible propen-
sities: if then in our journey through life, we fall in with a chosen few,
whose sensibility of mind and disposition accord with our own, let us
highly prize them imparting our most secret thoughts, taking counsel of
each other, and blending as it were our very souls together become as
one. These my dear Alfred were the genuine ideas of the generous the
feeling Octavious: how sensibly then must such a one feel to discover he
had placed his utmost confidence and shower'd[99] unbounded generosity
on unworthy ungrateful objects; for whom he would have sacrificed his
hearts best blood; and thought the action too insignificant for the world
to observe; such was Octavious. We are sometimes led away by apparent
acts of kindness and liberality, things in themselves when duly considered,
so trivial, that it is astonishing we should not view them rather as every
day occurrences: such as Octavious justly observes, prevalent ideas of
misplaced generosity which ideas, he himself has most sedulously avoided,
has[100] in more illiberal souls, had the baneful effect of so hardening the

---

98 'The cause of the fatherless': Jeremiah 5.28; and cf. Job 29.13: 'I caused the widow's
    heart to sing for joy.'
99 'Shower'd': 'd' added later and above the line to original 'shower'.
100 'Has': 've' added later and 's' crossed through.

hearts even of those *accounted* generous; that many, many worthy objects
are passed hastily by, and unjustly exposed to the suspicions of those,
who have it in their power to lend a helping hand. It is an acknowledged
and I think an exceeding correct opinion indulged in by most prudent
parents that an extensive acquaintance for youths of either sex, is far from
being desirable, this idea naturally arises from young people not being
supposed to be capable of judging of the equalities essentially requisite;
to good order in youthful society, so much depending on early impressions; those opinions imbibed in youth often lay the foundation for their
future government in life, and is the cause of unceasing sorrow or on
the contrary, of lasting happiness according[101] to the principles instilled
in their tender breasts. for as the twig shoots so will the tree incline.
It becomes then a subject of the most serious consideration to parents
and guardians; as well as to those who have any controul over youth, to
carefully and kindly point out to them the consequences that may arise
from the associating with evil company, too often met with under the
denomination of young friends: it was well observed when inquiring the
character of a young Man, tell me his friends and I'll tell you his true
character; for you may indeed nearly judge of a mans predominent dispositions by the choice of his acquaintance; I would then recommend the
most careful discrimination in the choice of those you would wish to
make your bosom friends, Petrarch[102] says obtain for thyself friends who
will follow thee in adversity, and who doth most diligently frequent those
houses which fortune hath forsaken, and not such as Horace observes
who when the lees wax dry in the Cask take their departure.[103] To quote
another of Petrarch's[104] where he says, who so findeth *one* good friend
through a long life, is accounted a very diligent traveller in such matters;
to have a multitude of mere acquaintances, is unworthy a mind capable
of employment; one approved friend is a precious jewel, but common

---

101 'According': originally 'acceeding', the 'ee' crossed through and 'or' added later.
102 'Petrarch': originally 'Petrach'.
103 Horace, *Odes*, 1.35. The MS shows 'lees' written over 'bees'. The writer of this essay
     appears to have relied for this passage on Susannah Dobson's *Petrarch's View of Human
     Life* (London: Stockdale, 1791), pp. 65–66 which includes an English version of
     Petrarch's dialogue 19 in *De remidiis utriusque fortunae* (available in modern English
     translation in Conrad H. Rawski, *Petrarch's Remedies for Fortune Fair and Foul* (Indiana
     University Press, 1991), pp. 55–59). Susannah Dobson's version violates the divisons
     of Petrarch's dialogues and continues almost immediately to the passage from dialogue
     50 noted below.
104 'Petrarch's': originally 'Petrach's'.

friends, busy themselves in worldly matters, and will not know thee but in prosperity, for led by vile interest and envious opinions, they neglect so dear so precious a commodity: if then thou hast so divine a thing as a friend, be diligent to preserve such a treasure, love thyself if thou will be beloved, and never shrink from such a jewel.[105]

It is painful to observe what trifles amongst friends will sometimes breed the most inveterate and deadly hatred; this shews clearly a great want of natural good disposition, a forbearing conciliating manner, will at one dispel such unpleasant occurrences, and pluck out discord in its very bud, to bear, forbear, and forgive, is a maxim should ever be uppermost in our minds: for as Socrates that ancient and much admired moralist remarks; How few things there are worthy our anger, and again, do nothing in a passion, for why should we put to sea in the violence of a storm.[106] We certainly do not know how to justly appreciate the benefits and comforts arising from a course of lasting happiness in social Friendship, we suffer our passions to carry us so far out of our depth, neither are we deserving of its comforts, yet I agree with Octavious, that allowances to a degree should certainly be made for our natural predominant dispositions: but he was always at a loss where to draw the line, they whom nature in her various gifts hath not blessed with a sweetness of disposition free from those violent bursts of temper, which plunge them in a sea of trouble, and as a tempest on the angry ocean hurls to destruction all objects opposed to its fury, would do well to make it their constant study to curb well their unbridled temper; and endeavour to counteract it by reason and application, and by opposing to it those ideas which will naturally arise in their calm and sane moments.

> Is aught so fair
> In all the dewy landscapes of the spring,
> In the bright eye of Hesper or the morn
> In natures fairest forms is aught so fair
> As virtuous Friendship, as the candid blush

---

105 This long sentence is a quotation, with some errors ('acquaintances' for 'acquaintance'; 'busy' for 'bury' on Susannah Dobson's rendering (pp. 65–67) of Petrarch's dialogue 50 from book I of *De remidiis utriusque fortunae* (Rawski, *Petrarch's Remedies*, pp. 157–60).

106 Socrates' refusal to be made angry is cited in, for example, James Beattie's discussion of anger in *Elements of Moral Science*, 2 vols. (Edinburgh: Constable; and London: Cadell and Davies, third edn, 1817), I, p. 248: 'It is said of Socrates, that, when greatly provoked, he became instantly silent [...].'

Of him who strives with Fortune to be just?—
The graceful tear, that streams from others woes?—
Or the mild majesty of private life,
Where peace with ever blooming olive crowns
The gate; where honour's liberal hands effuse
Unenvied treasures, and snowy wings
Of innocence and love protect the scene.[107]

T.—October 1818.

An Ode to the PASS[108]

When music, heavenly maid, was old,
Near Jacobs Well, as I've been told,
A place renown'd in ancient story,
When Britain was in all her glory
(Not that in sacred writ explain'd,
Nor to such eminence attain'd,)
But that which joins to Barbican,
Where stood Queen Betsys vatican,
And which was then the town's Court end.—
But to my subject now attend.[109]
This Jacobs Well was near Hare Court,
        And there her ardent vot'ries met,
'Mong other temples, here they sought,

---

107 Mark Akenside, *The Pleasures of the Imagination*, Book I, in *The Works of the British Poets*, ed. Thomas Park, 42 vols. (London, 1805–08), XXV, p. 33; the passage as quoted in the Mental Exercises varies in punctuation from this edition and contains other small errors.

108 PASS: unidentified. This poem is highly intertextual: the opening parodies William Collins' 'An Ode for Music' (1746): 'When Music, heavenly maid, was young.' The shift into fairly low comedy in the later part of the poem, however, is a departure from Collins' classical allegory. Collins was very popular at the beginning of the nineteenth century: between 1800 and 1815 eight editions of his *Poetical Works* were published, and Collins was a staple of the many collections of English poetry produced by publishing houses from the 1790s to the mid-nineteenth century (St Clair, pp. 527–50).

109 Jacob's Well was in London, in the Cripplegate district just north of Cheapside. The Faraday family lived in Jacob's Well Mews from 1796. Hare Court, mentioned in the next line, is a little southwest of Jacob's Well.

To woo the maid; a vocal sett,
Tho' she was worship'd at this place,
    Sometimes she smil'd, but often frown'd,
And few among this roaring race,
    She with the bay or laurel crown'd.
How long ago this heavenly maid,
First began her charming trade,
    Another Bard hath sung;[110]
And how the passions felt her power
As o'er her lyre each rul'd an hour,
    While thrilling raptures rung:
But now, I sing another strain,
Tho' *he* had pleasure *I* have *pain*,
    In tracing her decline;
And tho' like us, she once was young,
Her face by discords often stung
    Confess'd the wrinkled line.
Like other maidens change of place,
Makes wond'rous difference in her face
    She knows when she is pleas'd
But some will say, *she* like a prude
Will be by *any* body woo'd
    But long will not be teas'd;
The fact is this, her ear is chaste,
She loves the lyre of attic taste
    The softly swelling song;
And when her lovers rapturous strain,
Smoothes her brow from discords reign
    Ah! *then* it is she's young.
One Evening which was set apart
To practise in the tuneful art,
When all were pew'd, and in due order,
The table round, a pretty border;
They first invok'd their guardian power
To grant her presence at this hour,
And that she might propitious prove,
They chose a tune they thought she'd love;

---

110 I.e. Collins.

A well known piece, which was the rule
Of this sweet phil-harmonic school.
But first the president was seated,
And wip'd his brows being over heated,
He then gave out instead of grace,
This tune well known with serious face.
Cecilia's deputy that trod,[111]
The pews between, a demi-god
Now seized his pipe, & blew a blast
So sweet, so low[112]—Oh could it last
'Twould save their hearers many a pang,
Themselves a Curse—or go and hang!
Thrice did he blow—when with a shout
The notes came pouring bravely out;
Now Minims, Crotchets, quavers all,
Were mingled in the mighty bawl;
Bass, trebbles, tenors kept together,
Like pigs when drove in thirsty weather,
"Where'er prophetic sounds so full of Woe"[113]
  For this repeated thrice,
  Because they thought it nice.
Swell'd high their bosoms with a rapturous glow.
Now as the Cadence died upon the ear
  Their anxious looks were fix'd on high;
Th'expected guardian should now appear,
  Attracted by their harmony.
But thus, the Maiden, in her native spheres,
  Bespoke her Choristers around.
"Friends[114] I'll descend, for well we know that tears
  Enhance our joys profound;
As Ease is soothing pleasure after pain,
  So shall this visit be to me;
When from these mortals I return again,

---

111 St Cecilia: the patron saint of music. The essay-circle author follows Collins' example in mingling Christian with classical references.

112 Cp. Collins, 'An Ode for Music', l. 44: 'And blew a blast so loud and dread.'

113 Quoting 'An Ode for Music', l. 45: 'Were ne'er prophetic sounds so full of woe.'

114 The quotation marks appear to have been added later.

Oh charm me into ecstasy."[115]
Diminuendo like, then down she fell,
     Light as a fairy hover'd o'er the crew;
Attentive list, to what I here shall tell
     For I was present in a dark side pew.—
Now the quaint Master with an iron smile,
Turn'd from the trebbles, stalk'd along the isle;
Lean'd o'er the pew, in attitude the best,
And thus in deep-mouth'd tones the chair address'd.
"Sir, with your leave, we'll now the voices try,
Which bass will suit, or which for Alto high;
For tenors who, and who for first soprano,
Can shout the loudest, or touch off piano;
Then next the lessons, for to sing at sight
"Is[116] quite essential on our extra night."
Soon various octaves, sound throughout the place,
With various efforts made and notes of grace.
One from lower G ascends with rapid ease
And in the lower parts is sure to please;
Another ventures up the higher tones,
And grumbles o'er them like a dog with bones,
In false chromatics some the next would call,
For like a Cat upon a neighbouring wall,
(Just then that pip'd a most enliv'ning air,
To soothe an amourous tom in mute dispair,)
His octave ran; in unison so new,
Two peas alike could scarcely be as true;
Loud peals of laughter, echoed thro' the room,
Order! the chair commands—go fetch a broom;
Dislodge the beast, who dares our peace invade,
And mock the tones Apollo's sons have made:
As Greyhounds loos'd the younger Sons begun
To issue forth and stir the noisy fun.—
Scour round the pews, then up the gallery stairs,
While through a broken pane the cat repairs;
Thus safe from harm he turn'd himself around,

---

115 Again, the quotation marks appear to have been added later.
116 Quotation marks appear to have been added later, and in error.

Peeps thro' the pane, then happy gains the ground;
Altho' the scent was strong, they lost the game,
Gave up the chace and down the stairs they came.
Pray said a Wag, who lov'd a timely jest,
Which Mr. President was it sung the best:
Th'important hammer now in anger rose,
And claim'd due order by repeated blows.
During the bustle, which before prevail'd
Oh Music! heavenly maid, thy spirits fail'd.
For as she hover'd o'er the noisy band,
Her nerves were shook, she lost her self-command;
She flutter'd, sunk, and on the board of sound,
Fell for a time, which kept her from the ground.
But as the solos now began to rise,
Like water bubbles upwards to the skies,
She gently rais'd her head and languid eyes;
No discords now—she felt herself reliev'd,
And smil'd at times, if I was not deceiv'd;
Now these arranged to shew their various skill,
Each tun'd his pipe and chose a tune at will.
'Till pass'd that time when sober folks should go,
Home to their wives to tell them what they know;
One member wish'd to try if they could sing,
In numbers sweet; a charming hymn to spring;
Oh fatal wish! oh worse than woful spight,
To tempt that dangerous lay so late at night.—
The pipe was seiz'd, and thrice in anger blown,
Then flew the wooden tube in thunder down;
The Song was sung—but as the growling notes
Ascend the air, and harsher discord floats
Along the board of sound—the maiden shook
A chilling tremor came—a ghastly look
Pervades her frame—Oh! now she lifeless falls
While rattling screams repel her from the walls:
Low at the bottom of the deacons seat
She prostrate lay, devoid of sense and heat;
When quiet 'gain resum'd her peaceful reign,
She wak'd, reviv'd, and stood upright again:
But ere she spread her wings to mount on high,

To'[117] enjoy the chaste celestial minstrelsy;
She thus address'd the gaping group below,
Who stood entranc'd to hear such music flow.
"Mortals, Vot'ries of Song, who worship here,
      'Tis music now commands your stay;
Altho' my suff'rings and this trickling tear
      Accuse your inharmonious lay;
Anger can ne'er my placid mind possess,
Nor thro' my veins his active poison press:
Lull'd by my charms his nervous arm's unstrung,
      His language chang'd assumes a tone,
As mild, as gentle as the sirens tongue,
      He sinks in languor at my throne;
The tear of sensibility is shed,
And proves at once the boist'rous spirit's fled.
All ye who wish to taste th'extatic bliss,
      The thrill which feeling Souls enjoy;
Now mark me, Mortals, for it is not this
      Which lately did my frame annoy;
No intermitting, shrill, or cracking squalls,
Should e'er be heard within these sacred walls.
But gently swelling on the buoyant air,
      The liquid sounds must float along,
And thus in melody each note with care,
      Should join with ease throughout the song;
For tones staccato have a harsh effect,
And sure the wand'ring discord to detect.
Thus harmony, the greatest care should claim,
Of all who wish to join in concord here;
And rules for time, of various styles, the same:
From want of feeling there is most to fear.
But courage now—this time I will forgive
The discord past—in future learn to live
As ye profess to be, choice sons of harmony."
      Thus spoke the heavenly maid, and spread her wings
'Midst dewy odours, then aloft she springs;[118]

---

117 'To" presumably for 'T".
118 Cp. 'An Ode for Music', l. 94: 'Shook thousand odours from his dewy wings.'

Th'astonish'd crow'd[119] in dumb amazement stand,
As in the air, they hear a vocal band
A Chorus Chant—the maid to welcome home;
Sweet music fills th'etherial starry dome,
Then less'ning dies away—'till not a sound
But gentle breathings now are heard around.

October 1818.

Garreteer's Epistle[120]

Honest Sec.

I have just set myself down with a great deal of Self-complacency, to inform you of the happy termination of a War which has been carried on for sometime by a particular friend of mine against your humble Servant; you should know Sir that I am a young Man about twenty, with all the becoming Vanity generally attending this Age; but to strike closer to the foundation of the subject now before you, I should tell you that I went early to School, at a small distance from Town, where I have continued nearly up to this period. About four years ago I enter'd upon Terms of Friendship with a Gentleman about my own age, who not[121] having paid so early attention to Education as myself, could not of course enter so deeply into matters of Study as I did; and as our circle of acquaintance was one and the same, he sometimes appeared to a disadvantage in my company, this he bore with becoming fortitude for some time, but latterly it seem'd to sour his disposition, and (I am sorry to add) occasioned him many unhappy moments. It happened Sir to be acknowledged by a party of friends in his presence that I had a talent for poetry, this I observed seemed to vex him in an unusual manner when I might reasonably expect his congratulations, however he soon told me that two Suns would not shine on the same scene,[122] and at the same time discovered to me that

---

119 'Crow'd': transcription error for 'crowd'.
120 'Garreteer': a person living in a garret; thus, often, a literary hack (OED). For a reply from another member of the essay-circle see below, p. 118.
121 'Not' inserted above the line.
122 Two suns cannot shine in the same sphere: a fairly common aphorism: e.g. William Hazlitt, 'On Actors and Acting' (1817): 'We have not, neither do we want, two Shakespeares, two Miltons, two Raphaels, any more than we require two suns in the same sphere.'

he had an inclination if not a talent, for satire, since that period he has not ceased to gall me in his malice; but I have affected every degree of good humour; appearing not to feel the weight of his lash, and at the same time practising such Artifice as to draw him into such an exposure of his own faults, that time and his absence only can deface them, I have repeatedly shewn him Pieces of my own Composition interspersed with extracts of eminent Authors, by which means some of the finest pieces have fell under the merciless stroke of his Malice, and thus I have heard Shakespeare, Dryden Pope and Thompson, accused of the[123] very opposite extremes of their general Characters.—I need not tell you his confusion on the day of reckoning, but the hope that such abilities may be applied for instruction, rather that the pitiful venom of bickering, will be ever entertained by

     Your humble Servt.
     Garreteer.

P. S. Poor Bismuth's gone to Bath.

October 1818.

A Mathematical Love Letter
MF[124]

Hypomochlion of my Life,[125]
   A *quantity* of the *multiplied* glances, *impelled* from the external *hemispheres* of your Eyes, have enter'd *perpendicularly* into my heart, to

---

123 'The' is a later insertion above the line.

124 Faraday's initials appear in a different ink and hand from the title and body of the letter. As with the initials appearing similarly at the start of 'On Argument' (p. 49), it is impossible to know when they were added to the manuscript.

125 Hypomochlorion: a fulcrum (OED). This letter, an exercise in mathematical puns, reflects the (non-punning) sample letters published in collections such as *The Complete Letter-Writer: Or, Polite English Secretary, Containing Familiar Letters on the Most Common Occasions in Life* [...] (London: Crowder, and Collins, 1772), which includes, for example, a letter 'From a Respectful Lover to his Mistress' (p. 112). Faraday was at this time entering into the writing of serious love letters on his own account. The first letter in *Correspondence* from Faraday to his future wife, Sarah Barnard, dates from 11 October 1819: it consists of four stanzas in amphibrachic tetrameter renouncing another poem he had written in which he criticized romantic love (*Correspondence*, I, p. 183). Faraday was very fond of puns and recorded many in CPB. Also in CPB is a

the destruction of that *equilibrium*, I was so proud to maintain in it; and the *inversion* of all its *powers*.—Long did I endeavour to *annihilate* these *singular* effects, by a *transposition* of my thoughts to some other *centre*, than yourself, but *directly*, as were my efforts to *extirminate* all Ideas of You, *so was* the continual recurrence, of your *figure*, to my imagination; 'till *rais'd* to the *apex* of misery, by the *repetition* of *similar* Ideas, I resolved to exert the *highest powers* of my mind, and *demonstrate* to you, by a declaration the *unlimited* devotion, and *infinite* attachment of him, who once stood firm and *vertical* as a *pyramid*, but who now, is laid *horizontal*, by the *momentum* of your charms, and is *reduced* to the *level* of a slave.—

Madam, you are the *co-efficient* of my being,[126] 'tis in your *power* and in yours only, to *add* the *fractions* of my heart together, and restore it to its *integral* and *pristine* state: then those *powers* which are now *involved* together, shall be brought into an *equal* and *similar* state;—shall be made to *quadrate* together and *exert* in *equilibrio* to the due performance of their *functions*: then all my *problems* shall be *solved*, all my *queries* attain *solution*; my conduct shall be as a *right line*, my happiness unruffled, as a *horizontal plane*.

But, permit me *exponent of my faculties*, to reason awhile, and endeavour to propitiate you, by *substituting* argument for declaration: as a *postulate*, allow me that all mankind should be happy, and as an *axiom*, that no one can be so, who is miserable; then it follows, that you, who *circumscribe* all my thoughts, and whose name is *inscribed* in my heart, should *reduce* your views to my *level*, and go *parallel* with me, in the *Line* of life.—

It is *demonstrable*, by the strictest *rules* of *analytical reasoning*, that we ought to be *added* together, for as *Binomials*[127] are the *quantities* intended to be brought out by the *addition* of the *factors* on this our *sphere*; and as each *binomial* should have a *positive value*; therefore U and I should be *added* together; for as I *minus* heart, am *negative*, and you *plus* said heart, are *doubled in value*, we should be *ranged* on the same side of the *equation*, to be *equivalent to the end required; therefore we ought to be added &c* Q.E.D.—hence it follows, that no lady should be hard-hearted to a sighing swain.—

I have endeavoured, by an *infinite series* of attentions, and the most

---

parallel to this, a 'Chemical Love Letter' (I, pp. 424–26), which begins: '*Essence* of my Happiness / Almost *decomposed* by the *brilliant radiations* from the *globules* forming a part of that *substance* called your head […]'

126 'Co-efficient': a number multiplying the number following it.

127 'Binomial': consisting of two terms (OED).

rectilineal and *perpendicular* conduct, to attract your notice; but the most *acute* observation, has still been *in-efficient*, in *extracting* comfort from your behaviour; you leave me at a *tangent*, and each action appears to me, *equal* to a refusal.—I *multiply* my thoughts on the *case ad-infinitum*; but being *dissimilar* and *unlike*, the *product* is *negative*; nay worse, since it *tends* to *involve* my mind in a *sphere* of trouble; my *actions* the *signs* of the thoughts, are *diametrically opposite to each other*, and *denote* the *unequal* and *reduced state* of my intellectual *powers*; my thoughts like Comets, *rotate* in *excentric orbits*, but they respect your image as the *focus* of their curves. You are indeed the *common measure* of every thing, by which I exist.—But why do I endeavour to describe to you my state; *simple terms* will not express it, nor is it possible even to *approximate* to it; I am *involved* in a *hemisphere* of doubt, my *horizon* is black dispair, all joy is *extirminated* from my breast. But perhaps my *results* are too gloomy; perhaps the *product* of my hopes and fears will be the *highest sum* of happiness, an *unknown quantity* of bliss: The *chords* of my heart *vibrate* at the idea its *perephery* becomes enlarged; and its *capacity* increas'd; Its *powers* are *extended*, its *exponent raised*, and I feel, that as a *like quantity* it will be worthy of yours. *Add* then these *two prime numbers* together, and *as like signs produce positive results*, our fame shall be *produced* through all generations, until the *remainder* of Days is past. But should you refuse, should your feelings be so *obtuse* as to remain unruffled by my *acute pains*, *then*, *as* my hopes *are to* your merits, *so shall* my vengeance, *be to* your refusal. The *base* on which my hopes are *founded*, is your humanity, their *altitude* your heart; should you *bisect* them, the *division* would go to the *centre* of my soul; a *frustrum* of life only would *remain* to me;[128] my *powers* would droop, I should be *extirminated* from society by a *general expression*, and become a *mere cypher* among the numbers around.—

Euclid.—Nov.r 1818.

---

128 'Frustrum': 'The portion of a regular solid left after cutting off the upper part by a plane parallel to the base; or the portion intercepted between two planes, either parallel or inclined to each other' (OED).

On seeing a Rose in the Possession of a
Lady at the SMHPABNASL[129]

Dec.r 6. 1818.

Emblem of thee, O lovely maid
In blooming youth & sweetness grown;
Tho' Roses every season fade,
Thy virtuous beauties have[130] not flown.

Ah lovely flower! why now appear
To trust thy tender blossom'd form,
The Winter's chill dost thou not fear
Or shun the nipping frosty morn?

Considerate Rose, and didst thou dread
Ere summers Sun should see thy bloom,
A fairer flower might grace thy bed
And throw thee in continual gloom?

But whilst thou'rt cherish'd by that love,
Which greatly press'd thee to her breast;
And whilst thou'rt fondled as the dove
A sacred emblem from the nest,[131]

Thy sweetness never shall depart,
Thy innocence, sweet emblem, rest,[132]
Of her who, dearest to my heart,
Hath softly press'd thee to her breast.

T.—Dec.r 1818.

---

129 SMHPABNASL: unidentified.
130 'Have': a later correction above the line of original 'hath'.
131 A later hand has proposed a revision to make this line read 'An emblem sacred from the nest'.
132 Cp. William Herbert, 'Stanzas' (1799), ll. 3–5: 'This humble flower the modest virgin chose, / Pure, as herself, and delicately fair. / Sweet emblem of the maiden most admired.'

On Courage

As our conduct and happiness in life depend materially upon the principles we imbibe and the habits we acquire in our youth; we should be careful while we are young and conscious of it, to confirm ourselves in those that are not meretricious, and such as will not forsake us when the decripitude and satiety of old age, shall have deprived us of the inclination or the power to enjoy with our early zest, the bustling scenes of the world and the morning pleasures of our existence.

There are principles which we imbibe and habits which we acquire, that although they may not appear to be absolutely, or essentially necessary to us in the decline of life, yet are so, when we reflect, that the peace of our latter days, is influenced much by the line of conduct which we have adopted; and that, in the evening, when the winds have subsided, and the heavens are serene, the safety of the vessel depends upon the manner in which she has weathered the storm.

There is one principle of quality of the mind, which in its various modifications is peculiarly necessary to a young man who is endeavouring to form or give a stability to his character; it is that which imparts to him, a proper reliance on himself, decision in judgment and firmness in action;—it is Courage.

When we recollect how great are the advantages gained by the possession of this quality; and how much we lose by the want of it; that without it we seldom venture to place ourselves in a situation in which we never were before, and that it is always the concomitant of great actions, but generally absent, in those that are mean; we shall acknowledge it is a subject which deserves our closest attention.—

Courage, or a proper Confidence, not only renders a man capable of placing himself in perilous situations, and conducting himself in them with propriety; but it enables a man to resist the fascinating temptations to indolence and vice, to repel the taunting shafts of ridicule, and to refuse to be a partner in those actions, which he feels are contrary to the dictates of his conscience, and which he would blush at in performing. He will not be afraid to acknowledge a virtuous man in poverty or distress or deny a vicious man who is rolling in riches, and whose nod is the nod of power. Courage is not incompatible with modesty for they are nearly allied, they are brother and sister; but it is the cure of Mauvaise honte; possessing it, a man's character is elevated, his resources are encreas'd, he surmounts difficulties and dangers, he commands his fellow Creatures, and is capable of performing those actions which among the ancients would have raised him to the rank of a deity; without it, a man becomes a slave to a mean, a weak, and a pusillanimous spirit,[133] his hopes are poisoned, his prospects are blighted, his exertions are paralised, he is despicable among men, and is only fit to become a hewer of wood and a drawer of water.[134]—

There are situations in life, where Courage is absolutely requisite, and in which it becomes a profession, as in the army and navy; in these the possession of it commands universal respect, and the want of it general contempt; The flattering distinction with which the former is treated, particularly by those who are destitute of this qualification, often raises a feeling of jealousy in the breasts of many; among whom are some whose chance of life, deeper reflection or keener sensibility, has prevented them from entering into such a profession; yet it cannot be asserted that to take them as a whole, they possess more true Courage, or that it is more inherent in them, than in any other Class of mankind; but under what denomination their Courage is to be placed, in general, we will leave, to the close of this paper.[135] We cannot however, wonder at the admiration which this quality or its resemblance excites in the human breast; how natural it is for us, to pity, to love and to cherish such of our fellow Creatures, as have been in wondrous perils, and had hair breadth escapes: The sailors shipwreck, the soldiers battle, and the travellers wonder, each take their turn, each creates an interest for his fate, and, as is the Sensibility of mind and warmth of imagination in his hearer, so will be the pity and admiration which it will excite; we substitute ourselves for the hero, we think for ourselves, and feel as if we were placed in the same situations. How often are we attach'd even to inanimate objects from their possessing imaginary qualities; we handle with affection, a walking Cane or Snuffbox, perhaps the legacy of a friend; it has been half round the world, in the Indies, at Quebec, weathered Cape Horn, and round to Peru or elsewhere; it was lost, and almost miraculously found; the value which many sett upon such things, is natural and very great, and is proved every day; it is a social and pleasant sensibility, and can be productive of no harm, but of good to the individual and to the Community. From

---

133 'Weak, and a pusillanimous spirit': cp. *The Spectator*, no. 576 (4 August 1714): 'What greater Instance can there be of a weak and pusillanimous Temper, than for a man to spend his whole Life in Opposition to his own Sentiments?'

134 Deuteronomy 29.11: 'from the hewer of thy wood, unto the drawer of thy water.'

135 'Paper': the term used, most famously, by Addison and Steele for the numbers of *The Spectator*.

hence we may trace, the variety of histories, and adventures of animal, vegetable, and mineral travellers which has been presented to the world by authors of various celebrity; and of much of the interest with which the museums of ancient fragments are inspected;—they are things of other days, have existed long; have witness'd many changes, they[136] possess imaginary qualities, and various are the sensations produced by this train of moral association.

As we perceive that such advantages are derived from the possession of Courage, the question with respect to its nature becomes important to us; whether it cannot be acquired, or how[137] far it is a property of the mind or the effect of habit?

If we endeavour to trace it to its source we shall find, that it depends, partly on habit, much on strength of nerves or constitution, but much more on the reasoning powers of principle. Courage from any source may be exerted either in a good or a bad cause, as man can reason either virtuously or viciously, correctly or incorrectly; it is the same in Erostratus who fired the Temple of Diana to perpetuate his name,[138] as it is in Howard the philantrophist, who visited dungeons and hospitals the abodes of misery and contagious distemper;[139] it is as conspicuous in the North American Indian who is led an undaunted prisoner to the Stake, where he is to suffer excruciating torments; as it is in a regiment of Seapoys,[140] who would make an attack at the very front of a destructive battery without shrinking; although the one is the result of superstition, and the other of the doctrine of fatality; it is the same in the man who first ventured to soar above the clouds by the help of a flimsy machine filled with rarified air, where he might meet with effects and situations entirely unknown to him, as it was in an engineer in the Peninsular War, who while following with others, in the Ammunition train, observed a bomb thrown by the enemy, fall into a waggon full of rockets, shells and other combustibles, he immediately leaped into the waggon and threw

---

136 'They': originally 'the'; the 'y' added later.
137 'How' inserted above the line.
138 Erostratus, sometimes called Herostratus, burned down the temple of Diana at Ephesus in order to secure the immortality of his name.
139 John Howard, 1726(?)–90: penal reformer who visited almost every county prison in England and Wales in the 1770s.
140 Sepoys: Indian soldiers under British officers. Such troops were praised for their courage in, for instance, an article on the history of the Bengal Native Infantry which was published in the *Quarterly Review* in May 1818 (vol. 18, no. 36, pp. 385–423); this article immediately follows the *Quarterly*'s review of *Frankenstein*.

it out while the fusee was burning, and at the very moment it might have burst and blown him to atoms, besides causing the destruction of all in its neighbourhood. These examples are among the thousands, which might be adduced, and which occur in a greater or less degree of importance every day; not from the effects of habit, but from the result of an operation of the mind. Erostratus knew what must inevitably be the consequence of his action; he was not enabled to do it from habit, for he had never been placed in a similar situation; he evidently came to a decision upon it after having reason'd for and against the act. The same with Howard, but his motive had a better foundation and his duty or benevolence to his fellow Creatures, was the basis of his conduct; yet he must have known his danger, but to him, his reward appeared in the distance and overcame it. Whether we brave extreme danger by an implicit belief in fatalism, or from superstition, or from a sense of our duty, our confidence will be derived principally from the reasoning powers; and this is undoubtedly the case where men act singly, without compulsion, in situations unknown, where use or habit cannot have blunted their feelings, nor ignorance thrown a veil over the dangers that are before them.

Habit produces a great degree of firmness; but we cannot term that which is the result of Habit, true Courage. (I do not refer either to good or bad actions). A veteran going into battle will feel less than a recruit, or he will be more able to overcome his feelings; men working daily at a gunpowder mill, which perhaps has been blown up every few years and their predecessors killed; and men accustomed to all the terrors of a storm or other sublime effects at sea: these are among the numerous instances of the result of Habit: but these men, are not in general, more courageous than others; for place them in different situations; send one down in a diving bell, one up in a balloon, and the third where he believes he shall be visited by Ghosts or supernatural appearances, what will then become of their Courage; they will feel as other men or more acutely. It is the nature of the mind that whatever idea it has entertain'd for a lengthened time, or repeated often the feelings on that subject will have lost their poignancy and produce little effect, whether it relates to grief, Scenes of horror, or of imminent danger. We soon speak with tranquility of the death of the dearest of our friends, and of every minute circumstance relating to it; Surgeons will describe an operation the most appalling, without one feeling being stirr'd except that which is connected with the success of their profession, and Old Age will contemplate with serenity its near approach to dissolution, while Youth can scarcely reflect upon it without shuddering.—

The Courage then, which is acquired by habit, is the same in mankind, as it is in those animals, which we train to face dangers or objects of which they are naturally afraid; Use strengthens the nerves, it brings on a want of consideration or thoughtlessness, and when it has reconciled us to a particular danger, it is not then Courage which supports us; it acts as an opiate, it lulls the feelings, produces a species of delirium, and inattention to our situation, which should of all things be avoided, and be guarded against by careful vigilance and presence of mind.—

With respect to the natural Courage in the constitutions of some men, though there are very few who cannot be class'd under the head of habit, we must acknowledge, there are some born superior in this, as in other qualities of the mind; fearless in danger, yet careful to provide against contingencies, firm in decision and prompt in execution. This is desirable, but it is the birth-right of few, and that which we *can* acquire by reason and perseverance is more praise-worthy. There are some who have had the character for superior firmness, and who untill the hour, when the trial has come more immediately to themelves, have supported it well; but then,—have trembled at the impending stroke and the weakness of their nature has triumphed over their utmost exertions. But to expose the meretricious nature of habitual Courage, or natural strength of nerve, let us give those men who rely upon it, time for reflection, when placed in situations of greatest danger, and if they have any sensibility they will then acknowledge the weakness of their support: In the solemn stillness which precedes a storm, in the dark dead hour of a night, which is to usher in a day, when Death shall ride triumphant over the prostrate bodies of thousands of mankind,[141] perchance themselves among the gory heap, among that heap of which they could not say, there lies one to whom they bore the smallest enmity; nay, had they they but have known them, might have become their bosom friends.

There must then be a something to which we must have recourse in lieu of this;—let us reflect, let us reason, let us form a judgment before action, surely this is a good method—but the vicious man will do so also, and the result of his arguments will be equal to his view of the question,

---

141 Cp. Revelation 6.8: 'And I looked, and behold a pale horse: and his name that sat on him was Death, and Hell followed with him. And power was given unto them over the fourth part of the earth, to kill with sword, and with hunger, and with death, and with the beasts of the earth.'

and he will be supported by it in the same degree throughout; but he will not have such a foundation for his arguments, as the man who acts from a sense of justice, or from a sense of the reciprocal duties of man. To fulfil *that* duty with justice, which may devolve upon us by the laws of our fellows, in particular situations of life, often becomes extremely painful; but let us recollect, that we are indued, by an all-wise though incomprehensible Creator, with an innate knowledge of right and wrong; possess'd of which if we do not rebel against the dictates of our conscience, and if we keep in mind, that golden rule for our conduct "Love thy neighbour as thyself" remembering that we are of the same fallible race, we shall be able to preserve ourselves from indecision of character and vice.[142] The thorny path of life will become tolerable when we are supported by the consciousness of having acted, with correct intentions towards our fellow Creatures, and with becoming humility before our God.—

R. Nov.r 1818.

Irritus to the Manager

Sir.

I am one of those beings the world commonly calls crabbed old Fellows.[143] Having spent the greater part of a long life with material inconvenience to myself and the great annoyance of my numerous friends I have just set about the hopeless search of a Remedy to retrieve that character which I can scarcely recollect to have inherited

I was Sir in my earliest days the favourite or as others say the darling of my parents being the youngest of a large family nothing particular transpired at that period worthy of relation except that (as I am told) my sweetness of disposition sanctioned every indulgence that could have been granted me but as I grew into more mature years those little marks of kindness not being sufficient to gratify my desire of novelty my Parents found it imprudent to shew me that favour which my ingratitude daily learned to abuse here my temper became soured my playmates forsook every game that I interfered in my brothers were always anxious to leave the room in which I chose to sit from the various provocations that I

---

142 'Love thy neighbour as thyself': Matthew 19.19, and elsewhere.
143 This contribution spoofs the papers in *The Spectator*, *The Rambler* and other periodicals, which take the form of letters from imaginary and dislikeable readers.

continued to give nearly the whole of the Family got early settlements and I finding myself left alone with no other to quarrel with I set about making my father unhappy which doubtless hastened the termination of a valuable life that was an ornament to all that part of the country. Since that I have gone through the various offices of life prescribed by nature and upon looking back can scarcely recount any thing to endear me to the circle that interest or affection has placed about me. To enumerate all the mischiefs in which I have played principle would indeed tire you but a few instances will suffice to shew the ill effects of such a wretched temper. I have six several times turned an affectionate daughter from my doors without any other fault than the ill choice of her companions the peculiarity of her head dress or the reading of an old fashionable novel I have discharged fourteen servants in as many weeks and have carried on suits at law with vicars lawyers and burgesses in every city within a hundred miles of my estate My dearest child is in a rapid decline from grieving and within these ten days I have laid an unhappy partner in the dust I would not have troubled you with such a doleful story but under the hope that some of your round-table friends may be able to define the original cause of such a disposition and point out by anatomical or mental explanation the happiest remedy for those who in future may be so troubled—I should further mention that none of the family but myself were so disposed and that I have not to lay it to the charge of want of Education or of Health.

If it were possible for me to be happy I should be grateful to acknowledge an obligation which your reply will place me under as long as the miserable existence shall continue of

   Yours &c
    Irritus.

Marriage is Honourable in All[144]

Much having been offered in every age by learned and pious men of almost every country on the delicate subject now before us it would be seeming vanity in me to expect I should be able to come in competition with those learned ones or vainly to imagine it would be in my power to

---

144 Hebrews 13.4: 'Marriage is honourable in all, and the bed undefiled: but whore-mongers and adulterers God will judge.'

elucidate or throw any new light on the important subject on which I
am about to treat. What I would more particularly in the first place wish
to draw the attention of my readers to is a few remarks which I will class
under the head of early and late marriages.[145] While I proceed to commit
to paper the effusions of a mind somewhat at war with opinions often
asserted and as confidently maintained by parents as to the conduct proper
to be pursued by children when having arrived at the age of maturity and
which opinions are held sacred by them from a sense of filial duty permit
me generous readers if in the perusal you should imagine me capable
of endeavouring to alienate the duty of children by presuming to point
out a new source of argument and opinions tending to counteract those
instill'd into their tender bosoms by prudent and wise parents permit me
to assure you my object is in part to endeavour to shew the fatal error
many parents fall into through mistaken ideas by an over-ruling and I
may add a too frequent indiscreet assumption of that power vested in
them over their children as relates to the choice of a partner in life.

Young people are too often brought together through interested
motives suitable only to the pride the avarice or the private views of
those under whose guardianship they may be placed to be brought up
and introduced into the world and not from any previous attachment
softened by friendship into sympathetic and affectionate love which is
so beautifully depictured by our much admired Poet speaking of the love
and attachment which should exist—says—it should be that thought
meeting thought and will preventing will with boundless confidence for
nought but love can answer love and render bliss secure[146]

Future happiness in the married state depends upon long previous
knowledge of the party beloved for it is impossible that in a short courtship
minds can sufficiently display themselves ideas should assimilate opinions
and sentiments should be in unison kindness gentleness and forbearance

---

145 Malthus's *Essay on Population* (1798) gave impetus to the national debate over the
advantages and disadvantages of early marriage. In 1818, for instance, George Purves's
Gray Versus Malthus: The Principles of Population and Production Investigated (London:
n. publ., 1818), subtitled *Should Government Encourage or Check Early Marriage?*

146 James Thomson, 'Spring', in *The Seasons* (1730), ll. 1120–22, on happy marriages:
'Thought meeting thought, and will preventing will, / With boundless confidence:
for nought but love / Can answer love, and render bliss secure.' These lines, and the
larger passage from which they come, are quoted in a work of 1813 by the Dissenting
minister John Ovington on *The Duties, Advantages, Pleasures, and Sorrows of the
Marriage State* (London: printed for the author, 1813), pp. 91–92. Ovington's book
begins with the epigraph 'Marriage is honourable in all.'

should be reigning[147] features in those who aspire to that much to be respected state matrimony

Early marriages can only generally speaking be desirable when the parties have been long acquainted when the families have been united by the closest ties of friendship as in this case a much greater probability exists of the younger branches perfectly understanding each others predominant dispositions.[148] We must be well aware lovers always endeavour in the company of each other to sett themselves off to the best advantage; those foibles and weaknesses of the mind which in the domestic circle too often display themselves are carefully hid from those in whose eyes they themselves would wish to appear in the most favourable light. A heart-rending trial must it be to the tender maid whose affections are placed on an object not sanctioned by the parent the struggle between love and duty must indeed be most severe Many instances do we hear of in life of this unhappy circumstance plunging whole families into the utmost distress. Wise parents will see the propriety of a reasonable forbearance in the exercise of their authority and not by endeavouring to turn the flowing stream of their childrens affections into a new and self interested source so rendering miserable their existence in their journey through life. On the other hand many difficulties arise from young people not acting with that open and candid conduct which will oft secure the wished for object. Children should look up for advice and counsel to their parents 'tis due to them for the many anxious hours they have watched over their tender infancy when every future hope in life and every comfort must spring from that source gratitude alone then will teach them what is due for all their various kindnesses. The angry brow of a severe yet tender father or the dread of reproof of a loving and affectionate mother has oft driven the lovely fair one to deeds most imprudent and much to be deplored a secret possession having invaded that once peaceful seat of harmony and love to obliterate which not even the duty and gratitude due to parents will avail We hear of females taking the most unadvised steps on account of those on whom they have placed their affections. Here we observe constancy to be one of the many brilliant and amiable features in our fair Country-women what trials and difficulties will they not encounter for the man who has won their too susceptible hearts by vows of honorable and most fervent attachment. Here is the trial here the bitter pangs between love

---

147 'Reigning': this word is unclear in the manuscript.
148 There may be an allusion here to the Sandemanian practice of intermarrying.

and duty warring against each other in barbarous succession they are imperiously called upon by the parents to renounce[149] for ever the object of their attachment or quit the roof the paternal roof under which they in their tenderest infancy were taught to hold sacred the commands of their parents.[150]—Ye who are blest with daughters lovely in person and with each grace adorned pause ere ye pronounce your cruel sentence O pause ere ye inflict the unhealing wound already opened by the unerring shafts of love.[151]

Celibacy is a state which I will venture to assert very few aspire to but the fates having so ordained some to that banishment much against their will prompts me to become their advocate A single man or to use the more common phrase a Bachelor is as little respected as any class in Society this I think generally arises from the belief they are so from choice which I will venture to say is not the case with one in five thousand numerous causes producing their various effects upon these unfortunate outcasts of Society. Misplaced affections in early life have no doubt often checked the aspiring youth and given a cool timidity to venture again into the fields of love. Let disappointed lovers attentively peruse the following chaste and elegant extract from Dodsley in which he depictures the charms of a virtuous woman "When virtue and modesty enlighten her charms the lustre of a beautiful woman is brighter than the stars of heaven and the influence of her power it is in vain to resist. The whiteness of her bosom transcendeth the lily her smile is more delicious than a garden of roses the innocence of her eye is like that of the turtle simplicity and truth dwell

---

149 'Renounce': originally 'remove', the 'move' crossed through and '= nounce' added above.

150 'Barbarous succession': cp. the description of the mental agony of the new widow in Robert Blair's 'The Grave' (1753), ll. 78–80: 'busy-meddling Memory / In barbarous succession musters up / The past Endearments of their softer Hours.' The poem was frequently reprinted in collections such as *Elegant Poems* (Gainsborough: Mozley, 1814), pp. 63–84. The line including 'barbarous succession' is described as 'particularly happy' by the anonymous editor (p. 60). 'Quit the paternal roof': cp. Mrs Taylor, *Reciprocal Duties of Parents and Children* (London: Taylor and Hessey, 1818), p. 31: 'Perhaps your children will shortly quit the paternal roof, and enter on the busy scenes of life [...].'

151 'Lovely in person': a common formula for female beauty in early nineteenth-century writing. 'Unerring shafts': often linked to Cupid in eighteenth-century poetry; for instance, in the Dissenting poet John Hughes' 'Greenwich-Park', ll. 36–37: 'But Cupid shows the nymph a nobler Game. / Th' unerring Shafts so various fly around, / 'Tis hard to say which gives the deepest Wound' (in *Poems on Several Occasions*, 2 vols. (London: n. publ., 1735), I, pp. 106–10.

in her heart The kisses of her mouth are sweeter than honey the perfumes of Arabia breath from her lips. *Shut not thy bosom to the tenderness of love* the purity of its flame shall ennoble thy breast and soften it to receive the finest impressions"[152]

It has been observed the happiest days of a man's life are those generally which pass in Courtship provided his passion be sincere and the party beloved kind with discretion If the laws of this country were such as to render it necessary a certain time should be required wherein love and affection should be offered to the object addressed it is possible it might have the effect of saving many bitter pangs to the tender hearts of our fair country-women if it would save even *one* sigh of sorrow it would be well worth the adoption perhaps it might be a very essential clause to insert that during the period of courtship the conduct of a man should be subject to the minutest scrutiny by the authorities might not this precaution guard against the many unmanly advantages taken of the fair sex might not this also serve as a check to those headstrong youths whom fancy in her most glaring colours paints to the mind the form the elegance and the richness of the casket whilst the jewels the hidden treasures within seem minor objects of consideration To shew the beauty and brightness of this Jewel I need only quote Pope's picture of an estimable woman

> Oh blest with temper whose unclouded ray
> Can make tomorrow chearful as to day
> She who can love a Sisters charms or hear
> Sighs for a Daughter with unclouded ear
> She who ne'er answers till a husband cools
> "Or if she rules him never shews she rules
> "Charms by accepting by submitting sways
> "Yet has her humour most when she obeys.[153]

If it should be a received opinion that the days of courtship are really days of happiness it may not perhaps be foreign to my subject to notice if such is the case it might be well if the fair sex would encourage a

---

152 Robert Dodsley, *Oeconomy of Human Life [...]*, 2nd edn (London: Cooper, 1751), p. 42. The passage as given in the Mental Exercises differs considerably in punctuation and layout from this edition, and contains occasional errors. St Clair includes this book among the 22 'produced in the largest numbers' in the Romantic period (p. 131).

153 Alexander Pope, 'Epistle to a Lady: Of the Characters of Women', ll. 257–64, with punctuation adapted.

prolongation of that happy period might it not put them in possession of facts which time only can furnish that on the one hand they might by frequent opportunity of conversing elicit that which set their fluttering hearts at rest as to important points many of which there are or doubtless *ought to be* which should be carefully cleared up and on the other hand they might spurn from their presence the man who by his profligate conduct might heap sorrow and affliction on the head of his hapless victim

It has been observed those protestations of love offered in earliest days to the object of our regard are by far the most sincere and the least changeable and indeed I am not prepared to differ in that opinion yet must observe if they are the most sincere they are too often to say the least very unadvised very imprudent and the source of many bitter pangs to the parties but if their conduct is marked by reason and propriety sanctioned by prudent parents and grounded on pure love and the truest affection I do not see any objection there can be in that case to their embracing that looked-for happiness and domestic enjoyment in each others society even in early life let them first well know each others heart let truth and candour be reigning principles and not by mean subterfuge and deception too highly colour circumstances which at first sight may appear conducive to their views but in the sequel will prove misery and torment in the breast of the husband grief and disappointment in the once loving and affectionate wife

It is certain much may be advanced for and against early marriages but we do not often find that young men sufficiently weigh the matter but imagine that having arrived at the state of manhood it becomes a matter of course they enter into matrimony; without first considering if[154] their affections are placed on a worthy object,[155] if the object beloved taking a correct view of the important change about to be effected is so confident of the mutual affections being so closely united that no circumstance through life whether disappointment of prospects in business poverty nor sickness can dissolve the tye.

I have heard it argued thus as a reason why young men should enter at an early period into Matrimony viz that being naturally of a gay turn of mind led by the enticing scenes around entering them and partaking of their too often poisonous qualities they become as it were insensible to

---

154 'If': 'whether' inserted above the line.
155 'Or' inserted above the line.

the charms of the soft and tender endearments of an amiable woman This is a doctrine not exactly in unison with my sentiments neither indeed do I consider it far removed from an insult offered to the fair sex what if a man's predominant disposition is such as to carry him so far out of the line of prudence and discretion is he to seek shelter from the impending storm in the bosom of a charming woman is he to risk the further peace and happiness of a tender female reason answers no but rather let such an one appeal to the Monitor within him that will tell him first of all to prove himself worthy the regard and affection of her he would call his wife and by a continuance of the practice of honorable conduct shew himself worthy the name of husband.

Ah! gentle fair ones pause ere ye assign over your dearest and most valuable rights and when the eyes of men gase on ye[156] with delight O hear with caution their alluring words guard well thy[157] heart[158] nor listen to their soft seducements.

Remember thou art made mans reasonable companion not the slave of his passion the end of thy being is to assist him in the toils of life to sooth him with thy tenderness and recompense his care with soft endearments.[159]

Late Marriages says Dr. Franklin are often attended with this inconvenience that there is not the same chance that the parents shall live to see their children educated and "late children" says the Spanish proverb "are early orphans".[160] There are as many objections which could be advanced against entering late into the marriage state as there are of embracing it at too early a period

I should think there is scarcely a man who having arrived to that age when it is prudent to make choice of a wife but what has had some opportunity of making advances and may no doubt have retired from the scene stung with remorse at having found on closer inspection and acquaintance a total absence of those qualities more particularly

---

156 'Ye': crossed out and 'thee' faintly inserted above the line; 'thee' crossed out too. Marginal note: 'plural'.

157 'Thy': crossed out and 'your' faintly inserted.

158 'Heart': 's' faintly added to 'heart'.

159 'Gaze on thee [...] soft endearments': quoted, with inaccuracies, from Dodsley, *Oeconomy of Human Life*, pp. 45–46.

160 Benjamin Franklin, letter to John Alleyne, Esq., in *The Private Correspondence of Benjamin Franklin [...]*, third edn, 2 vols. (London: Colburn, 1818), I, pp. 7–9 (p. 8).

requisite,[161] from a vain opinion entertained of a superior discernment in matters of this kind over those rash young men who hastily enter into the happy state and repent at their leisure

It has been often asserted that a reformed rake makes the best husband[162] A more pernicious and indeed a more barbarous idea cannot be disseminated these loose and unguarded remarks have a very injurious tendency on the minds of youth by a frequent repetition they lose the literal signification. It is needless I trust to attempt to refute such reasoning Thomson has most pathetically given a true picture of that description of love which should harmonise our souls when he says it should be that thought meeting thought and will preventing will with boundless confidence for nought but love can answer love and render bliss secure[163]

T.

Friendship

On thee O Friendship sweet my pen shall dwell,
And all thy sweetness all thy virtues tell;
Fail not my Muse while I this task perfo*rm*,
Or[164] leave my feeble efforts quite forlo*rn*.[165]
Well do I prize a truly generous mind,
Adorn'd with every virtue, and refin'd;
A friend sincere a noble candid heart;
And one who acts a Brothers, Sisters part.
If in this World at happiness we aim,
Why seek we it, in riches or in fame
Why do we search in chambers of the great

---

161 'Requisite' appears to have been added later into a gap in the manuscript.

162 A widely repeated and widely disputed saying: e.g. John Hawkesworth's essay 'The Ladies Directed in the Choice of a Husband. Good Nature Described' (1753), which appeared first in *The Adventurer* but was often excerpted, for instance in vol. 23 of Chalmers' very large collection *The British Essayists*, pp. 192–98: 'With the ladies it is a kind of general maxim, that "the best husband is a reformed rake;" a maxim which they have probably derived from comedies and novels [...]' (p. 192).

163 The author reverts to the quotation from Thomson's 'Spring' (see above, n. 147).

164 'Or': 'n' added later at the start of the line.

165 The italics appear to be drawing attention to the misrhyme of 'perform' and 'forlorn', and are thus perhaps the scribe's rather than the original author's.

Or crave the highest honours in the state[166]
Give me true Friendships bond, and social tye
For happiness in these alone doth lie
O Friendship sweet delightful flow'ry charms,
How highly do I prize thy savory balms;
With thee could dwell in rural rustic bowers
And happily pass the sweet the enchanting hours
The fleeting hours of morn which glide away
And bear us joyful to lifes evening day.
O could I find in some sequester'd place
That form I oft have pictur'd to my mind
Sweetly adorn'd with ev'ry virtuous grace
Accomplish'd manners amiable chaste and kind
A form Angelic innocent as the Dove,
That Friendship sweet might kindle into love.[167]

T.

On Mind and the Duty of Improving It[168]

Associated together in Man by the strongest ties, still no two things are more distinct from each other than Mind and Matter. We cannot in any way assimilate them, or make them identical; nor can we confound their relations, or trace them to one common origin. Every effect, or motion, or change dependant on the one part, or the other, carries with it that mark of its source which it is impossible for an *indifferent* mind to mistake; and even Materialists are spited by their very reasonings proving in each step of their progress the opposite of the conclusion which *is* to come.

It may be assumed that the material part of man is merely a convenient vehicle or machine in which the mind may exist and by which it may

---

166 This couplet may be faintly remembering part of the 'Sleep, gentle sleep' soliloquy from Shakespeare's *Henry IV*, Part 2, III.1: '[...] in the perfumed chambers of the great, / Under the canopies of costly state.'

167 The poem contains so many common phrases and clichés of eighteenth- and early nineteenth-century *belles-lettres* that it is impossible to trace individual sources. In this last couplet alone, 'innocent as the dove' and 'kindle into love' are each to be found in numerous contemporary writings.

168 This essay shares some interests in the divisibility of human nature with *Frankenstein*, published in the same year that 'On Mind and the Duty of Improving It' appeared in the Mental Exercises.

demonstrate its powers. This assumption may be made without any reference to a future state, and simply as it concerns present existence: It is of very ancient date, and as I think, by much the noblest way in which man can be considered; And, yet, perhaps, it will not be allowed me; for whilst such a vast portion of the practice of the world is in opposition to it, I have no right to suppose that that portion will condemn itself by admitting the above assumption.

Though on being asked the question of what is the relative situation of Mind and Matter in Man, every one who understood it, and there are few that would not in its simplest terms, would be ready with an answer; yet it may be justly doubted, whether the answer would accord with the opinion induced by a short succeeding consideration of the subject. The question is put to every man every moment of his life, and he acts in consequence; indeed, actual life is nothing more than a continual answer to it. The *nature* of Man consists in the union of mind and matter; and he would think the question of his moving, thinking, and living, according to his *nature*, ridiculous, because he can have no other object: Yet the terms of this ridiculous question include those of the one asked before, and if it is absurd to ask him whether he lives according to his nature, it is as absurd to ask him what that nature is.

Considered in this way, things appear confused. Man doubts not for a moment that he acts correctly; but to act, he must think; and to act correctly, act according to his nature; he must know his nature, therefore, as well, and as readily as he knows how to act; and, yet, when asked of his nature in abstract terms, his answer is doubtful; and in most cases, the more he thinks, the more it varies from that we should deduce from his usual habits.

The cause of this confusion arises from the very nature of man, existing in his twofold state; and I think, may be explained thus. The two parts of which man is formed, are not associated in any of their proper habits, pleasures, or perceptions; but have distinct objects, distinct modes of action, and distinct gratifications. They *are*, however, associated together in one being; and may be said, to a certain extent, to have a common existence, in consequence of the relations and connections, which in that being are found necessary between them. The line, therefore, which may be supposed to divide the two sets of relations and habitudes belonging to Mind and Matter, has no existence; for whenever we presume to draw it, it trespasses either on the one set or the other. In enumerating and associating together, the modes, affection, and dependancies of the mind;

we should at once claim the Judgment, Memory, and Imagination, with their Progeny,[169] and we should reject Solidity and Extension, with the qualities Opacity, Hardness, Mobility &c dependant on them;[170] But in gathering up the strings which tie Mind and Matter together, doubts would arise respecting their place, and consideration would only render us more undecided. Sensation,[171] for instance, would at first be given to the corporeal system; but, surely, *all* sensation is not corporeal; or if you affirm that it is; inform me where sensation terminates, and how, and when it is, that mind aids and at last makes the pleasure. The votary of sound is enchained by the charms of music, he knows not how, or why; and, without any apparent exertion of his will, is forced into all the various moods of feeling, and into every state of passion, at the pleasure of the demi-god that rules over him. The God, 'tis true, is earthly, is material, and influences only by material means; but mind is connected with the matter he governs, and mind is active in the sensations produced. On the contrary, what can be conceived more intellectual than the Poet's existence. When he leaves his thoughts to commune with the things about him, he scarcely remembers them, so strange are they to him: he eats, he drinks, and he clothes himself; but his only object seems to be, to preserve the existence of his body because mind inhabits it; and he appears in doing so,[172] to play an unwilling tax to nature, who has oppressed him with matter. The moment necessities are supplied, he reverts to intellectuality,

---

169 Cp. John Prior Estlin, *Familiar Lectures on Moral Philosophy*, 2 vols. (London: Longman *et al.*, 1818), I, p. 10: 'To the *Understanding* likewise belong the powers of *Judgment, Memory*, and *Imagination* [...].'

170 Solidity and extension are standard attributes held in eighteenth-century physical science to be characteristic of 'body' (i.e. matter). Opacity and hardness were similarly standard characteristics of metals (e.g. Samuel Parkes' popular *Chemical Catechism*, fourth edn (London: printed for the author, 1810), p. 291: 'The general characters of the metals are, hardness, tenacity, lustre, opacity, fusibility, malleability, and ductility'). On mobility, see for instance the 1814 English translation of the first volume of Simon Laplace's *Mécanique céleste, A Treatise upon Analytical Mechanics*, trans. John Toplis (Nottingham: for Longman *et al.* and others, 1814), p. 125: 'mobility is the characteristic property of fluids.' But alongside these specifically scientific usages, the passage seems to owe a good deal to Locke's distinction between the ideas 'peculiar to spirit', viz. 'thinking and will', and the ideas 'peculiar to body', viz. 'the cohesion of solid, and consequently separable, parts, and a power of communicating motion by impulse.' Locke ascribes 'existence, duration, and mobility' to both spirit and body (*Essay Concerning Human Understanding*, book II, ch. 23, §17–18).

171 'Sensation': originally 'Sensatition', the 'ti' crossed through.

172 'In doing so' inserted above the line in original scribe's hand.

the only state in which he seems to possess existence; and there gives to the mind unbounded liberty, in which she indulgies even to extravagance. But, analyse these sensations, and follow them by the most rigid rules of assimulation, still they will descend towards matter. Some, 'tis true, preserve their mental character unsullied; for being in their nature perfectly abstracted from matter, they cannot be associated with it; but, these are few in number compared with the rest, and belong rather to the Philosopher than the Poet; and all those fine raphsodies on the Passions, all those enchanting views of nature, which emanate from the Poet like the aura of a deity, are only so to *material* beings, and owe their beauty, and even existence, to a material nature in the world around.

It is in consequence of this combination of mind and matter in so many of the actions and states of life, that, the question asked at the commencement of these observations, receives such unsettled and various answers from different men. Say unto a person directly in words "which is superior in your nature, Mind or Matter?" and if a man of the least thought, he would say *Mind*. But obtain your answer from observation of his actions, and it is *matter*. Point out the apparent contradiction, and he will at first deny its reality; urge him to consideration, he will either refuse the subject altogether, or doubt his first answer; but oblige him to pursue it, and you come to this result: He perceives the inconsistency of his conduct in the pursuits and enjoyments which engage his attention, and which in almost all cases are sensual and subservient to materiality; and correcting such habits commits himself to the guidance of reason rather than sensation and employs himself in tendering, cultivating and improving the powers of the mind; he becomes in pleasure more independant and more refined; his artificial wants diminish; and finding more resources within himself than he had at first supposed, or than man can have in his material nature; he perceives the completeness of his nature in himself, he goes less abroad for aid, or engagement, or any requisite of life, gains a superior and independant station, and is able, where he before stooped to receive; to dispense of the abundance of things he finds within himself.—Or finding that he cannot justify he practices and habits by the intention of his nature, as reason immediately explains it to him, he doubts the conclusion he has drawn with her aid and again and again defers to decide on the change he should make: inclination urges him to resort still more frequently to the material sources of pleasure, and existence and the more degraded and inefficient they become the more eagerly does he resigns himself to them: At each fresh thought of Mind he preserves less respect for it, and willing to believe that its irksome reproofs are unjust, he doubts it right of judging the man, and either succeeds, in forgetting it altogether, or satisfies himself, (too easily satisfied), that it is a mere bundle of useless habits, and antiquated notions.

Such then is man; and such the result of his efficient or inefficient view of his own nature. When first organized and subjected to the laws of Society and the Universe, he is unconscious even of his own existence. As his faculties dawn, they are employed, rather in perceiving the existence of other beings, than of himself; and the sole wish of the infant seems to be, to be like others. An artificial and adventitious character is stampt on him, before he perceives the state which nature intended for him; and when he assumes individuality, and independant existence as his right, and acts in consequence, 'tis in the form and by the rules which the world has previously given him. Drawn on through every moment of his existence by the example of Society, and threatened with expulsion if he does not accommodate his manners to the general usage, he never considers until life is finished, the accordance of its intention, and its reality; and then perceives, when too late, that he had mistaken its object.—If, perchance, the attention of the individual is either from accident, from friendship, or from strength of mind, drawn towards a consideration of himself, and the intention of nature in him; then, as I have before stated, is he either degraded or exalted from his first state, according to the result of his thoughts and practices: If he fails in producing within himself, a full conviction of the inversion by Society of the natural laws of man; or of establishing within himself, the proper subordination of body to Mind; then he falls even from his first humble state; and voluntarily falls the lower, that he may never come within the sphere of that consciousness, which would inevitably reproach him. But if he succeeds; he immediately disembarrasses himself of the trammels that opinion had laid on him; all the imaginary objects attached to his former state disappear; phantoms and shadows no longer amuse and cheat him; he secures an infallible test for the propriety of every intention, and every object; his thoughts have but one subject, mind; and though he may, and must be retarded by the ruin of the habits he had before so eagerly accumulated, yet still he will make constant advances towards that state of unity, of dignity, and of happiness, which belongs to the pure and uncorrupted nature of man.

In thus giving utterance to these general opinions on the nature of man, I beg leave to attach to them a justification of myself in *presuming* to do it, and in thus doing it.—Without any intention of considering man in a moral or metaphysical state, I have tried to throw a few thoughts together in such a way, as to illustrate what I have further to say about the mind and as might be agreeable, or fit, in our confined circle. Though considering the nature of Man, I do not profess to consider his whole nature, for my subject does not require it. I have aimed, also, more at utility than perfection; and, I did not think it required of me in composing for our Circle, to compose for critical, methodical, abstract, moral philosophers.—Thus I justify my presumption:—And with respect to the *way* in which I have done it, I have first to remind you of what with me is a principle, the separation of morality from Religion.[173] Wishing to be understood to the full extent and acceptation of my words, I wish nothing *added to* them: and where no meaning is expressed, claim that none be assumed or implied. I have not mentioned Religion nor have I thought of Religion, except to prevent its introduction here: at the same time, I have not substituted for it, but have considered duties and states independant of it, and for this to me,[174] plain reason, that I think too highly of Religion to regulate it by mere moral duties, or to subject it to the weak powers of reason which I or any man can exert. What further regards my way of considering man will I hope require no explanation.

If I succeed in gaining an assent to the superiority which I have given to the mental part of man over the material, and, I can hardly fail where the mere enunciation of the proposition, where added to actual, though depraved existence, must carry its affirmation with it; then, I want also to succeed in calling attention to the difference between that assent, and the general practice in life. This I do, merely for forms sake; for though I have assumed the right, in considering the nature of man generally, to doubt a consciousness of that difference, yet I should be ashamed to suppose that any one who attempts to improve himself as we profess to do, had not for himself anticipated all that I have said: and I wish you to recall the result of those presumed reflections to your minds, only that you may perceive more readily the propriety of enforcing the duty of improving the mind.

That the powers of the mind are capable of Improvement, is I think unquestionable. Indeed, some have gone so far as to assert, that all

---

173 Cp. Faraday, letter of 11 October 1812 to Abbott: 'I find I am passing insensibly to a point of divinity and as those matters are not to be treated lightly I will refrain from pursuing it—all I meant to say on that point was that [...] I appear moral and hope that I am so tho' at the same time I consider morality only as a lamentably deficient state' (*Correspondence*, I, p. 39).

174 'To me,' added above the line.

the superiority which Genius appears to possess over ordinary under-standings, is owing to an accidental and fortuitous improvement, to which a common mind has been subjected by the peculiar circumstances and situations of life.[175] That this is the case; that all minds are equal in infants and equally capable of improvement in men, I am not presumptuous enough to assert; but modified and reduced into a less startling form, I will, encouraged by the company of many others, support the possibility of improvement in them, even great improvement, and I venture to promise even in this book an illustration of it both in theory and practice.

I think every mans experience will furnish him with illustrations of the proposition asserting the possibility of improving the mental powers; for though, perhaps, every individual has some part of his character to conceal, which if exposed would exhibit a wide and barren waste of uncultivated mind, yet still every one will in other parts of his character offer proofs of its truth. It is not my object to find a being who in every thing has thought and acted correctly, who has wasted no portion of time, who has neglected no power in his possession; for though such a being would prove the point I want to establish, yet he would destroy the general interest of my subject, by shewing it was not necessary for, and did not apply to him. I can as well succeed by gathering from different persons different evidence, so as to prove in turn, the possible advancement of every part of the mind; and at the same time that this is done, the deficiencies we meet with on other points, will offer the strongest reasons for agitating this subject and recommending the particular improvements that come before us for general imitation.

Instead of seeking out for the brightest and fairest examples to illustrate what has been advanced I will revert to the meanest and most degraded wretch I can find: fully convinced that he will afford me abundance of aid, and trusting that such an example of the facility with which it may be supported will ensure a ready reception and acknowledgment of this point of my subject. This witness shall be the good liver, the Gourmand. the Gourmand is a being, in which mind exists in union with matter in the lowest state of degradation; and it seems almost entirely absorbed and swallowed up, in the sensations, affections, and feelings of the material

---

175 Cp. Johnson, 'Life of Cowley', in *Lives of the English Poets*, in *The Works of Samuel Johnson*, ed. Arthur Murphy, 12 vols. (London: Nichols *et al.*, 1810), IX, pp. 1–71 (p. 2): 'The true genius is a mind of large general powers, accidentally determined to some particular direction.'

part. The highest pleasure this being feels, is in the gratification of a sense entirely[176] bodily and sensual, and the only object he seems to have, is the artificial excitation of it. He waits not until nature calls for food, but forces it on to her: Or if he waits, it is not in obedience to her dictates, but opposing her salutary precepts and admonitions, he excites those feelings to the utmost, which were never intended to have a primary influence: and, merely for the enjoyment of appeasing them. That the habitation of the mind may not fall to decay, during the refined and intellectual employment of its spiritual inmate, nature has furnished it the means of making known its want of repairs; these consist in slight involuntary pains, which disturb faintly the general pleasure of the system and which disappear when nature is supplied. But the *eater* has formed to himself new but meretricious pleasures, and in these involuntary sensations, which in reality are so many proofs of the *imperfection* of our present nature; and their apparently adventitious accompaniment taste, has founded the *highest* and most *exalted* of his enjoyments—At times, when by habits of repletion (which even he confesses to be bad, but only because they have rendered torpid the feelings which delight him,) he has so far changed and debased his state, that the system refuses to furnish those admonitory tokens of its wants which did belong to it; and when natural appetite with him is a mere name; then does he force the enslaved mind to the degraded office of suggesting means to create an artificial one, and though employed in this unnatural manner so opposed to her own nature, yet the practices so common in great cities, prove the efficacy, the sad efficacy of her exertions.

Of all the Senses taste stands lowest with relation to Mind We can with difficulty, only, conceive the possibility of its furnishing a single idea which the imagination can take up and make its own, and the judgment will scarcely at any time deign to take cognizance of them. Yet, this is the sense which to the good liver is as a God. This is the Source of his pleasures, the object of his greatest solicitude. It is practiced and varied in a thousand ways, it is modified, inverted, and so that this sensation be pleasurable, though death be in the morsel it must be eaten.

In fine the eater is a being whose actual existence is material, whose pleasures consists in bodily sensation, whose care is solely to supply matter to his system, and whose occupation is the return of animal matter to dust again. He moves in the same sphere with the worm, and has not higher thoughts; and yet this being will prove the possibility of

---

176 'Entirely': originally 'entirely and', the 'and' crossed through.

improving the mental powers. Though the mind be totally enslaved to the body, though never exerted but to supply its desires, though not one native thought allowed it; still it evinces the privilege of improvement, still it is progressive; but, alas, how progressive; the farther it proceeds the more it departs from the course assigned it, and the more it embarrasses its own return.

If asked to shew the mind thus employed, I must confess my inability; but I am glad of it, for I would not willingly be acquainted with one so debased. But I have seen such pass by me, and I refer you to modern feasts, and modern feasters, in illustration of what such minds have and can do. Observe the multifarious ways of dressing food, the astonishing variety of forms in which the same viand can appear; observe the disgraceful refinement in wines, the disgusting variety in the sauces, the complex nature of the accompaniments; and for this I think I need not refer you to French Cookery, which has a list of 200 Sauces, which describe 40 ways of dressing oysters, and between 70 and 80 different methods of cooking mutton, for the experience of an Englishman, though far beneath this, will[177] be sufficient.[178]

When we consider the whole quantity of *refinement* of this kind, (I am obliged to use that word,) and the multitude of distinct steps required in it; it will be evident, that it is so great, as to exceed the comprehension of a single human being. If, then, we turn our thoughts towards an estimate of what can be done by minds which endeavour to act consonantly to the dignity of their being, and to improve the very essence of their nature, the conviction must arise that it is almost unbounded.—What can indeed confine the mind willing to improve, but the shortness of time and the weakness of the body; and whilst time continues, and beings succeed each other, she must ever be progressive where the inclination exists.

It frequently happens that men answer remarks, saying, "I am not competent", "I cannot"—"I shall not be able"—"I have not the abilities".—Idleness most frequently dictates these answers, though sometimes interest, and sometimes other causes suggest them; but no man in his heart thinks he cannot improve himself; there is no man who has not the vanity to suppose he might be good, or wise, or learned, if he would exert his powers and resolution, although to the present moment something has

---

177 'Will': 'still' inserted in a different ink above the line.
178 The fact that during his tour on the Continent in the mid 1810s Faraday experienced French cooking at first hand supports L. Pearce Williams' attribution of this essay to Faraday.

intervened to prevent him: And the result of the Mans thoughts are right, though, perhaps illogically obtained; for there *is no man* who might not better his principles, his judgment, or his information by exertion, and the great and injurious error is in his *delaying* to do it.

I do not believe that any feeling of the breast is more general, or more ready, than the consciousness of a capability of Improvement: but it rarely seems present to the mind at the right moment. To be useful, it should be active when the opportunity and time exist; but it is generally recalled to the mind, only, when the reward of merit is bestowed on others; and, instead of causing previous excitement, so that the reward should be contested for; it only comes to give birth to vain regret and self reproach.

Both Reason and Instinct (if I may be allowed to use that word) point out the principle of *Improvement* in the Mental powers, and yet in the common usage of the world they are both overpowered. Reason points it out from the consideration of the relative situation of Mind and Matter and their respective properties, but is overpowered by Sensuality.— Instinct does it by an innate internal feeling, which, however, through idleness and habit, loses its power.

The man who admits that the Mind is superior to the body inasmuch as it controuls and directs it, must of necessity admit the propriety of its improvement; but he who remembers its exalted and superior character, not only admits it, but feels it incumbent on him to cherish it to the utmost. As possessing a consciousness of its own existence which the body does not, and as including the end and aim of our being, it becomes of such inestimable value, that reason dictates every possible care should be taken of it; and, when by a consideration of itself it perceives the existence of many powers and properties, which are not only competent to form its present state, but to extend it much farther; it seems to the mind treason against itself not to cherish and extend those very powers, by which it exists. This duty presses more urgently on the reason from every Essay of the mental powers, for still with improvement is the nature of the mind rendered more perfect, and the greater the advancement the more powerful the consciousness that the state arrived at is the true and fit one for the existence of the faculties.

The result which reason offers therefore to the meditative man, is, the duty of mental improvement; and the influence which directly opposes this stimulus, is the corporeal sensations. *How* they oppose has been noticed before, but I have yet to point them out as forming one of those obstructions which are to be removed. As long as they exist in full plentitude of power, they will effectually mar any efforts at improvement, and the first thing, therefore, required, is to impress on the mind a full, firm, and perpetual consciousness, of the superiority of the mind over the body; the constant preconsideration it ought to gain; and the absolute subordination in which the body ought to be to it.

The almost innate idea which I before referred to, of the possibility of self improvement, and which I ventured to call instinct, persuades us that we could have been superior to what we really are, if we had endeavoured to be so. It would hardly be consistent to offer reason in favour of this idea, supposing it instinctive, and, as, if it is not so, it must be the result of vanity, it will in that case not be[179] worth a reason The most important point, however, the existence of the idea, may be established either by self examination or by general examination, and its influence in numerous cases is also undoubted: By continually, but modestly, recurring to it, it would tend to give a confidence to the mind, of great importance in its attempts to elevate itself; and by degrees would remove the idle habits which chain it down in self willed inaction.

I have now stated the *possibility* of improving the powers of the mind, and the *propriety* of doing so: there now only remains, to render this subject usefully complete, a statement of the best means of doing so. What I have already stated, are merely points of opinion, but this is a matter of practice; the others are preparatory, this the result to be obtained; the others I have urged to raise attention and excite interest, this is offered for exercise as a source of positive and permanent benefits. I will not stop at present to notice more than one or two general principles deducible from what has been said, and which I think should be impressed on the mind; they are such as these. We should acquire[180] an habitual and perpetual consciousness of the high value and dignity of the mind, and of the state for which it is competent; and we should cherish a modest but firm conviction that we are equal to nobler and better things.—These are a sort of preparatory means, which used enable us, directly, to follow those instructions which apply immediately to a system of mental discipline, and which whenever earnestly used must be productive of valuable results.

Perhaps I may be tempted to resume this subject at a future time if for no other reason, for this; that it holds my own thoughts to the subject. I shall think myself at liberty to pursue my plan in a way which may appear

---

179 'Be' inserted above the line by the original scribe.
180 'Should' inserted above the line by the original scribe.

to me useful, rather than logical, for as we have not merely to move a machine which is already in order and perfect in every part, but have to correct one which is deranged and moving in a wrong direction; so it is not theoretical views and ideal impulses of the mind that will suffice, but such immediate and peculiar applications, as will at the same time that they originate a right impulse, overcome those which are wrong.

A word for Page 73[181]

It appears by a Letter signed Garreteer[182] that a certain Gentleman of our Picknick[183] Class is favoured by a generous Muse in his own estimation, we should be doubtless happy in the perusal of his handy works,[184] but he must not think to disarm us in Criticism by pretending to throw a stumbling block in our way, for if he is willing to throw the Gauntlet in the ring, he may not go far to find a Combatant, at any rate if he is the author, of a certain long and laborious Ode or the *then then* style of a trifle called Agis.[185]

On the Early Introduction of Females to Society

> O, friendly to the best pursuits of man,
> Friendly to thought, to virtue and to peace,
> Domestic life in rural leisure pass'd!
> Few know thy value, and few taste thy sweets,
> Though many boast thy favours, and affect
> To understand and choose thee for their own.[186]

There is a most lamentable practice among society, viz, that of introducing the rising generation at too early a period into mixt company; or what

---

181 Page 73 of the original MS contains the first page of 'Garreteer's Epistle'.

182 See above, pp. 88–89.

183 'Picknic': originally 'picknick', the 'k' crossed through. Picnic: 'something which has multiple contributors or sources; a miscellany, a collection, an anthology' (OED).

184 'Handy works': handiwork.

185 'Ode': perhaps 'An Ode to the PASS'; see above, pp. 82–88. 'Agis': see above, pp. 74–75.

186 William Cowper, 'The Garden', book III of *The Task* (1785), ll. 290–95; punctuation altered.

is more fashionably termed "bringing them out" at a period when the youthful mind is most liable to imbibe false ideas, when it is acted upon in a truly alarming manner; the result of which is seriously injurious, rendering them unfit for those stations they may be called upon to fulfill in the world, in[187] the more happy enjoyment of Domestic pursuits.

Independant of the destructive inroads late hours and a continued change of pleasures and amusements make on the too delicate constitution of these tender plants; it engenders an unsettled habit, a dissatisfaction of home, and of the solid comforts there only generally to be met with; they do not feel the value of their own innocent domestic circle.

A reflective mind cannot but shudder at the idea of a beautiful and innocent female introduced into mixt society "where weeds and flowers promiscuous shoot;"[188] however the susceptible heart may be delighted by their charms, or the wanton eyes of men gratified by the splendid beauty of these youthful, and I may add unblown roses, what'ere the gratification to be allowed the honour of introducing to the gay assembly or in the happiness of receiving their fair hand "as with smooth steps, disclosing motion in its every charms they swim along and swell the mazy dance"[189] for beauty is their own,

> "The feeling heart, simplicity of life,
> "And elegance, and taste: the faultless form;
> "Shap'd by the hand of harmony; the cheek
> "Where the live crimson, through the native white
> "Soft shooting, or'e the face diffuses bloom,
> "And every nameless grace; the parted lip,
> "Like the red rose bud moist with morning dew,
> "Breathing delight; and under flowing jet,
> "Or sunny ringlets, or of circling brown,
> "The neck slight shaded, and the swelling breast;
> "The look resistless, peircing to the soul."[190]

However their fascinating charms may inspire us to the most tender

---

187 'In' crossed out, and 'and' inserted in a different hand above the line.

188 Pope, *Essay on Man* (1734–35), l. 7.

189 Thomson, 'Autumn', in *The Seasons*, ll. 594–96: 'with smooth step, / Disclosing motion in its every charm, / To swim along, and swell the mazy dance;' (on the appropriate femininity of British women).

190 From 'beauty is their own' to the end of this quotation: Thomson, 'Summer', in *The Seasons*, ll. 1580–91; punctuation altered.

feelings; so soon as our ideas cease to be acted upon by those feelings, and we awake as it were from a pleasing dream we give vent to serious thoughts, which although irrelevant to the gay scenes around, are natural as they are becoming; for on viewing these "Daughters of mirth" as in succession they pass along the mazy throng O how striking the change, how altered the features of some of those of our early acquaintance, who for Beauty of countenance, and expression could be compared only to the splendour of the Rose; but now alas! must be classed with the Lily, when exposed to the rude touch of the offending hand it falls, it withers long before its time. Hearken ye Parents guardian protectors of these your charming Daughters; should disease, premature affliction be the consequence of this early initiating to the gay and destructive amusements of the Town; or should misplaced affections in simplicity of heart on an unworthy object be the consequence; will ye not then in bitter agony disclaim the practice and as tender plants watch over their innocence with unceasing care that in successive years they may blossom out, and prove the joy and pride of thy last evening days.

T.

Memoranda

A Man should be tardy in the choice of his friends, but lasting in the remembrance of them.

Paris is all Superfluity, London all Solidity.

Many fools travel in Foreign Countries in search of new Wonders, without being acquainted with half the Curiosities of their own.

My friend has but few faults, but wherever he raises a Storm the bolt is sure to break on his own head.

The Son of Napoleon is more legitimate on the throne of France than the present Dynasty on that of England.

Cassius would fain degrade the great Julius for his want of bodily strength, but the World will ever remember that to that alone they owe the enjoyment and Instruction that his Commentaries afford.[191]

We are all clever in our own Eyes.

---

191 Julius Caesar wrote commentaries on the Gallic and Civil Wars. In *Julius Caesar* I.2, Shakespeare has Cassius recount episodes of Caesar's relative lack of physical hardihood, to suggest that Caesar's supremacy is illegitimate or delusory.

Whatever is great and noble in the Acts of Men may be found in the history of ancient times, and whatever is mean and despicable will be found among the moderns.

To read the various Histories of the ancients seems like breathing the Atmosphere of Health and Liberty, but when we come down to the relation of our more modern exploits it seems like being shut up in some monkish Cell, and sometimes affects the head with a feeling that we experience in Childhood at the recital of some gothic story some dull old fashioned Mansion, or the dreams of such in the Nightmare.

Got a long & tedious poem in hand, wonder if it will ever come into the Class-book.

I have received repeated injury from a Man who has long professed to be my friend; lately having detected him in several treacherous transactions I resolved to be revenged on him, when in the height of passion, I thought of a more glorious revenge and so forgave him.

It is a hard matter to proclaim an Error universal, yet there seems to be something very like it when we see the difference paid to natural Abilities over acquired. A Man who is born with good natural abilities with very little Industry or exertion attain much Celebrity, while those who are of a dull disposition naturally with every care and desire to amend, will scarcely find half the encouragement in the World.

On prematurely Forming Opinion of Characters

There is perhaps, not a more evident mark of the vanity of the human Character, than the facility with which men flatter themselves, they can discover the train of reasoning, and the bias of judgment of others, by the smallest exertion of their *own* minds, or by little more than simple perception.

That mankind do, in various degrees, possess an intuitive knowledge of temper, from phisiognomy, will not be disputed; but we are continually reminded, in our intercourse with the world, of the fallacy of such impressions, and of the danger of forming connections on such unsubstantial and unreasonable cases. Under the most forbidding countenance is often found the best regulated mind, and he whose face, is a sufficient introduction wherever he enters, is frequently discovered to possess none of the qualities which insure the continuance of goodwill and respect, or that prevent ultimate disappointment.

If then, from various causes, the mind is altered from its original character, and can assume any other, it must be hazardous to form an estimate of man's opinions or principles, from a few sentences, or from a slight acquaintance—Yet how often do we perceive in Society, the ill effects of this premature decision; were youth the only cause, it might be considered in some degree excusable, for then prepossession is powerful, and credulity is generally the companion of inexperience; idle scandal, fancied matrimonial schemes, or a pretended dislike to them might perhaps be their principal topics, and from them we do not expect serious consequences. But on more important subjects, we often see the man condemned, who has not been tried, because he appears to doubt whether the opinions advanced are consistent with reason; and merely differing is made a sufficient crime to be punished by misrepresentation—Eugenius in the company of Bigots questioned the power of the king under some peculiar circumstances, and considered that a Monarch is but a Man, who is elevated to his rank by the general consent of his fellows not to debauch himself with the luxuries which his high station could command; but to be an example to others, the arm of power for the administration of the laws, and the fulfilling of justice, the source of honour to reward meritorious services done for the Country, and the fountain of mercy towards those, to whom, although condemned by the laws it was thought it might be extended. For saying so much Eugenius is condemned, as a democrat, a leveller, one who wishes ill to his Country, a dangerous man and a revolutionist. This takes wind and Age cautions Youth; beware of Eugenius he is a tainted man, a man who professes his sentiments, is[192] not under the influence of any moral obligations. Thus the illiberality of forming opinions from slight circumstances proves often the most serious consequences, and generally originates either from the careless habit of a shallow or conceited mind, or from one under the influence of prejudice. Prejudice either for or against any subject, throws over it so thick a veil, which is difficult for the rays of truth to pierce, and we too often find it, not only preventing but actively operating against it by repelling the rays. Were we carefully to investigate the state of mind which the person is in, who seems to take a pleasure in traducing the principles of others, or of speaking lightly of them on serious subjects, we should find that they had perhaps thought less on that subject than any one, but were[193] merely

---

192 'Is': originally 'and is', the 'and' crossed through.
193 'Were': originally 'where', the 'h' crossed through in different ink.

Chaff driven before the wind,[194] or a straw on the surface of a stream at the mercy of the waves.

It is a question, whether it is more noble and consistent with the dignity of man, to bring into action that superiority, which the Deity for the most exalted purposes has given him over all created Nature, or to remain with a mind capable of the highest improvements, innert, inglorious, in mental slavery?—When we arrive at a certain age we are immediately considered by our friends and by the laws of our Country, accountable for our actions and principles; this being the case, we should make ourselves competent to answer when asked, why do you act thus, what reason can you give for entertaining such and such opinions?—Yet in endeavouring to improve ourselves in youth if we adopt the mode of putting questions to the *ability* of those with whom we converse, it is *then* that liberality is wanted; instead of *concluding* from the *tenor* of the questions, what the principles of a person are, they ought to consider them only as the means adopted to elicite sentiments, and or the elucidation of the subject discussed. This disingenuous[195] mode produces the worst effects; it prevents a communication of sentiments, which might be the means of proving that the parties approached nearer in opinion than they first thought; it makes some suppose, that as their questions are avoided or as they do not *get* reasonable answers, they *cannot be* reasonably answered, and thus it too often prevents the correction of youthful errors and fancies.

Y.—February 1819.

---

194 Psalms 35.5: 'Let them be as chaff before the wind [...].'
195 'Disingenuous': originally 'disingenous', the 'u' inserted above the line.

On the Death of the Princess Charlotte[196]

Who can repress the sympathetic tear,
Oe'r youth, and virtue, on the mournful bier;[197]
Stretch'd pale by Death in earliest ripen'd years
Britons repine, and melt in sorrows tears,
Yes Albion weep, your brightest hope is fled,
For lovely Charlotte joins the band of Dead;
With her youth, Beauty, loveliness are gone
And hapless Britons left in gloom forlorn,
Without a youthful race to wear the Crown
Illustrious and to name her great renown,
But ah! our lips shall sing her every praise
And to the skies such virtuous goodness raise.

T. 1817.

Affectation

In submitting to my friends the few following remarks, it will be immediately perceived how little capable I am of treating with sufficient rectitude a subject, that is at all times open to the observation of every individual, the errors and good qualities continually in exposure, and at the same time so much spoken of abstractedly, and seldom wrote[198] of at large, yet I have no apology to offer, but on the other hand would wish, that every one who has an Argument to offer, for, or against it, will advance it as free[199] as I do, for as it will be doubtless an elucidation, I shall be proud to see this Essay fall, either a victim of refutation, or the text of better works.

---

196 Stephen C. Behrendt's study *Royal Mourning and Regency Culture: Elegies and Memorials of Princess Charlotte* (London: Macmillan, 1997), highlights the very large quantity of texts produced in response to the death in childbirth of the daughter of George IV. Princess Charlotte died in November 1817, presumably between a year and 18 months before this entry was made in the Mental Exercises; as the date at the foot of the poem indicates, the author wrote the poem shortly after her death and contributed it to the essay-circle the following year.

197 'The mournful bier': a phrase frequently occurring in elegies and drama concerning mourning in the eighteenth century.

198 'Wrote': 'written' inserted above the line in a different hand.

199 'Free': 'ly' inserted above the line.

Affectation is a Word that needs no definition, it is a virtue or vice (according as it is used) to which we are all subject either more or less; it is a habit that seems so general among mankind that few if any ever escape it, and perhaps its origin was no later than the Age of our first Parents,[200] it may also be perceived in other members of the Creation, as the artificial Grandeur of the Peacocks plumes, or the well trained speed of the Horse, it is so nearly allied to the vice of pride, and so invariably attendant on it, that it is scarcely possible to be proud without being affected.

It may appear rather paradoxical to assert that what is a Vice can also be Virtue, although I am not the first that ever advanced such an Argument, and although I have the authority of a very renowned writer,[201] I will not pretend to determine, but by comparison and observations will endeavour to place them in such in manner, as to facilitate the decision of all[202] who may be pleased with the practice of the one, or detest the appearance of the other.

If a Man is born with certain ill qualities, as uneven temper, or bred with others, as deformity of gait, or harshness of speech, the acquirement of better although it may be affectation, is at all times truly laudable,[203] but there are a race of beings in the world, who in spite of every endowment which they may have received from nature, or of every Instruction which good Education can possibly bestow, or of every opportunity that offers itself for ripening the Judgment, they will take so great a degree of pains to deceive the world, and to hide their true Character, that the dissimulation gaining so great[204] a power, does not fail to affect even the minds of themselves, when we view it in this light—we can no longer wonder why the ancients tell us that it is the hardest thing in the world for a man to know himself.[205]

I have seen (says an Author) a Man who possessed of every degree

---

200 I.e. Adam and Eve.
201 Perhaps Alexander Pope, *Essay on Man*, epistle II, ll. 195–200: 'Extremes in Nature equal ends produce, / In Man they join to some mysterious use; / Though each by turns the other's bound invade, / As, in some well-wrought picture, light and shade, / And oft so mix, the difference is too nice / Where ends the Virtue, or begins the Vice.'
202 'All': 'those' inserted above the line in a different hand.
203 We might think here of Faraday's attendance at Benjamin Smart's Royal Institution lectures on oratory (or elocution) in 1818: see Hamilton, pp. 135–36.
204 'Great' inserted above the line in different ink.
205 Probably a reference to the injunction 'know thyself', often ascribed to Socrates.

of learning that a long duration at College[206] could attain, with all the experience of many years travelling, and perhaps with good natural temper, yet he had so great a portion of affectation as to make himelf almost continually unhappy. He had a remarkable good ear for Music, was an excellent Theorist, and played several Instruments, yet he could not bear to hear one[207] word uttered in praise of any one but himself, sometimes he would spend hours or even days in dividing the particles of a small morsel of Earth, while if he had lived contempory with Julius, perhaps they would have found very little difficulty in leveling all the Mountains in Italy, this is a sort of affectation that is scarcely pitiable.

There is another degree of this ill Quality which is truly the pest of all civil intercourse, it is a sort of fear or dread of being known in our own Characters, and it is generally so ill managed, that in the attempt to hide one failing there are fifty virtues concealed—I was lately favoured by a piece of information from a friend who as a Philosopher is a great observer of human Nature, and particularly of the action of those who he may with justice consider within his own sphere. he observes

I was the other day invited to an entertainment at the House of a Friend, and having arrived among the earlier part of the visitors, I took my station in a part of the room distant from that which is generally appointed for the ceremony of Introduction, and being rather left to a better share of quiet than most of the Company, I had a good opportunity of indulging my favourite Study "velute in speculum".[208]

At one time there were three or four Gentlemen ushered in with so much ceremony as almost to amaze the whole company present, for while I endeavoured by enquiry to find out who they were, but none seemed disposed or able to satisfy me, and having failed in my repeated attempts, I resolved to collect as much as I could from quiet observation, at one time I heard a voice between half whisper and general tone, mention something about a deceased Uncle Sir Matthew, at another time the mention of a large Legacy was pretty loudly leveled at my ear, at another time I observed that one of those Gentlemen had more attention paid him than the rest, which in the end I discovered to be the rich spoken of young Baronet, but seeing the company rather throng about him at every motion of the entertainment, I began to think there was something

---

206 'College': originally 'Colledge', the 'd' crossed through.
207 'One': 'any' inserted above the line before 'one'.
208 'Velute in speculum': the correct Latin is 'velut in speculum', meaning 'as in a mirror'.

remarkable in his manner or that he was better informed than most of our Beaux, this raised a degree of ambition in me to be a little acquainted with our illustrious Visitor[209] after some time I found means to get an Introduction to him and having seated myself beside him, I ventured to address him on the subject of general Philosophy, and though the speech was delivered with as much Eloquence as I was master of, yet I considered that it was language not unfit for any one, possessed of moderate Education to use, in this I was deceived, for a while he seemed rather embarrassed and after some deliberation he told me that it was some time since he was at College, and when he was there he paid so little attention to his learning as not to be able to converse in any other languge than his mother tongue, at the conclusion of his reply he turned his head to a Gentleman on his other side and made some very appropriate remarks on the races that they were at last, at this moment I felt all the vexation and disappointment naturally incident to such Circumstances and having quitted my seat for one at the opposite side of the room, I entered into conversation with an elderly Lady who seemed in some measure concerned for the hasty departure of a younger Ornament of her Sex, this was a Lady appearing to be about the Age of twenty, whom I several times indulged myself with glancing at, she had entered the room about the same time as our all accomplished Baronet, and being placed by our worthy hostess between two elderly Gentlemen, was so eclipsed by the corpulent carcase of the one, and the forward gabling of the other, that few took any notice of her, this I observed with a less degree of wonder, in consideration that she had none of those costly ornaments about her dress that so invariably attract the eye of fashionables,[210] upon further enquiry about her I found that she was one of those affected beings that will at all times raise admiration in the virtuous and envy in the wicked, her knowledge of the languages of literature and science generally, are extensive she is quite conversant in natural Philosophy the arts and music, and her Fortune is great, and still she is of a retiring disposition in mixed company, and only shines where she thinks she can be of real[211] service or entertainment to her Friends, you may suppose this made me leave the room with a little more satisfaction, and I returned home to contemplate the false Colours in which all Mankind appear at one time or other.

---

209 'In me to be a little acquainted with our illustrious Visitor': inserted above the line in the same ink and hand.

210 'Fashionables': as a noun, dating only from c. 1800 (OED).

211 'Real' inserted.

On Conscious Approbation

Elevated as is the character of Man, still he is but a mere bundle of Ideas, and Ideas differ nothing in their nature from dreams and phantoms.— He may think and reason for ages, were his existence to extend through them, without advancing one jot in the knowledge of that existence; and he is obliged at last, to remain in passive ignorance of it. The common observation made by every idle, thoughtless being, when any thing novel or intricate appears before him, may with great propriety be adopted by the Man of thought; nay more, he is *obliged*, when considering his own nature and existence, to cry out "I cannot believe my senses". All that a man, or any multitude or series of men, could of themselves ascertain, without information from a superior power; would be, that he or they *were*, and had existence; and the whole of that existence would be comprised in the sensations of which they were conscious. What that was in which the sensations existed; what those sensations were; or how excited; they could not tell: nor could they have the least idea of any thing external to the sentient power. The internal proof which a man has of his own existence, is his consciousness of it; and it is the only proof he possesses; but this not being in his power as it regards other beings, *he* really has no proof that they have an existence similar to his own.

The perceptions however which a man has, make up his existence, and whether those perceptions relating to society are founded on the real & external existence of beings similar to himself, or are caused in any other way, still they are to be the rule of his conduct; and the internal monitor[212] he possesses, is as much to be attended to, on the idea of his being an insulated being,[213] as on that which makes him one of many individuals: A point of great importance however I think is gained, by the consideration that a man has no proof of the external existence, of what appear his fellow creatures; namely, that he should in every case of conduct, first gain the approbation of the being he knows to exist i.e. *himself*; before he submits himself in subordination to the opinions of those creatures who perhaps have merely an apparent and fancied existence.

Those who sacrifice their internal and conscientious views of right and wrong, either for the sake of gain, or credit, or honor, or any other motive, in reality sacrifice them to the respect, the approbation, or the applause

---

212 A common formulation in early nineteenth-century writing on morality.
213 Another common formulation in this period.

of others.—It must be acknowledged that in every point of view this is wrong; but it not only appears wrong, but ridiculous and absurd, when it is remembered, that the man who offends himself, and who acts against his conscience, knows nothing of the beings he does it for.—who perhaps are nothing more, than the vapours and phantoms of his imagination.—Such a man is a sort of madman; no certainty exists that his views are real or unreal, and his senses are on a level with those of the lunatic who worships a straw as his god. The only difference is, that the mans madness is common to the whole race, and is therefore not perceived by any of them, whilst the Lunatic's differing in its direction and objects becomes observable.

I must beg it to be remembered that no reference has been made to revealed knowledge:[214] that I am concerned only with what man can ascertain by his own powers: I dare not venture to argue on that which the goodness of a supreme being has made known to us by revelation. Such knowledge is to be received by his creatures according to the conscientious feelings of their own breasts. It concerns them with their creator and not with their fellow creatures. Though of this very superior nature, it does not interfere with or contradict the rule of life, which each[215] has in his own breast; and in the attempt I have made to establish the propriety of self approbation, I have taken this as my guide.

April 5th 1819

The Origin of a Critic—A Fable

A little learning is a dangerous thing
Drink deep or taste not the pierian spring.
Pope.[216]

How oft mankind aspiring efforts make!
How oft thro' fear their flatt'ring prospects shake!
Their Castles built in air confess their base,
For shook by Fancy's breeze they change their place:
At their creator's will, these fabrics are,
With every beauty deck'd and proof to care;
By the same powers, desponding vapours rise,

214 I.e. religion. Cp. above, p. 112.
215 'Each' inserted above the line in same ink and hand.
216 Pope, 'Essay on Criticism', ll. 217–18.

The prospects intercept & cloud the skies:
'Till Reason's Sun, darts thro' the mazy gloom,
His powerful rays the brightened Skies illume;
And then no more, deceitful visions play
Which led the wanton mind so far astray.
Perchance inlieu of scenes from fairy land,
Corrected Vision finds a cottage stand;
More humble notions now possess the mind—
With bitters, sweets, with roses thorns we find.
How oft in Youth, the vigorous passions press
To find expression in poetic dress;
And warmth of feeling, then 'tis thought might claim,
A lenient hand to raise the trump of fame.
But only those should try this stormy sea,
Who are well rigg'd with wit and vanity,
Who for their ballast, learning take in store
Their Pilot Prudence, and of Classic lore
A cargo such as good returns will make
Of ample profit for the ventured stake—
Let those who are not fitted out this way
Steal round the shores, or on the rivers play.
In still domestic lakes, their vessel try
Where partial breezes, make a cloudless sky.
For Nature made not all who write in rhyme,
To muse in raptures or to soar sublime
Will each the magic of th'harmonic thrill
Confess he feels or can express at will?
When Nature would their Art will not comply
And Art once gained then Nature oft is shy
Yet some will venture out to meet the storm
Of adverse winds from every Critic form,
Press'd on by Pride they seek the port of Fame[217]

---

217 Cp. Paul Whitehead, 'Honour: A Satire' (written 1747), ll. 137–44: 'Thro' Life's wild
Ocean, who would safely roam, / And bring the golden fleece of Glory home, / Must,
heedful, shun the barking *Scylla's* roar, / And fell *Charybdis'* all-devouring shore; /
With steady helm an equal course support, / Twixt Faction's rocks, and quicksands of
a Court, / By Virtue's beacon still direct his aim, / Thro' Honour's channel, to the port
of *Fame.' The Poems and Miscellaneous Compositions of Paul Whitehead* (Dublin: Price
et al., 1777), pp. 81–97 (p. 89).

Nor think aught wanting or themselves to blame
Before their reeling bark has found too late
The crowded vortex of a common fate
Thus prove their wants of genius or of art
Oblivion seek—or act a Critic's part.

       The sapient bird of night as fables say
Once slept thro' shade, and hail'd the morning ray
With cheerful wing, he wanton'd in the air
And join'd the feather'd choir in carols there;
Long had he liv'd by friendly crowds carest,
Long happy liv'd if with contentment bless'd
But in an hour, a fatal hour, t'is thought
He drank of a spring with wond'rous powers fraught
On whose gay banks such tempting flowrets grew
That thirsty Souls flock'd round it not a few;
Crowds came on crowds and sipp'd & sipp'd again
But as they only sipp'd it caused them pain
For of that potent stream, if those who drink
Dip round the edge or at the flow'ry brink
Quaff but a potion²¹⁸ for their puny thirst
As not to quench or lay the fiery dust
Or only tease, intoxicate their brain—
But listen now the fable makes it plain.
For know, this spaient bird was one of these
And dipp'd his beak so far his taste to please
And to imbibe enough, to raise weak passions
Puff up his pride to head seducing fashions
To emulate the king of birds in flight,
And meet the godlike Sun in equal height
The morning blush'd—his head was whirling round
He left the spring and spurn'd the dewy ground.
On high he soars—the Sun viel'd by a cloud
The Eagle mock'd but scorn'd to laugh aloud
Now reach'd a height—too much for dizzy brains,
He thought he felt the cure for all his pains,
Just then the Sun gleam'd full upon his head

---

218 'Potion': originally 'portion', with the 'r' crossed through.

He flutter'd shriek'd and toppling fell as dead
Thro' th'expansive air, no more to rise,
The Eagle laugh'd his laughter fill'd the skies
Down by a ruin'd wall the Culprit fell
In a dark hole he crept and curs'd the well
From which his sorrows sprang; but still he feels
The potent liquid, and his blood congeals
For now no more he shews his face in day
But skulks in hollow trees his hours away
'Till night comes on, and that bright sun descends
That caus'd his fall; soon as the moon attends
He ventures out, then o'er the fields to roam
And slay the sleeping warblers in their home
Or lonely flitting o'er the shaded Vales
He hoots harsh Critiques on the Nightingales
While mimic echoes from the woods around
Detect his screams—but still repeat the sound.

March 1819—Y.

Reflections on Death

The Man how wise who sick of gaudy scenes
Is led by choice to take his fav'rite walk
Beneath Death's gloomy silent Cypress shades
Unpierced by Vanity's fantastic ray
To read his Monuments—to weigh his dust
Visit his vaults and dwell among the tombs!

Young.[219]

Where is the certainty of things
On what in life can we confide
The like attends the Sovereign Kings
The blooming Youth the lovely bride

---

219 Edward Young, 'Night V. The Relapse' in *Night Thoughts on Life, Death, and Immortality* (1742–46), ll. 310–16: 'The man how bless'd, who, sick of gaudy scenes, / (Scenes apt to thrust between us and ourselves!) / Is led by choice to take his favourite walk / Beneath Death's gloomy, silent, cypress shades, / Unpierced by Vanity's fantastic ray; / / To read his monuments, to weigh his dust, / Visit his vaults, and dwell among the tombs!'

Death looks around his victims fall
The high & low his summons 'tend
Both rich & poor obey his call
At his command all humbly bend
No earthly ties of dearest kind
Of youthful wife in brides attire
Or children loved in whom we find
All the fond heart can wish desire
Not Parents, Brothers, Sisters dear
Or those we love; Nor[220] with tender sighs
Nor tears avail when Death draws nigh
Vain all their sorrow vain their cries
The unwelcome Messenger of fate[221]
Walks o'er the land with rapid stride[222]
Each memory quick his deeds relate
Our humbling fear we cannot hide
And when he calls us to our home
Calmly resigns us to the grave
We seek the rude wide world to roam
And yet a little longer crave
We fain would stay still longer yet
We cast a lingering look behind
As if t'were pain that world to quit
Where nought but care and grief we find
We dare not think our end is near
But with the constant stream of joy
Repel the sickening thought of Death
Drink pleasures cup without alloy
We swirl in the tempest roar
The wirlwind rushes o'er the main
Destruction waits us at the door
We ne'er can think time's on the wane
Till Death grim Death his arrows throw

---

220 Semi-colon and 'Nor' added in different ink.
221 Cp. Hester Thrale's comic poem 'The Three Warnings: A Tale' (1766), which calls
Death 'Th'unwelcome messenger of Fate'. The poem was included in anthologies such
as Francis William Blagdon (ed.), *Flowers of Literature; for 1804* (London: Crosby,
1805), pp. 220–24 (p. 222).
222 'Stride': originally 'strides', the 's' crossed through.

Then Man collects his scattered thoughts
Truly forgives each injured foe
Feeling the stream of life cut short
He vainly thinks O could the times
In each successive year return
That he might take the sacred lines
And from that holy volume learn
That it contains the truth reveal'd
That hope of comfort to the heart
The bulwark strong the mighty shield
Able to quench the fiery dart
Which wicked Men in wrath have[223] thrown
Against that holy sacred book
Who cruel brought to nought God's own
All his wise Counsel hath forsook.
O may man then take prudence[224] way
And seek forgiveness for the past[225]
That he may be give for every day
A suitable account at last
Sleep steals at length o'er life's worn thread
No earthly power now can save
Gently reclines his peaceful head
And softly sinks into the grave.[226]

---

223 'Have': originally 'hath', the 'th' crossed through and 've' added in different ink.
224 'Prudence': 'wisdom's' inserted above the line in a different ink and hand.
225 'And seek forgiveness for the past' inserted in a different ink and hand between the
adjoining lines; evidently the scribe accidentally skipped this line.
226 Cp. the deathbed scene in George Crabbe's 'The Village', book I, ll. 294–95: 'He
ceases now the feeble help to crave / Of Man; and sinks into the grave.' *Poems*, sixth
edn (London: Hatchard, 1812), pp. 1–40 (p. 20).

On Avarice

Curst be the gold & silver which persuade
Men to follow far fatiguing trade!
The lily peace outshines the silver store
And Life is dearer than the golden ore;

Collins[227]

Of all the passions which exist in the human breast, & of all the vices which infest civil society, none appear to me more despicable and dangerous than avarice. It is very usual for persons in advocating the cause of the poor and needy to inveigh with bitter invectives against the gay and the profligate. It does to be sure seem inconsistent that one man should be rolling in the utmost gaiety and pleasure, enjoying all that gold can purchase or the world produce, whilst perhaps a being of the same make and species shall be calling upon him in the name of all that is good and sacred to behold his wretchedness and to bestow some small pittance towards alleviating his miseries and supplying against hunger & nakedness.—But what I propose to consider in this little paper is, which is the most injurious to Society, the man of gaiety, pleasure, and fashion, or the avaricious man, whose sole aim it is daily to add to his coffers, whose gold is his god, and who denies himself the common necessaries of life in order to amass that wealth which is of no real utility to him or the society to which he belongs.—The striking contrast between the two characters will facilitate our disquisition of them.—

Let us first view the spendthrift as he is termed by those who now call penury by the new but irroneous name of frugality and would almost commend it as a virtue. Let us notice the man whom fortune has placed somewhat above the generality of his fellow creatures, in rank, title, and property. In the first place we find him possessed of a very large mansion whilst (it may be said) a much less one might do, & not contented with this he must have other residences in the country which probably he seldom visits.—But what of all this does he not keep a large establishment in each place, are not many employed & provided for in the capacity of servants, are not many tradespeople assisted by supplying him with the variou articles of life, and is not society in general benefitted by the diffusion of his income.—But I must confess that he falls very short

---

227 William Collins, 'Hassan: Or, the Camel-Driver', in 'Oriental Eclogues', *The Poetical Works* (London: Sharpe, 1811), pp. 19–23 (p. 20), punctuation altered.

of the performance of his duty, unless he contributes very bountifully to his distressed fellow creatures either through some charitable institution or by more direct means.—

On the other hand we find the avaricious man (either as the merchant, retail trader or whatever be his situation in life its effects are equally the same) using every means that art can suggest to increase his wealth and decrease his expenditure. The comforts & health of himself & his familly, all social intercourse with his friends & neighbours are sacrificed to the desire for gold he never thinks he has enough for[228]

"Riches still what mortal can resist?"[229]

The Avaricious man reminds me of the simple but instructive fable of Aesop respecting the dog in the manger that would not eat the hay himself nor suffer the ox to eat it.[230] So is the Miser and his gold he will neither use it himself nor let others use it. It is really extraordinary to see as we sometimes may do, an aged man loaded with infirmities[231] (who according to the course of nature cannot expect to remain much longer on the stage of life) hugging his gold to the very last moment, and perhaps deferring medical assistance when nature requires it, in order to avoid the expence.—

Are not such beings a pest & a disgrace to our species, are they not far more injurious to Society than the most profligate spendthrift? Far be it from me to censure either prudence or frugality (the times in which we live require them both)[232] but I detest to hear as we sometimes may do, penury miscalled frugality and generosity condemned as extravagance.—

On Tradesmen

Among the various observations that are continually being made among mankind there is none more universal than that which touches on the circumstances of individuals, or their poverty, or riches, we find it so

---

228 After 'for', the manuscript has 'riches' but this word is crossed through.

229 Young, 'Night VI. The Infidel Reclaimed' in *Night Thoughts*, ll. 496–97: 'Riches enable to be richer still; / And *richer still* what mortal can resist?'

230 In e.g. Robert Dodsley (ed.), *Select Fables of Æsop and Other Fabulists: In Three Books* (London: Edwards, 1800).

231 'Loaded with infirmities': a common formulation in eighteenth-century writing about the elderly.

232 The late 1810s were a period of poor harvests and economic hardship in Britain.

much the task of the historian that even the commonest narrator is not without this as the chief topic of relation whenever the subject is the actions of men.

It is the duty of all those who read to judge of what they read, & it is a duty which all seem in some measure to act up to; who peruse the actions of men in the histories of their times. It may seem presumptious for men who have but a moderate education, and a very abstract authority to judge of events that happened thousands of years before their own Era, & yet we find that[233] occurrences every day, there is no one who reads, who does not say that Alexander was ambitious, Areistedes just,[234] Crassus avaricious,[235] Cornillus great, or Corialanus proud,[236] these are decisions which may be made by every one, & in every age, but what is more to be observed with wonder is the very easy manner in which states would be disposed of by the modern commentator, as the actions of Scipio, of Hannibal of Pericles, of Darius, or of Ptolemy, will alike bear his censure or praise, forgetting that he may have just caught an hours glance of them as a relief to some other study.

It is a very natural & equally common practice among us, when we find our own characters attacked, to question the authority of the accuser as if any one says we are all fools, we immediately enquire the source of wisdom, that has discovered what we were not able or willing to believe, & by duly supporting ouselves in the argument, it is rarely that we can complain of inequality in the conflict unless it is by our own faults, or ignorance of the subject we would wish to support, & if we fall it is by the right of power, & our sufferings should be without murmur,[237] but who will not mark without[238] indignation the dastardly attacks that are continually making on the characters of departed men, who are known to us by their superiority over us, & whose greatest faults were but small in comparison with our own.—

Rabagir is a Tradesman of some celebrity, but is no historian. I have seen this nimble fingered Artisan, after some hours play with the pointed steel,[239] leap from his shop board and catching at the first book that came

---

233 'That': crossed through and 'these' inserted above the line in a different ink.
234 Aristides, known as Aristides the Just, was a renowned Athenian statesman.
235 Marcus Licinius Crassus, a Roman triumvir.
236 Coriolanus: an early Roman general.
237 Philippians 2.14: 'Do all things without murmurings and disputings.'
238 'Without': 'out' crossed through.
239 I.e. a needle.

to hand, & sitting down with as much dexterity as he would mend a coat, to tear every character that our age contains in such a manner that if we were to believe all he uttered, Orpheus would yet have been pent up in hell, or Helen in an eggshell for want of music or of charms, at one time we hear him condemning the rashness of Leonidas from a christian principle, or the Patriotism of Cato from the same, & in fact judging men by Jewish Pagan or Christian laws, without the least discrimination whatever, but here the presumption does not end, we agree that Alexander was a great man and so was Phillip his father, but he will sit down to search the records of their times, and with much composure parcel out provinces, divide armies, and tell us that if they had acted so they would have been beaten or so and their victories would have been more compleat, the arrogance of this fellow is boundless as his impudence, he is found meddling with every one's concern, interfering in all matters moral or political, & is known at the head of those abstract statesman who suppose they are at all times doing right, by the support of men in power (these *things* in Affairs are generally of two classes the one from interest or place-hunting will follow the chase thro' thick and thin, and the others are rather passive than active, and are found from ignorance or indolence unable to judge of the passing events of the Day, and having form'd one opinion in their lives are for ever harping on a system that they do not understand) I would ask this modern Solomon, this exemplary manager what he has done for himself in his lifetime, he has, it is true been managing for every one else & giving advice, particularly where it was not wanted, he has play'd the beacon to a hundred vessells[240] that would have sail'd as well without, and at last finds his own where it was fifty years ago, from these and other circumstances I have been led to observe how much a man may be known by the management of his Possessions, & by that it may be seen in whatever capacity he may be, whether he has lived for any thing at last.

As there are many who seem to scoff at the idea of being Tradesman without the support of reason on their side, I shall take occasion for some observations on this head, but it is not my intention to enlarge much upon this opinion as there are but few in my circle of acquaintance of this stamp, & none in the number that this is intended to address. Every man must be a Tradesman for the time being who is engaged in any trade or traffic whatever, whether a noble lord who deals in Members

---

240 'Vessells': the second 'l' crossed through.

of Parliament through the borough-mongering system, or the Israelitish
tribe who hawkes oranges or old cloathes in the streets, & there are few
who can say they have never in their lives, engaged in any sort of dealing
for the sake of gain, if it be the artist, the man of literature, or the man
of science each will vend some time or other the produce of his hands, or
his intellectual labor, and as it will be seen that all are so engaged (unless
thro' the prevention of indolence) from the Monarch down to the lowest
subject, the plans & conduct of every individual must become the objects
of censure or praise according as each may have played his part in the
world.—

The Wheel of Fortune (says an Author) is continually going round,[241]
& the credit is not to him that is always at the top but to him that shall
get up as often as he is thrown down, this is the true sentiment of the
Speculator & should not be held out in defiance of all prudence, but
as there are those who are unhappily endowed with too much of this
precious virtue to their perpetual misery & those who have none at all.
I must say that they are happy indeed who can steer between the two
extremes, to know the enjoyment of life while they live, without either
squandering away their own substance, or that of their friends in foolish
or unmeaning extravagance, or pinching themselves & their dependants
to gain an hereafter, going through a voluntary season of misery, in order
to know[242] how to live, which before they have learnt find themselves
called from the world & their taper is burnt out while they are vainly
imagining it is yet to light.[243]—

In the few years that have granted me experience in life, I have
observed managers of every class that I could suppose the world capable
of producing Men whose only enjoyment seemed in the pursuit of gain,
men whose pleasures were so inseparable with their increase of power,
that every one must fall before them or meet their utmost hatred &
revenge, men whose foresight is of such little value that they will share

---

241 E.g. Dobson, *Petrarch's View of Human Life*: 'the wheel of fortune turneth continually'
     (p. 250).
242 'Know': crossed through and 'learn' inserted above the line in different ink.
243 Cp. Anne Lee Wharton, 'Verses on the Snuff of a Candle, Made in Sickness': 'See
     there the taper's dim and doleful light, / In gloomy waves silently rouls about, /
     And represents to my dim weary sight / My light of life, almost as near burnt out.'
     Reprinted in, for example, Horatio Walpole (ed.), *A Catalogue of the Royal and Noble
     Authors of England, Scotland and Ireland*, enlarged by Thomas Park (London: Scott,
     1806), III, p. 303.

their fortune with the first friend they meet, at the cost of their happiness for ever, & others whose shuffling artifice under the cloak of Charity or Religion, have lulled themselves in false security and whose fall must be desperate at last.—

Among the multitudes who are continually appearing in the character of Tradesmen, there is such a great variety in the difference of their dispositions and consequently such a difference in the management in each ones affairs, that if we were to divide them into a hundred classes, we should find some without the pale of either one or the other, so that to take them in three degrees will almost be sufficient for general remark, to begin with the extravagant spendthrift who finds his ruin much sooner than he ought reasonably to expect to rise in the world, then to take the opposite extreme the man whose avarice prevents the enjoyment that should result from the sweats of labor, & then those who pursue the midway course & meet that constant pleasure, that the other two will not taste without a too great ballance[244] of pain. The motives that generally induce a young man to expend more than his income, on his entering life are in some instances, the want of due consideration, with miscalculations, in others the great prevalance of certain certain untimely[245] which should have been in the duty of parents to suppress. When a young man arrives at an age fit to judge what may be his interest & welfare, he begins to judge of the conduct of others, if he observes his Parents in comfortable circumstances, he thinks that his amusements ought to be more, his purse should be more liberally supplied, & his affairs should in general bear some comparison with the prosperity (not the inclinations) of his parents & when he finds those little bickering checks on his comforts which are as imprudent as frequent bestowed by the unquestionable right of a father, he naturally hardens into a sort of distrust of the superior power that is destin'd to rule over him, & though the spirit of disobedience seems not to find existence in his breast, his heart is ever watchful for a happier state, so that every pang is treasured up in evidence against that day that breaks the bond for ever.—

Alphus was a man of good natural parts, his heart was ever open to the interest of his fellow creatures but the controuled manner in which he had been prepared to take his part in the great Theatre of the World, caused his utter ruin, his father had amassed much Wealth by his strict

---

244 'Balance': second 'l' crossed through.
245 'Untimely': 'Passions' inserted above the line in different ink.

attention to business & wishing to instill into his son an equal love of gain, he began by teaching him to part with little money while he was young, in order that he might act so when he grew old, his pocket was closely restricted, & the enjoyments of his own purchase were certainly few, but as he was destin'd to move in a higher sphere, he was always surrounded by a number of young friends, whose apparent kindness to him was rather the effect of Prudence & Foresight than good natural disposition, whatever were the amusements among them Alphus could always share them & though he often blushed for the meanness of his Parent, he promis'd himself a day that should banish every stigma from the name; soon after the age of twenty one he found himself possessed of a very large fortune, without any restriction of his management of it; he first began to question the propriety of saving what he could not live to enjoy, then he thought of the manner his parents had wished him to spend his life, & after a due consideration of the matter he thought that the precepts held out by them rather the effect of inexperience & miscalculation which he would endeavor to correct in himself, every benefit he had from his friends was doubly paid every want that he observed in the circle of his acquaintance & his dependants, or even in the poor of his district was immediately attended to from the sudden change in his affairs his generosity overcame his prudence, and nothing seemed more certain than his utter ruin, but at the moment when his inkhorn would have fail'd, he lost his life endeavoring to save that of an ungrateful fellow who had known & abused his kindest services all his life it will not be needful to enter much in detail in the different characters who play the slavish part opposed to this, as we all know there are men whose gains are more than ten times their expenditure, & whose meanness is proverbial, though they are countenanced by some from interest, some from affection and some from the common principle of charity and allowance to be made for the imperfections of our nature, but[246] they are despised in the hearts of all.

For the general tradesman or the man who steers the midway course (& of which sort I hope there are by far the greatest number) much is to be said, on entering the world he sits down to consider the extent of his capital, the way he is to employ it for the best, the restrictions requisite to impose upon himself, that he should not outrun that capital, & the general plan he should pursue for the support of that name without which

---

246 'But' inserted in different ink.

he can do no good in the world, from the adoption of the first idea he begins to have his multitude of advisers, & how to listen to one without offending another is among his first perplexities, one stands forward with all the apparent wisdom of a sage, with the old thread-bare maxim "no one can do good till he is married" to which he adds "take assistants, article Clerk Premiums &c"[247] in a week he calls to know what business is done, and quarrels[248] that the returns are not a hundred pounds, after some other illnatured remarks, as it were the words of a controller rather than the adviser he breaks with him in a pet. Another presumes to dictate and perhaps with equal sincerity but in all points a perfect contradiction of all the former precepts, so he will find so many opinions to listen to, that unless he has judgement of his own he must (like the old man with his ass) be ruined by the abundance of good council;[249] on his first making his way up in the world, whether he should be successful or otherwise his lot is by no means to be envied the caution used by those who have to deal with him, bears so much the appearance of suspicion that he will oftentimes question his own character to find what has[250] given rise to a supposed dishonesty of which he had no thoughts the strange mixture of opinions he hears on all occasions, the difference of tone of the pretended friend and real the real one,[251] and the contradiction so truly apparent in the former of these, for a while staggers his judgement he thinks, for a while no truth of sentiment can be found, & no one advises but[252] from some distant source of interest, but he will at last learn like all others, that those who are the first to advise are the last to assist.

---

247 Articled clerk: a clerk bound to the tradesman by articles of apprenticeship. 'Premium': the money paid to secure an apprenticeship.
248 'Quarrels': originally 'quarrells', second 'l' crossed through.
249 The story of the old man who, walking with a boy and a donkey, follows the contradictory advice he receives from strangers as to who should walk and who should ride, and finishes up carrying the donkey himself, is retold in, for example, the thirteenth number of Robert Dodsley's *The World* (29 March 1753), itself reprinted in Chalmers, *The British Essayists*, vol. 26, pp. 61–67 (pp. 66–67).
250 'Has': originally 'has has', second 'has' crossed through.
251 'Real the real one': a transcription error in the manuscript.
252 'But' added in different ink and hand.

On Laws

Laws are very convenient things, and yet those that are bound by them are seldom satisfied. All agree that laws are useful; all find pleasure in making them for others; and, all dislike the constraint they impose on themselves. It is a question, certainly very difficult to be resolved, whether, in the droll and unnatural state into which a great part of the world has now sunk, more evil would not arise from the perfect fulfilling and completion of the laws imposed by compact and force, in society and in legislation; than does accrue at present from the evasion of them. The evil which arises from the evasion of them, consists in the necessarily imperfect execution of those plans suggested by the wise folks of the times for the improvement of man and Society. The evil which would accrue from obedience to them, would be owing to the vanity, the prejudices, and the ignorance of those wise folks, who not able to understand and govern themselves, still pretend to comprehend and direct the world.

The importance of this question is such, that I shall leave it to my brothers of the class book to discuss; and I think this the wiser plan, because each of them is in possession of data, which at all events will be sufficient to introduce the question, though they may be too scanty for its resolution. It can scarcely be necessary for me to explain, that, by these data, I mean the little code of laws we have amongst ourselves for the management of the class book, and our observance of them.[253] Thus, there is a *law*, that each member shall take charge of the book for *two* months; another, that all the papers for the period shall be given in by the end of the first month; and a third, that the book shall be delivered up at the end of the period of two months to the next member in rotation who is to take charge of it: and as to our obedience to them, I may just observe, that I had not the book until some time after my period commenced; that all the papers ought to have been given in by the end of last month, though even now June 26th I have not received one; that my period finishes in 4 days, though it is impossible I shall be able to get the book ready in that time.[254] Now, though it is a sad falling off to descend from General Jurisprudence to the arrangement of our

253 See above, p. 40.

254 The table indicating which periods are to be scribed by each member of the essay-circle (see above, p. 39), indicates that from May to July 1819 was to fall to Faraday. The reference (below, p. 156) to the period from July to September 1819 being scribed by Deeble suggests that the members adhered to their original schedule. Thus, it would

class book, yet still I think we may with great propriety inquire, whether most good would result from keeping or does result from breaking our laws; whether our design of improvement is forwarded or retarded by our insubordination; and, whether we are not like the rest of the world, willing to avoid ourselves that law which we would impose upon others.

1819.

On the Changes of the mind[255]

It is said that the human body undergoes an entire change of matter in the course of a certain time[256] Whether this be truth or no it may perhaps be difficult even for philosophers to determine but let a man examine his mind and make a comparison of periods between which seven or ten years have elapsed and he will find so considerable an alteration especially in youth that was it not for the important associations of his material part with the changes that have taken place in his mind he might often doubt whether he was the same creature so continually progressive is the mind in the acquirement of knowledge[257] Our ideas our opinions our feelings and too often our principles change as the gleams of reason succeed each other[258] It is not for Man to say here will I rest satisfied no more shall my abberrations unsettle my fixed resolves—no. when our opinions are not founded on a basis of demonstrable truth they are always liable to change like the ridges of sand on the sea shore each succeeding wave

---

appear that this piece reproaching the members for not having submitted their essays is by Faraday.

255 The author of 'On Laws', immediately above, complains that no one else has yet sent him their contribution: it therefore seems likely that this essay is by the author of the last. Thus, if 'On Laws' is by Faraday, this one is also very possibly by him, as the lack of punctuation and use of the first person, reflective style also suggest.

256 Cp. for example, 'Philosophical Reflections No. III' in the 'Juvenile Department' of *The Baptist Magazine*, 8 (London: Button, 1816), pp. 113–15 (p. 114): 'Many are of opinion, that an entire change takes place in the human body in the course of years, so that not one particle, that originally composed it, remains; [...].'

257 Cp. Watts, *The Improvement of the Mind*, ch. 16, section V: 'As method is necessary for the improvement of the mind, [...] so in all your further pursuits of truth and acquirements of rational knowledge, observe a regular progressive method.'

258 'Gleams of reason': cp. Johnson, *Irene: A Tragedy* (written c. 1737), V.5, in *Works*, I, pp. 223–323 (p. 305): 'The gleams of reason, and the clouds of passion, / Irradiate and obscure my breast by turns.'

drives along that ridge formed by the last and places a fresh one beyond it till progressive motion is no more

This unsettled state of the human mind in the thoughtless gaiety of youth when the ardour of curiosity is unsatiated is the great cause of our happiness for then we think we have time enough to make decisions and the pursuit of variety engrosses our attention

The endeavour to trace the progress of our intellect from infancy and the various changes of our opinions and feelings if not an entertaining employment is certainly an instructive one it is that species of self exami-nation which is well calculated to humble us in our present opinions and predisposes the mind to receive truth. The reflective mind will early begin to notice the weakness as well as the powers of its nature by the difference of effect which the world in its various parts makes upon it in its progress 1. There is the change which is produced by the repetition of visual objects—2 That which arises from intercourse with each other—3. That deduced from our our acquired knowledge of the consistency of the creation—4 That which is produced by our own imagination and specu-lations under the head of Philosophy or Theology.

That childhood is the happiest period of our life few will deny when they have arrived at an age when reflection takes the place of thought-lessness anxiety of gaiety or when the knowledge of mankind has dissipated some of the delusive beauties of the prospect Altho' we may smile at the recollection of the simple trifles which caused our happiness yet we cannot help acknowledging that the pleasure was as real as any we can now enjoy unalloyed and more innocent Memory whilst contemplating in the distance the Mists of infancy dwells upon the bright and agreeable spots with rapture and many at times would be happy to give up all their knowledge to be relieved of the anxiety which attends its possession and to be as they were in their youth unsuspicious open hearted and generous sympathising with the unfortunate and indignant at the oppressor but this is not the course of nature man is doomed to be convinced of his fallibility and of his innate disposition to err When intelligence first dawns in our countenance and reason appears in our actions we feel that happy confidence in and dependance on our parents which is natural to all animals and as our weakness continues longer we retain instinctively that affection and reliance to a much later period We look up to them as superior beings without doubting the correctness of their advice or actions and it is a happy circumstance to those who can still retain the same feelings when reason has rendered themselves also capable of judging

In childhood every fresh situation or object produces a sensation which it is impossible for us to enjoy when the mystery of novelty is gone. It is the time too when the social feelings and every thing favourable to virtue is in action interest has but little hold and vice is detested from the ignorance of the many alluring snares she lays for her victims and in proportion to the manner in which she has been depicted in their early lessons.

In the first few years of life man seems to possess microscopic eyes every thing around him is important and the beginning of existence appears like the beginning of eternity He is not aware of or able to comprehend mortality for every thing is new and produces a new joy and there appears to be no end to the succession of novelties. The return of a season which brings with it some decided change in nature or her productions when the memory retains but a faint idea of the former one becomes a grand epoch. For snow or hail is viewed with wonder and delight the first time or two it takes place in our recollection. We perceive something descending in a new form from the clouds and we feel as if it was an addition to our happiness—and thus it is with various fruits &c which are in season but a month or two in a year. The year then appears like our life and we examine with pleasure things as they happen and which we are hardly conscious are to happen again This will not appear imaginary to those who have a faithful memory to recall the occurrences of their infancy As we grow up we begin to hail the annual return of these seasons as the return of a happy time but this is from experience and is at that time unalloyed by satiety. The ceremony of a birth day or the remarkable era of casting our petticoats[259] are periods which when viewed at an advanced age will appear that they were then as important to the child as a wedding or burial to the man

Thus every substance or circumstance is of consequence till it has become common by repetition and the mind gradually begins to anticipate the arrival of future periods which are to bring with them some future good or happiness not before enjoyed. Our expectations are then founded on our intercourse with mankind and our opinion of the world is formed on the basis of social duty which we have enjoyed in our domestic circle. The changes of mind which now take place after experience and the fresh passions which are called into action I intend for the substance of another paper.

---

259 'Casting our petticoats': being dressed in boys' clothes rather than the unisex garments of infancy and very early childhood.

On Marriage[260]

To Dillemus

Since you have called upon me to commit to writing my opinions on the probable cause of unhappiness in the married state I beg to hand you a short treatise on that subject and must trust to your candour and known indulgence to pardon the want of perspicuity in the composition. My object will be merely to take a cursory view of things as they have appeared to my own immediate observation without diving too deeply into probable circumstances. I am well aware there is subject sufficient to be gleaned from the works of able authors but I feel you will most approve of my own unbiassed thoughts with the introduction of as little of extraneous matter as is consistent to the more clear and plain elucidation of the subject.

The probable causes of unhappiness and dissatisfaction in the married state are at once so numerous and complex that to strike at the root of the evil itself would require that experience in those matters which I am not in possession of I wish you to view these as the opinions I have imbibed by a silent and attentive observance of that class of Society In my view of the happy state (for such it is invariably denominated) I have generally found that those who married in their own immediate station of life have had the greatest share of connubial happiness and on this head I must declare I am favourable impressed with an idea that it is much more likely so to prove than when the contrary is the case. I have known those who were ever aiming at being united to families who were moving in a much higher sphere of life than themselves some from one cause and some another each having their particular object in view. I will readily give full credit to the wonders wrought[261] where pure disinterested love only is in the scale yet I do say that that man who can work by even honorable means on the passions of his fair object and so gain uncontroulable sovereignty over her tender heart is a base villain with all his triumphs unless he has duly and previously secured for her use for her convenience and for her immediate happiness those necessaries and comforts which from her superior station in life she has a right to expect

I am aware what a wonderful effect the tender passion will work It

---

260 'Marriage': originally 'Marrige', the 'a' inserted.
261 'Wonders wrought': cp. Acts 12.5: 'And by the hands of the apostles were many signs and wonders wrought among the people; [...].'

will lead us to think the most distant and unlikely things are within our grasp not bearing in mind at the same time how much we are deluded by our own sanguine imaginations. If it unfortunately happens a young man feels a tender passion rising in his breast towards one whose station in life is far beyond his own if he is possessed of one degree of firmness becoming a man let him collect his scattered and bewildered thoughts and consider how little *he may* make himself appear in the eyes of her he would hope to be prefer'd beyond all others should she with a proud look and contemptuous smile reject his humble though honorable suit.

To be continued[262]

> Tho' not to love be very hard,
>   Yet on my conscience I opine,
> 'Tis easier for the heart to guard
>   Than bid the Stomach not to dine.[263]

For May 1819

On Calumny

"Nothing extenuate—nor sit down aught in malice"[264]

I have often been at a loss to account for the great propensity which exists in the minds of men to censure one another. How many good actions may be performed by a man, which probably are never known or at least never spoken of by persons residing under the same roof: and yet should that man inadvertently commit an inconsistent action how soon would it be known to the whole world but in that exaggerated form that a person who might have known or seen the action originally would scarcely observe the least similarity between them.—It is quite proverbial that Report is a many-tongued Monster[265] & doubtless much mischief results

---

262 The essay continues below, p. 152. A different ink has added '[By F] [not in this book].'

263 These lines are written out in CPB (I, p. 329), with the citation 'Old ballad' and the heading 'Love': 'Though not to love be very hard / Yet in my conscience I opine / Tis easier far the heart to guard / Than bid the stomach *not to dine.*'

264 *Othello*, V.2: 'Speak of me as I am. Nothing extenuate, / Nor set down aught in malice.'

265 Cp. 'Induction' to *Henry IV*, Part 2: 'Enter Rumour, painted full of tongues.'

to society from the disposition there is among mankind to exaggerate whatever they may relate as having seen or heard.

But even this inconsistent as it may be is an impropriety trivial indeed in comparison with willfully and uncharitably censuring and criticising the conduct of all who do not see as exactly as they see or whose ideas and actions do not correspond with their own. But the most detestable part of the criticism of these odious critics is the base insinuations with which they attack worthy and laudable characters. Insinuations are always worse than a direct charge. But whenever some worthy individual is mentioned as having deserved well of his country or as being very charitable and serviceable to his neighbours, we invariably hear some expression of this kind from those sapient critics, "He is no better than he should be" or "The public do not know all they should know" thus insinuating there is something concealed which if known would stain his character. We generally find however that these creatures are seldom able with all their ingenuity to do any serious injury to the objects of their envy. They may indeed succeed in exciting doubts and fears which will float for a time in the minds of some, but must soon sink into oblivion for want of facts to support them. Let then the honest and virtuous continue to walk in that path of rectitude which they deem to be right,[266] and they will possess that which cannot be attained by their enemies, a mind happy, quiet and serene.

for May 1819

Letter to the Secretary

Mr Secretary,

Sir,

I know not what you will think of my assurance in daring to send you a riddle, of *all* things for insertion in Our Class Book. What (you will exclaim) a riddle among the lucubrations of Metaphysicians, poets and moralists? Yes, indeed, and it will be no uncommon thing either. What does the metaphysician, but continually form riddles in his brain which he cannot solve? For instance whether matter *is* or *is not*; or mind is matter or matter is mind or both no matter at all; or whether right

---

266 Cp. Psalms 23.3: 'he leadeth me in the paths of righteousness for his name's sake.'

may not be wrong and wrong, right (and in truth, for want of being kept seperate, they are often alarmingly confused)[267] or whether *all* is not wrong and *nothing* right: or that *man* is all *ideas*, that ideas are nothing and yet nothing *must* be something: and so *man* is *his* great *riddle*. Next come the Poets—and yet they are happy poor fellows; in their own vain imaginations: continually living on the productions of their fancies, altho' they may not produce that *material*, which is necessary for the support of their *visible* self; yet temperance surprizingly assists the mind in its extensive flights. they soon wing their way to regions of bliss; and delightful odours, delicious viands and celestial harmonies conspire to increase their felicity. The better the poet the longer he will live upon this unsubstantial ambrosia. But woe to those who soon feel the Cravings of their earthly nature. too much addicted to groveling, they cannot ascend high enough to weaken the earth's attraction: down, down they come, with broken wing, and a hobbling gait & dolefully discordant cries alarming all the neighbourhood, having solved *their* riddle and found that the flights of Imagination are only to be undertaken by strong pinions, and that they are of no real benefit, but as they are under the guidance of a well regulated mind.—

Now for the Moralists—far be it that I should attempt to prove all their doctrines riddles; yet as they are of mankind and mankind is a riddle (as proved before) so they are riddles.—*Their* spirit is willing, but their flesh is *too*—*too*—weak.[268] They are too often pointing out the road to others, with their finger over their left shoulder while they themselves are proceeding with hasty strides in an opposite direction. Why should Men, believing and proclaiming one path to be right, yet not have sufficient resolution, to lead on and explore its dark corners and intricate windings? So *they* too are riddles.—

Thus, Sir, having endeavour'd to furnish you with an excuse for having inserted my riddle, in case you should have to confront any angry brows, I shall now give it you, not with confidence, as a subject worthy of our Critics (whom I reverence and fear) but as a bone, with little meat upon it for them to pick; as a trifle humbly offer'd to amuse them when their lengthened cogitations on the elaborate lucubrations of the enigmatical gentlemen aforementioned, have began to have a

---

267   Cp. above, p. 125: 'Vice can also be Virtue.'

268   Matthew 26.41: 'the spirit indeed is willing, but the flesh is weak.' And perhaps cp. *Hamlet*, I.2: 'Oh that this too too solid flesh, would melt.'

soporific effect, on account of the difficulty of finding matter sufficient
for animadversion.—

> I am
>
> Sir,
>
> As you take me

Enigma[269]

I was born with mankind, and call'd forth to express,
More of evil than good and less joy than distress.
If Adam like us, e'er felt pain or surprize,
I was near to assist and first spoke in his cries.
Of all nations I am, and all languages know;
From Arabys deserts to th'regions of snow.
Of feelings so fine, that I'm sure to cry out,
From pain like an epicure twinged with gout.
Dame Nature's my mother tho' some folks assert,
That most of my brethren are the children of art;
But I, tho' oft heard in the earliest ages,
Ne'er made my appearance 'till the time of the sages:
Most certainly not, 'till long after the fall;
And now when I do, I'm oft nothing at all:
Yet indeed I am found in these modern times,
To multiply fast in European climes,
Especially since the bright Sun-beams of Science,
Dispell'd the dark gloom of the Gothic alliance;
When the planet call'd Earth, by philosophers rare,
Was prov'd to be much like an orange in air,

---

269 Enigmas were, as Austen's *Emma* illustrates, a popular form in this period. Faraday
was interested in them and recorded a favourite one in CPB (I, p. 322, with another
enigma in answer on pp. 334–35), wrongly ascribing it to Byron (it was in fact 'A
Riddle' by Catherine Maria Fanshawe). He also composed enigmas and riddles
occasionally, for instance in a letter to Abbott, 2 August 1812: 'What is the longest,
and the shortest thing in the world: the swiftest: and the most slow: the most divisible
and the most extended: the least valued and the most regretted: without which
nothing can be done: which devours all that is small: and gives life and spirits to every
thing that is great?' (*Correspondence*, I, p. 12), to which the answer was 'Time'.

'Twas then too found out to be also like me
Which (to speak was[270] you made) you would prove it to be.

July 1819.

On Marriage

Continued from Page 169[271]

Every Man possess'd of the least sensibility of mind must accutely feel the mortifying refusal coolly uttered from those lips which he was wont to praise, while with anxious look and throbing heart, he awaits the doom that is to pronounce him the highly favour'd & accepted Lover or that which[272] in a moment hurls him from comparative happiness to a state of misery bordering on frenzy itself.[273]

How little must a man know the heart of her to whom he offers his addresses how short sighted & inconsiderate must he be, who lays himself open to so mortifying a repulse. With all the little arts & cunning a female can practise is it possible she can hide from her lover the *true* opinion she forms of him. Surely a man *must* know if he is acceptable to the Lady to whom he pays his addresses. how is it then to be accounted for that so many mortifying refusals occur on the part of the females, which lead them to commit the most dreadful crimes even[274] self destruction I think, the origin[275] of the cause may be fairly divided between the two sex's for there are many females who take a pride in making conquests & so leading their admirers on from hope to hope till worn out by incessant importunities they sink under the weight of fatal disappointments that surround them, & at last fall a victim[276] to cruel & disappointed love. Is this a triumph ye fair Daughters of Britain is it, thus ye seek to trample on the fond hopes of the ardent lover let it not be said your tender

---

270 'Was': crossed through and 'were' inserted above the line in a different hand.
271 See above, p. 148.
272 'Which' inserted above the line in a different hand.
273 Characters in contemporary sentimental or Gothic novels not infrequently find themselves in states 'bordering on frenzy': for instance, Montgomery in Charlotte Smith's *Ethelinde: Or, the Recluse of the Lake* (London: Cadell, 1799), enters such a state on the heroine's being thrown from her horse (p. 167).
274 'Even': 'to' added and then crossed through.
275 'Origin': originally 'orrigin', second 'r' crossed through.
276 'A victim': 'a' crossed through and 's' added to 'victim'.

sympathising hearts can wound the honourable feelings of him who seeks to offer you the highest tribute of respect & honour a Man has in his power to bestow by the consummation[277] of those rites sanctioned by the highest authorities human & Divine. On the other hand the Man by his too often precipitate conduct endangers his peace of mind by aspiring to the hand of one who probably may be the last to give him encouragement what may in the eyes of their friends appear (& which in reality is) nothing more than the usual civilitys due from one to another is often magnified into a particular & marked attention by him who would wish to appear in a more favourable point of view this is a species of vanity so common & so troublesome to the females that it deserves the highest censure. I must acknowledge great allowances may be made where[278] a Man is deeply enamoured of a beautiful & accomplished Woman, whose fascinating manners are such as to gain her the esteem of all who have the pleasure of her acquaintance yet it may be many chances against him that he should be her choice above all others how cruel then must it be where[279] she is prevaild upon to sacrifice her feelings to his ambitious views, more than one instance has occur'd to my immediate knowledge & were such has been the case the parties have not been happy in the choice of each other as partners for life were[280] friends have consider'd it a desirable match they have officiously urg'd the propriety as they termd it of the female withdrawing her objections & which objections may have provd injurious to their own private interest.

We have often heard of females being cruelly intimidated into acts far very far from their own wishes by threats being held out that unless compliance was made to their request, the parties may probably become a victim to self destruction how cruel how ungenerous is this mode of obtaining the object of their love where the object is attained by this infamous & unmanly proceeding can it be expected true Love & affection can exist how careful then how prudent should the fair sex be how guarded in all their actions how essential is it to their peace of mind as well as the friends of him who possibly might be so rash as to lay violent hands on himself, not to give encouragement were[281] love or even an atachment is most distant from their thoughts as to buoy up with

---

277 'Consummation': originally 'consumation', the second 'm' added above the line.
278 'Where': originally 'were', an 'h' inserted.
279 'Where': 'when' inserted in different ink above the line.
280 'Were': an 'h' inserted.
281 'Were': an 'h' inserted.

hopes of future happiness in the atainment of his most anxious wishes when with their own hand they press the cup of delight to the very lips, and as it were in a moment dash it far away & leave not a beam of hope to comfort or solace.

Effeminacy & Luxury[282]

"Oh! listen not to that enchantress Ease
With seeming smile; her palatable cup
By standing grows insipid; and beware
The bottom for there's poison in the lees.
What health impaired & crowds inactive maim'd!
What daily martyrs to her sluggish cause
Less strict devoir the Russ, and Persian claim
Despotic, and as subjects long inur'd
To servile burthen grow supine, and tame
So fairs it with our sovereign & her train."[283]

Probably there are no evils more destructive to the happiness and prosperity[284] of nations than luxury, and effeminacy. Many sensible, and enlightened characters have censured in the highest degree the destructive principle of war. It is certainly extremely injurious to the public, and private happiness of mankind—it not only barbarously destroys thousands of our fellow creatures—it not only greatly exhausts the finances of a country—but it is highly incompatible with the mild,

---

282 Effeminacy and luxury were frequently associated in eighteenth-century and early nineteenth-century moral and even political writing: to take just one of a great number of possible examples, the archdeacon of Winchester, Thomas Balguy, observed in one of his *Nine Discourses on Various Subjects*, second edn (London: Rivington, 1817) that 'some applaud the industry and frugality of a rising people; and complain without ceasing of the effeminacy and luxury of more polished times' (p. 2).

283 Sneyd Davies, 'Epistle XVII. To […] Frederick Cornwallis' (written 1763): 'Oh! listen not to that enchantress Ease / With seeming smile; her palatable cup / By standing grows insipid; and beware / Perdition, for there's poison in the lees. / What health impair'd, and crowds inactive maim'd! / What daily martyrs to her sluggish cause! / Less strict devoir the Russ and Persian claim / Despotic; and as subjects long inur'd / To servile burden, grow supine and tame:— / So fares it with our sov'reign, and her train.' In *Bell's Classical Arrangement of Fugitive Poetry*, 18 vols. (London: Bell, 1790–97), I, pp. 140–44 (p. 143).

284 'And prosperity' inserted.

and genial principles of Christianity.—But I am inclined to think that in a political sense luxury, and effeminacy are quite as destructive as war to the prosperity of nations—When a country becomes effeminate she soon loses all love of liberty—her prince knows not the state of her affairs— her statesmen are actuated solely by self-interest, are continually guilty of innovations on her laws and constitution—and her people are wholly regardless of their lost rights, and liberties.—

One of the finest, and bravest armies the world ever witnessed commanded by Hannibal was corrupted, and destroyed by the luxury of Capua.[285] So soon as that place was taken Carthage felt a shock which it never recovered; This noble army caught the infection, became effeminate, and fond of pleasure, and luxury which consequently rendered them an easy prey to their enemies.

May we not attribute the decline of the republic of Athens to the conduct of Pericles who debased,[286] and debauched the people's minds with shews, and spectacles, and every species of luxury by which they were made slaves to dissipation, and pleasure, instead of being as many of their ancestors were patriotic friends to liberty—

The corruption of the manners, and finally the downfall of the Romans commonwealth may be dated from the victory over Antioch, and the conquest of Asia when luxury, and voluptuousness were introduced among Roman Citizens.[287] After this period that love of liberty, and justice, that attention to the public weal, that amor patriare,[288] that anxious desire to subdue all internal, and external foes, and many other virtues for which their forefathers were so notorious, fast declined among them, and this great city which had long sat as mistress of the world[289] was reduced to the wretched condition of submitting to any terms that an army of barbarians chose to propose.

History furnishes us with other instances of the injurious effects of

---

285 Cp. Oliver Goldsmith, *The Roman History* [...] (1769), which describes how the victorious Hannibal led his troops to Capua, which 'had long been considered as the nurse of luxury and the corrupter of all military virtue; [...] from being hardy veterans they became infirm rioters' (Dublin: Wogan *et al.*, 1799), I, p. 176. Hannibal is also mentioned above, p. 137, 'On Tradesmen' and discussed below, p. 156, 'Junius & Tullia'.

286 Pericles is also mentioned above, p. 137, 'On Tradesmen'.

287 Cp. Goldsmith, *The Roman History*, p. 231: 'Upon [Verus's] entering Antioch, [...] he rioted in excesses unknown, even to the voluptuous Greeks [...].'

288 Amor patriae: love of the fatherland.

289 'Mistress of the world': a frequently used epithet for Rome.

luxury to the prosperity of states, but sufficient have been adduced to shew that to states as to individuals temperance is safe, and beneficial, and luxury is dangerous, and destructive.

A Brother's Letter to Mr. Deeble

Sitting Room
Aug 23rd 1819.

Friend Deeble,[290]

I have not time at present to comply with the Spirit of our Laws relating to the class book[291] but willing to fulfill them to the letter beg thee to insert this Epistle as my contribution during thy period of thy[292] charge.[293] I hope at some time to be more troublesome to thee, and in the mean time, Am

thine in the Class book[294]
A Brother.

Junius & Tullia

In the year 543 of the building of Rome,[295] when Hannibal had led his conquering army, nearly over all Italy, and was then laying encamped on the banks of the River Arno about 3 Miles from the Capital the greatest Consternation prevailed among the Inhabitants within the walls;[296] in every part were to be seen Women walking about wringing their hands in

---

290 I.e. Edward Deeble, one of the members of the essay-circle and the scribe for this period.

291 See above, pp. 143–44, 'On Laws'.

292 'Thy' inserted in different ink.

293 The use of 'thee' instead of 'you' in this letter, and the use of 'Friend' as a salutation, indicate that the author was a Quaker, or that he intended to suggest a Quaker-like manner. Faraday recorded 'A Quaker's Letter' from the *Harleian Miscellany* (I, p. 366) in CPB (I, p. 381), which begins 'Friend John' and addresses its recipient as 'thee'. He seems to have thought the letter amusing or absurd, since he has underlined many phrases which express worldly intentions in a religious register.

294 Possibly an echo of the Puritan phrase for signing letters, 'thine in Christ'.

295 I.e. 543 *ab urbe condita* (from the founding of Rome): 211 BC.

296 This rather Gothic story is set around the second Battle of Capua, when Hannibal unsuccessfully tried to break the siege of Capua by attacking Rome.

the greatest anguish, and even the oldest generals then in the City seemed
to give up their country for lost, but Patriotism which was then as
prevalent as at any time of the empire seemed by one great, and energetic
glow doomed to work the happy change, one evening when the great
Carthaginian had seen his troops well provided for, and riding, round the
Camp he could not help reflecting on the difference between his Station,
and that of the enemy, and casting an Eye towards the City which was
then illumined by the last rays of the setting sun he seemed more than
ordinaryly delighted with the treasure he promised his men in the plunder
of it, and being prevailed on by his Friends to take a nearer Survey he
ordered a Troop of horse to attend him, and he accordingly made a
Circuit of the Suburbs this was beheld by the soldiers in the Watch tower
of the capitoline hill and immediately communicated to the Consul
Flaccus,[297] who growing indignant at the insult offered to their Misfor-
tunes, ordered all preparation to be made for giving the enemy battle
early the next Day, about this time there were a great number of youth in
the City who had not quite reached the military age, and consequently
could not be levee'd,[298] but many of them reasoning among themselves
on the value of life the Immortality of Fame, and the Virtue of Patriotism,
they determined to join the Army, and by example prompt the utmost
Effort of the Citizens, however their decision was not known in every
part of the City, and among those who were ignorant of the matter was
Junius a youth of Patrician rank, one who bore an excellent name among
his contempories, who was skilled in all the Military arts, he was at this
time betrothed to a young lady of exquisite beauty, and on that very day
in which the Armies engaged, their nuptials were to have been celebrated,
the Morning was ushered in by the sound of joy, in his circle of Friends
the voice of congratulation was quick upon his ear, the lovely Tullia, in
her tunic dress was led to the joyful place, the Priest with the accustomed
spear parted the flowing locks over her forehead,[299] and all things were
about to be concluded when the sound of trumpets roused the busy

---

297 Flaccus was not consul in 211; the source of this error may have been Appian's
    Hannibalic War (38–41).
298 Presumably from 'levée en masse', a mass mobilization, especially in response to the
    threat of invasion (OED); first recorded use of 'levée en masse' in English, 1813.
299 Cp. [Harriet English], 'A Tale', in *Conversations and Amusing Tales* [...] (London:
    printed for the author, 1799), pp. 65–87 (p. 76): 'The bride appeared. Her locks were
    divided with the head of a spear, as a sign that she was marrying a man of a martial
    race; [...].'

Throng, and Junius was called off to join the band of whom he was chosen chief, their disappointment at first seemed to be afflicting, but the spirit of the Soldier overcame that of the lover, and he prepared to take his Farewell, the sacrifice then burning on the Altar, seemed propitious to their constancy, and they agreed to make Oath of Fidelity before they parted, this was first adminstered to Junius, and while it was about to be echoed by the words of Tullia the flourish of Trumpets again called them away, and the youth had only the time to hear her swear to marry within a Moon, as they were only expected to part for a day or while the Enemy were under the walls, he flew with alacrity to his standard. The moment he was gone the Priest who had entered his Office wrongfully, and who had long entertained a wish for Tullia himself began to try all his Arts to wean her from the object of her love, he had a hope that the youth would be taken off by the enemy, or some chance of War would prevent his return, but the result of the day was not as he expected, after some skirmishing with the enemy they thought fit to retire, and the Romans followed them, past the river Turia, and leaving them returned to the Seige of Capua, where continuing some time, the period was nearly expired, that should have seen the marriage of Tullia concluded. It was a custom then among the Romans to have the words of an oath always recorded, and when taken in any temple or public place they should not in any way be deviated from, without supposing the presiding Deity would cause their immediate Death; of this circumstance the treacherous Priest accordingly availed himself, as the departure of Junius was too quick, and unexpected he had not the opportunity of knowing the exact words administered in the Oath, and did not return quite so soon as he might have done, during his absence the Priest endeavoured to keep current a report of the death of the youth, and at the same time had his slaves in attendance to watch his return, and prevent it, or prolong it beyond the time expressed in the Oath, during this time he took every opportunity of seeing the Maid, and taking the advantage of his official situation, remonstrated against the crime of breaking an Oath, and reminding her of the exact words expressed in hers, telling her that if her lover should not return by the time appointed it would be requisite to marry another for the due observance of the laws. One evening when he had taken an opportunity of seeing her alone in the garden of the Temple, he took her to the most retired grove where the flowing of a Fountain; and the hollow sound of secret cells of the grotto seemed quite calculated to inspire awe in the breast of the inexperienced maid, "Here" said he, "must I dear maid declare the will of the Gods who have long made me acquainted with your fate, and that of your lover, and to disclose this matter makes it first necessary that I should give you some extracts from the narative of my own life, in the earlier part of which I was much inclined to the duties of a soldier, and in every respect disposed like the unfortunate[300] youth whose face you must see no more, when I was about to join some troops destined to defend some distant part of the empire, and was just prepared to leave the city, the goddess Minerva appeared to me in a dream, and calling me to the Office you now see me hold, told me that this period was to elapse when a maiden whose name should be Tullia should join me in office, and should be granted Immortality for the saving of the state, since that time I have looked forward with patience for the time which seems at last arrived, the Goddess again appeared to me this morning and informed me of the death of the brave Junius who fell in a battle with the rebels of Capua. The time of his return as prescribed in the Oath is now nearly elapsed, and for the fear of those Deities, whom you have called on to witness your fidelity you must immediately be married, as I know the virtue of your heart, and the reverence you have for the Gods it is not necessary that you should live[301] to the World, nor that mankind should know it, but I will espouse you in secret myself, and this place which is sacred to the Goddess of Wisdom, shall also be sacred to the love I bear you. At this moment entered the vestals with their sacred train performing a solemn dirge, at the sound of which Tullia started, and asking for whom it was performed, was told it was for the unfortunate Junius who had met his Death before Capua. Nothing could exceed the anguish of her mind on hearing this, she seemed as if Death alone could relieve from it, and she was just about to sink on the ground, when the Priest (who was ever watchful of advantage) caused a large blue flame to issue out of one side of the grotto. At this time a hollow voice cried out in a strain as if more than mortal, that soon their mourning should be turned to joy, that Tullia must soon change her state, and the Gods would be propitious to her happiness, the Priest who had constructed all this himself was little aware how true it would prove in his disadvantage. The unhappy Tullia seemed about to comply with his request, the fire was then burning on the Altar, but the moment he thought to have made her his own, the sound of trumpets announced the

---

300 'Unfortunate' is an insertion in the same ink and hand as the original scribe.
301 'Live': this word almost illegible in the manuscript.

return of the conquering army, and Junius who was now at the gates covered with the spoils of a conquered Foe, rushed to the sacred grove, and caught the fading Tullia in his wellcome arms. The Priest after his consternation a little subsided still professed his friendship for them, and after uniting the happy pair, retired from the Office to end his days in misery.

A Ramble to Melincourt

Melincourt July 20th[302]

After dinner I set off on a ramble to Melincourt, a waterfall on the North-Side of the Valley, and about six miles from our Inn. I found the canal path very foul; the canal overflowing in many places from the rain and the river very turbid and swelled. I crossed the river by a tottering slippery bridge with more safety than I expected; and soon rambled my way out to the Village of Melincourt. Here I got a little damsel for my guide who could not speak a word of English. We however talked together all the way to the fall though neither knew what the other said.—I fancy it is not often she is elevated to the rank of guide for she seemed proud of her office and was extremely solicitous to fill it with honor. She carefully pointed out the dirty and clean places and ran on so fast in her spirit of readiness as to leave me far behind.—I was delighted with her burst of pleasure as on turning a corner she first showed me the waterfall and then ran along more and more rapidly that she might bring me under the stream before I could recover from the impression it had first made on me. There she placed me on a stone and then throwing her arms towards the torrent chattered most volubly in welch. I suppose about its beauties and its force. The stream had been much swelled by the rain and fell in grandeur over the abrupt rocks which terminated its higher bed. Here as

---

302 This entry is extracted from Faraday's diary of a walking tour he made in Wales with Edward Magrath, a friend from the City Philosophical Society, from 10 July to 3 August 1819. See *Correspondence*, I, p. 182, n. 1. The diary is in CPB (II, pp. 49–200; pp. 95–97). The version in CPB differs slightly in capitalization and punctuation from the one in the Mental Exercises. The diary is published in Dafydd Tomos (ed.), *Michael Faraday in Wales: Including Faraday's Journal of his Tour through Wales in 1819* ([Denbigh]: Gwasg Gee, [1972]). Melincourt is a village about 20 miles north-east of Swansea on the River Neath.

in almost all the other falls the stream descended freely through the air the rocks receding from it behind and leaving it to combat wind. The body of water was considerable and yet it became so minutely divided in its descent as to run like a mere film thrown before the cliffs and every leaf of the trees behind it could be distinguished. Its height was perhaps 70 feet but I found impossible to form a moderately certain estimate. Two or three light airy falls occurred at the sides of the larger one diversifying the rock and softening down its rugged character.[303] Whilst I was admiring the scene my little welch damsel was busy running about even under the stream gathering strawberries. When she saw me at leisure she gave me a whole handful and would not take one for herself. They were excellent I wanted to look down the river and she perceiving my intention waded to a stone, she was too little to jump to, and then pointed out where I might with safety put my foot. On retiring from the fall I gave her a piece of coin that I might enjoy her pleasure she curtsied & I saw her delight. She again ran before me back to the village but wished to step aside every now and then to pull strawberries I made out that at home she had some finer she would give me. Every bramble she carefully moved out of the way and ventured her bare feet to try stoney paths that she might find the safest for mine.—I observed her as she ran before me on meeting a village companion, open her hand to shew her prize but without any stoppage word or other motion. When we returned to the village I bade her good night and she bade me farewell both by her actions and I have no doubt her language too.—Sterne may rise above Peter Pastoral and Stoics above Sterne in the refined progress of human feeling & human reason but he who feels and enjoys the impulses of nature however generated is a man of nature's own forming and has all the dignity and perfection of his race though he may not have the refinement of art.—I never felt more honorable in my own eyes (and I have plenty of vanity) than I did this evening whilst enjoying the display this artless girl made of her feelings.[304]

---

303 'Character' inserted above the line. The word appears correctly in the CPB version.

304 Hamilton describes the passage about the Welsh girl as 'heartfelt writing, typifying the depth of response that Faraday could summon to the natural and human world' (p. 146).

On Triflers[305]

"Go fool; and arm in arm with Clodio plead"
"Your Cause before a bar you little dread;"
"But know the law that bids the drunkard die"
"Is far too just to pass the trifler by.—"

Cowper.[306]

The follies and vices of mankind, their struggles against inclination, and their rare attempts in favour of virtue, must continually be the subject of reflection, to those who consider them, from their powers, as distinct, from the other animals of creation. Can it be doubtful to the reasonable man, whether he ought to view them in a serious or a ludicrous light, whether he ought to assume the character of Democritus or Heraclitus?[307]—Be it as it may, it seldom happens, but, that train of thought, gradually brings on a serious and a melancholy mood.—At such a time the mass of mankind, appear like other animals or even like myriads of insects, rolling and struggling and toiling for objects which we cannot perceive, apparently without any thing to be attained, but to be kept in motion, until they are again mingled with the mass from which they were generated.—View'd individually the greater part are trifling away their lives as they would fire a squib, heedless how soon it may burst, to the danger of the hand which holds it; thinking only of the present, unconscious and unworthy of the dignity of their nature, which would lead them at least, to reflect upon the wonders of their existence, the importance of a futurity, and their dependance on an all-pure, infinitely incomprehensible Deity.

From whence proceeds this thoughtlessness? Let Us endeavour to discover, by taking a single object, draw it aside from the Crowd, fix it in the focus, and with microscopic eyes,[308] penetrate into and examine the motives and objects of his life.—This appears to be a young subject; so much the better there are thousands such, they must have all been young; and it is less capable of hiding its faults and deceiving; and could We hope to make any impression on the rest by an exposure, this gives us the best chance of success. First observe its general deportment and form; with what an air of haughtiness and superiority it moves; what a

---

305 Title added in a different ink.
306 William Cowper, 'The Progress of Error' (1782), ll. 197–200, punctuation altered.
307 I.e. the laughing (Democritus) and the weeping (Heraclitus) philosophers.
308 'Microscopic eyes': cp. above, p. 146.

listlessness in its action, and an affected contempt for all around. Is its form so superior to a thousand others as to warrant this behaviour, or did it make itself?—no, a deformity has arisen from its weakness, and its Vanity has been the father of its degradation: art has arrayed it in those stiff trappings of fashion, which are the objects of its love and admiration, the Gods of its idolatry; while that which Nature gave him, that fair, that noble mind, an intellect superior to its fate, lies uncultivated, like a land but shallow dug merely for the growth of gaudy flowers, and those choked up with Weeds and brambles.[309] What a false foundation for pride is dress! and yet we see what a self complacency it produces: Oh Ye noble men! ye demigods in Knowledge![310] ye benefactors of Mankind! ye care not for the outer case; of whatever country ye are, or Costume covers your nakedness, whether ye are of Icy Norway or the Regions of the Sun; stripped of all outward Signs of greatness ye are the same: but take this child of Vanity and Fashion, clothe him in the beggars garb and he sinks below his rags. It is too often ominous of poverty within, when so much pains is taken with the outside. Can that mind be contemplating subjects, for its improvement, or that are compatible with its duties, that can allow of hours wasted in the proper *wrinkling*, stiffening or tie or a Cravat, the adjusting of a waiscoat, or in the elegant *disordering* of an *overgrown* head of *hair*?[311] What can We expect from these? "the tree shall be known by its fruit and the well by its Water"[312] If the fruit turns out to be ripe, and the Water to be sweet, how agreeably disappointed should We be; for, from the rankness of growth in the one and the accumulation of Weeds and Vapour about the other We can only expect to find this barren and that stagnant and offensive.—

Shall we then allow this trifling to interfere in the momentous duties of Life;? shall We be idling about the meadows, chasing Butterflies, when We ought to be hastening to the brow of the Hill to catch a glympse of

---

309 Cp. Watts, *The Improvement of the Mind*, 'Introduction' (below, p. 214).

310 Perhaps cp. *Hamlet*, II.1, 'What a piece of work is man! How noble in reason, [...] in apprehension how like a god [...].'

311 Cp. Faraday, letter to Abbott, 11 October 1812: 'What am I to think of that person who despising the improvement & rectitude of his mind spends all his efforts on arranging into a nice form his body speech habits &c is he an estimable character is he a commendable companion no surely not nor will such ever gain my commendation' (*Correspondence*, I, pp. 40–41).

312 Luke 6.44: 'For every tree is known by his own fruit.'

the glories of the Setting Sun? what! polishing the shell, when we ought to be examining the soundness of the kernel?—

It is enough for dress, when it answers the purposes of decency, and is consistent with the circle in which we move; it is well not to disgrace ourselves or our friends in the eyes of those who know us not; we *must* sacrifice a little to the prejudices of the world; but let us not sacrifice our own time, that which we can ill spare from improvement and meditation.—Dress should occupy but a short time, a few minutes in each day and when once put on should for that day be forgotten.

To say, that Dress is the cause of all that paucity of thought and absence of feeling too generally to be observed in Youth, perhaps might not be correct; it may only be one of the numerous channels that lead off the stream of thought from its proper and legitimate bed; nevertheless it is one which is intimately connected with many others, usually proceeding from an undue opinion of Self. We love dress because it is a passport into the good graces of the World and into the circle of fashion; We love it because it procures us the glances and attentions of the other Sex; We love it because it really deceives us into a much higher opinion of ourselves than we deserve. False estimates of ourselves, particularly when We overrate our Value, are always dangerous; it lays us open to the machinations of Knavery and to the incursions of the most insidious Vices; it leads us into the meshes of inordinate desire; from dupes We become knaves: and after being ensnared and polluted by sensual delights, We unfortunately know not how to seperate ourselves from the seducer. Sooner than be upbraided or suffer alone We do our utmost to defend our conduct, making use of weak and paltry excuses, sophistic arguments and confident assertions, thereby endeavouring to make proselytes to our folly, to assist us in defending or to share in the reproach our behaviour merits. Thus, Dress, the love of Company, flattery, uncontroll'd longings after or indulgence in pleasures forbidden both by moral and divine law, are the great absorbents of the time, and of the uncertain and flimsy approaches towards reflection of Youth; these prevent them feeling and acknowledging the importance of that link, which they were ordained to fill in the great chain of creation.—Besides these enemies to, that *Dignity of thought*, for which I contend, there is another of perhaps more passive, uncertain, tho' I think scarcely less criminal nature—Vanity is the basis of this class as well as of those who suffer from the influence of the aforementioned. These are not pointed out by any gross derilection of duty, even good intention may be on their side; but they are found, supercilious, over polite, effeminate, their conversation particularly empty and Small, especially to females, full of exaggerated Compliments, but which when deliver'd, seem more to fill the kind coxcombe with self complacency at his own superiority, than as if intended to be received as truth by the person to whom they are address'd. These are despis'd by both Sexes of rational beings, in the midst of their delusion, and treated with contempt, in secret, when they are believing themselves the idols of love and admiration.—

What can palliate, this trifling, this thoughtlessness, this idiotism? nothing but want of intellect. Not even the business of life or providing for our sustenance, can be urged as an excuse for our ignorance of our situation, for our inattention to the duty of reflection on the importance of our existence, either present or future, Though the wonders of the universe are incomprehensible, they have the greater claim upon our attention; reason was not given us to be degraded; We are answerable for the talents lent us for use; we are not to[313] wrap them up in a napkin and bury them;[314] nor to prostitute them to purposes foreign to the design and to the honour of the Deity, Let us remember then, that this Giver of all things, is *always present* with us; while *We* are thoughtless, *he* is thoughtful, and though *We* think not of him, or ever scarcely recollect that We are indebted to any power for our existence, he fails not to watch our every thought word or action; our progress from nothing until We decay and are nothing *visible* again. When Man contemplates the deity, he becomes superior to this world, when he contemplates Man, he is still honorable & sustains his rank; but when he gives way to sensual gratification, he lowers himself to the brute._____

There is nothing perhaps which sooner disposes Man to serious reflection, than the idea of the Omnipresence of the Deity; it prevents many from continuing in the paths of Sin, and when conscious of the rectitude of intentions it inspires them with Courage and humility to go forward in life without fearing its ills in progress and without dreading its close.—The 139th Psalm being an admirable enumeration of *ye* powers of the Creator over the Creature, and entering so particularly into the subject, so[315] as not to fail making an impression where it is read attentively, I have been induced to attempt a version of it; not supposing presumptuously,

---

313 'To' inserted.
314 Matthew 25.14–30 (the parable of the talents).
315 'So' inserted.

that I should improve it, but merely doing it as practice, endeavouring to preserve, as far as I understood, the text, the sense intended—It does not appear all through to be fit language to come from erring Man, but to contain a typical application or prophecy.—Nevertheless the most part, may be used by and applied to ourselves with effect._____

Note.—By closing my subject with this I shall give myself credit for *two papers*, both on account of the length of this, and of my lesson in verse._____

139th Psalm

Lord, thou hast search'd me, and alone
To thee my wand'ring ways are known;
In day-light walks, or when at rest,
Thou know'st the thoughts that fill my breast;
And not a word can stir my tongue,
But ere it sounds thou know'st it long:
Such knowledge is so very high,
It doth my reas'ning powers defy.[316]

Where shall I from thy spirit flee?
Where from thy presence can I be?
Should I ascend up into heaven,
Thence are thy brightest glories given;
Or should I make my bed in hell?
There in thy terrors thou dost dwell;
Or deep in earth, or high in air,
Oh wonderful! thou still art there.

What, if I mount the morning's wings.

---

316 As a sample, we may compare this verse with the King James version: 'O Lord, thou
hast searched me, and known me. / Thou knowest my downsitting and mine uprising,
thou understandest my thought afar off. / Thou compassest my path and my lying
down, and art acquainted with all my ways. / For there is not a word in my tongue,
but, lo, O Lord, thou knowest it altogether. / Thou hast beset me behind and before,
and laid thine hand upon me. / Such knowledge is too wonderful for me; it is high, I
cannot attain unto it.'

And visit Ocean's utmost springs?
Een as I fly, or when I stand
I'm holden by thy mighty hand.
Surely, I said, the veil of night,
Shall hide me from his piercing sight:
Still all round thy glories shine,
The day, the night are equal thine.

My substance was not hid from thee,
When wrought in secret curiously;
Thine eye my unform'd figure view'd,
And in thy book my members crude
Were written; e'en before they were
Thou saw'st their form existing there:
And in the darkness of the earth,
I was, 'till thou didst will me forth.

Thee will I praise, for thou hast made
My Soul with wonder to pervade
The produce of thy mighty will;
When I awake I'm with thee still;
How precious are thy thoughts to me
(An atom of immensity!.)
Though I could count the sandy shore,
Oh God, thy wonders still are more.

The wicked surely thou will slay,
Who turneth from thy chosen way,
Against thee speak, and ne'er refrain
To take thy holy name in vain.
I hate them, Lord, who 'gainst thee rise;
I count them all mine enemies.
Depart far off, from me, oh then,
Ye wicked and deceitful men.

Search me, Oh God, and know my heart,
And try its core's most secret part;
And see if there be any thought,
Within its sphere by Satan taught:

Oh try if there be found in me
Or wicked way or vanity.
Vouchsafe O Lord an heavenly ray,
To shew the everlasting way.—

Infancy[317]

Oh enviable early days
When dancing thoughtless pleasures maze
To care to guilt unknown

Burns[318]

Of all the tender feelings Man is capable of possessing next to those towards lovely Women there is not a greater incitement to pure love & affection than that which the presence of Children inspires us with. they are indeed well calculated to soften the heart of the most obdurate and give a zest of true pleasure to the whole frame.

How void of all the finer feelings must that Man be who can look on the smiles of lovely Children without emotions of the tenderest nature, their little innocent play that gleam of youthful happiness & contentment which setts fix'd in their ruddy looks is surely calculated to awaken in the breast of hardy Man the most lively sensations When we reflect that their little minds are unadulterated by any sordid views such as too often govern the actions of man hard hearted[319] & rebellious man. O how precious should we consider these gifts of Kind Heaven pledges of connubial bliss the greatest treasures in reality of our Kind Creator. Children are sent as a Blessing the truth of which has been acknowledged[320] by all ages handed down by sacred writ & those who are honoured by being Fathers will agree that children are a real source of happiness & comfort the main spring of our solid enjoyments in the married life, hard indeed then must be the heart of that Parent who does not actually feel from

---

317 The spelling of 'setts' and 'tye' in this essay suggest that it may be by the author of 'Marriage is Honourable in All' (and indeed the author of this piece appears to class himself as a married man).

318 Robert Burns, 'Despondency: An Ode', ll, 57–59: 'Oh, enviable, early days, / When dancing thoughtless pleasure's maze / To Care, to Guilt unknown!', in Burns, *Poems, Chiefly in the Scottish Dialect* (Kilmarnock: 1786), pp. 156–59 (p. 159).

319 'Hearted': originally 'harted', an 'e' inserted.

320 'Acknowledged': originally 'acknoledged', the 'w' inserted.

the bottom of his heart that affectionate love & desire towards them that at once binds them by every tye as the greatest gifts bestowed Oft have I in raptures press'd these little innocents to my heart & fondly wish'd their[321] days might prove & all their actions this life be guided by motives as pure & as unerdulterated as those which at that moment of adminis-tration inhabit their little hearts nay I have been tempted to wish it were possible they should remain in that state of infantine least[322] by snares of the world & the various temptations they may be exposed to they loose that native goodliness and as a tender blossom fall away when touched by the devouring blight. But such an idea would be weak & could only be pardonable in consideration of much affection for these sweet infants; being contrary to the course of nature & in defiance to the will of Him who hath created us for his own[323] wise purposes A lovely race of Children are[324] calculated to inspire the mind with awe and respect for the Deity, the sacred duties a family impose upon Parents are such as to draw their serious attention to the means of their future happiness & as early as their little minds are capable of knowing good from evil & initiate them into the principles of religion. A Family of young children is, perhaps the greatest incitement to industry & perseverance and many a parent may doubtless date his prosperity from that moment when with raptures of the tenderest love he clasps his little innocents to his heart & says what would I not endure for your sakes for your future comfort for your prosperity If there are those whose acutest feelings of sensibility are roused in affectionate regard towards these dear pledges of love who are alas doomed to drag on a miserable existence in single life & know not the real & substantial enjoyments of loving their own offspring how much more then must Parents appriciate these gifts of Kind Heaven. It is not surprising that those who in the Married state are not bless'd by a race of their own should by the adoption of anothers offspring seek happiness from a source deny'd them by that power above whose dispensations[325] are inscrutable[326] It is a well authenticated fact that much unhappiness

---

321 'Their': originally 'theirs', the 's' crossed through.
322 'Least': lest.
323 'Own' inserted above the line in a different ink and hand.
324 'Are': 'is' added above the line in a different ink.
325 'Dispensations': originally 'dispenstions', the 'a' inserted.
326 Faraday's marriage to Sarah Barnard was to prove childless; the couple brought one of their nieces to live with them in 1826.

has often arose[327] in the married state caused by the absence of these sweet pledges of connubial Bliss. What indiscribable pleasure must it be to the Parents of a lovely race of children to watch over their youth to form and mould their little minds & to prune away all injurious buds and branches & ingraft the true and genuine species that as the plant grows up to strength and maturity it may prove it has not been foster'd by any unskilful hand How very beautifully does Thompson[328] treat this subject speaking of the delightful enjoyment derived from the watchful care over children my readers are no doubt aware of the beauties of this passage to need other than a short[329] quotation

> "Delightful task to rear the tender thoughts
> "To teach the young idea how to shoot
> "To pour the fresh instructions ore the mind
> "To breathe the enlivened spirits and to fix
> "The generous purpose in the glowing breast.[330]

At a Village on the Dunchurch Road

At a Village on the Dunchurch Road,[331]
    Between two well-known towns
There lives a man—deny't who can:
    With kindness he[332] abounds.

His house, his[333] fare, and[334] fireside,[335]
    Are open to the weary—

---

327 'Arose': not crossed through, but 'arisen' inserted above the line in different ink.

328 'Thompson': originally 'Thomson', the 'p' inserted.

329 'Short': this word barely legible in the manuscript.

330 Thomson, 'Spring', ll. 1149–53: 'Delightful task! to rear the tender thought, / To teach the young idea how to shoot, / To pour the fresh instruction o'er the mind, / To breathe the enlivening spirit, and to fix / The generous purpose in the glowing breast.'

331 This untitled poem was published as 'The Sign of the Four Crosses, at Willoughby, Northamptonshire', in *The Gentleman's Magazine* (GM) for November 1819, p. 449, signed 'Thomas Deacon'. In the published version the punctuation is altered.

332 'He': 'who' in the published version (GM).

333 'His': originally 'and'; 'and' crossed through, 'his' inserted in different ink.

334 'And': originally 'his'; 'his' crossed through, 'and' inserted in different ink.

335 'His house, and fare, and his fire-side' in GM.

The rich, the poor, the destitute—
    He makes them all like cheery.[336]

'Tis said that Swift, St. Patrick's Dean,
    That satirical old sinner,[337]
When on his journey to the North,
    Here stopp'd, and took his dinner.

The sign by which the house was known
    Was called the Three Crosses;
But not I trow because mine host
    Had met with many losses.

However, be that as it may,
    The present Landlord's thrifty;
Though in the house he has not liv'd
    Years counting up to fifty.

It happen'd on a busy day,
    Mine Host was in the cellar,
When Swift began to rant and rave,
    And like a calf did bellow.

"Why am I thus to sit alone,
    "By Host and Hostess slighted;
"If this is all respect you show,
    "I'll have your house endicted.

"Dean Swift's my name; and, Madam, you
    "Should first wait on your betters;
"Before you serve the common folk,
    "Tend well the Man of Letters.

"And when a person of my rank
    "Graces the country round,
"In courtesy and humble mien

---

336 'He makes alike all cheery' in GM.
337 'That old satiric sinner' in GM.

"You always should abound.
"Go where I may, my Cloth commands[338]
      "Respect the most profound."

But Swift soon found the angry Dame
      Was not to be so humble;
For, in her rage, she told the Dean,
      To quit, or cease to grumble.

"Odds bodikins!" mine Hostess adds,
      "The Dean has lost his reason!
"To speak or look but at his Grace,
      "He'd make you think was treason!"

The Landlord from below had heard[339]
      A bustle and disorder;
Quickly ascended to the bar,
      To put his dame in order.

Swift's ready wit soon subject found,
      And taught the dame a lesson,
That from his lips not to expect[340]
      A prayer, or yet a blessing

Says Swift, "upon your casement, there,
      "A legacy I leave you:
"'Tis to your wife I do allude;
      "Let not the subject grieve you;

"For there you'll find a ready plan,
      "To reckon up your losses;
"Though, by my faith, in doing so
      "You'll sure increase your Crosses."[341]

_____

338 'Cloth': '_cloth_' in GM.
339 'The Landlord who below had heard' in GM.
340 'She from his lips could not expect' in GM.
341 'Crosses': '_crosses_' in GM.

Legacy.

"Good Master Tapster, I observe
        "Three Crosses at your door:
"Hang up your odd, ill-tempered wife,
        "And then you will have four."

N.B. Previous to this visit of the Dean's the house was known as the three Crosses; but was immediately altered to the Four Crosses, as it at present appears.[342]

---

342 This note does not appear in GM.

Part Two: Contexts

Faraday and Self-Education

Faraday, from the *Correspondence* (1812–16)

[The friendship between Michael Faraday and Benjamin Abbott was thoroughly rooted in their shared commitment to self-education and self-improvement. The two men met in or before 1812 at a lecture given by John Tatum, the London silversmith whose City Philosophical Society and scientific lectures played an important role in Faraday's education.[1] Abbott was two years younger than Faraday, and a member of a Quaker, rather than a Sandemanian family. He was working as a clerk in the City when he met Faraday, but later went on to found a school in Bermondsey, and eventually became headmaster of a Quaker school in Hitchin. During the 1810s, Abbott was one of Faraday's most frequent correspondents (see above, p. 3, for discussion of the circumstances of the correspondence), though most of his replies to Faraday have been lost. In this very early letter, Faraday discusses the stylistic faults he sees in his own writing and rather playfully explains his hope that writing letters will cure him of them, citing the recommendation of the highly influential eighteenth-century Dissenting minister and writer on education, Isaac Watts, to support his arguments.]

From a letter to Benjamin Abbott, 12 July 1812:[2]

I was lately engaged in conversation with a gentleman, who appeared to have a very extensive correspondence: for within the space of half an hour, he drew observations from two letters that he had received not a fortnight before; one was from Sicily; and the other from France. After a

---

1   See Frank A. J. L. James, 'The Tales of Benjamin Abbott: A Source for the Early Life of Michael Faraday', *British Journal for the History of Science*, 25 (1992), 229–40.

2   *Correspondence*, I, pp. 3–5.

while, I adverted to his correspondence; & observed that it must be very interesting, and a source of great pleasure to himself: He immediately affirmed with great enthusiasm that it was one of the purest enjoyments of his life: (observe he like you and your humble servant is a Bachelor.)— much more passed on the subject, but I will not waste your time in recapitulating it; however let me notice, before I cease from praising and recommending epistolary correspondence, that the great Dr. Isaac Watts, (great in all the methods respecting the attainment of Learning;) recommends it, as a very effectual method of improving the mind of the person who writes, & the person who receives;³ Not to forget too another strong instance in favour of the practice, I will merely call to your mind the correspondence that passed between Lord Chesterfield & his Son: In general, I do not approve for the usual tendency of Lord Chesterfields Letters, but I heartily agree with him respecting the utility of a written correspondence. It, like many other good things can be made to suffer an abuse, but that is no effectual argument against its good effects.

I dear A—, naturally love a letter, and take as much pleasure in reading one, (when addressed to myself: and in answering one as in almost any thing else; & this good opinion which I entertain, has not suffered any injury from the circumstances I have noticed above: I also like it for what I fancy to be good reasons, drawn up in my own mind upon the subject: and from those reasons, I have concluded, that letter writing improves; first, the hand writing, secondly, the—... At this moment occurs an instance of my great deficiency in letter writing: I have the Idea I wish to express full in my mind, but have forgot the word that expresses it, a word common enough too: I mean the expression, the delivery, the composition a manner of connecting words. thirdly, it improves the mind, by the reciprocal exchange of knowledge. fourthly, the ideas: it tends I conceive to make the ideas clear and distinct, (Ideas are generated or formed in the head, and I will give you an odd instance as proof). fifthly, it improves the morals: I speak not of the abuse, but the use of Epistolations, (if you will allow me to coin a new word to express myself)⁴ and that use I have no doubt, produces other good effects. Now, I do not profess myself perfect in those points, and my deficiency in others connected with the subject you well know; as Grammar &c therefore it follows that I want improving on these points, and what so natural in a disease, as to revert

---

3   I have not been able to find the passage Faraday refers to here.

4   The OED has no record of 'epistolation'.

to the remedy that will perform a cure; and more so when the Physic is so pleasant: or to express it in a more logical manner, and consequently more philosophically, MF is deficient in certain points, that he wants to make up. Epistolary writing is one cure for these deficiencies, therefore, MF should practice Epistolary writing.

Seeing that I have thus proved, from both Reason and Logic, and the last is almost equal to Mathematics in certainty; that I should Write Letters; it merely remained to obtain correspondents: Now do not be affronted Mr. Abbott at my looking towards you before you have heard my reasons; I am happy to say that my disposition is somewhat like your own, Philosophically inclined; and of course I wish to improve in that part more than in others: you too have I presume time to spare now & then for half an hour or so: your Ideas too I have ascertained while conversing with you, are plentifull, & pretty perfect; I will not say quite, for I have never yet met with a person who had arrived at perfetion so great as to conceive new ideas, with exactness & clearness. & your—vide above, where I failed; your composition, or expression, pleases me highly. for these reasons I have presumed to conceive, that the interchange of ideas & Information would not be unpleasant to you, & would be highly gratifying to me. You may if you choose take this (insert some word here) as a specimen of what mine would be, & return me an answer similar to what you have promised me, before *Yes* or *No*.

On looking back I find dear A—, that I have filled two pages with very uninteresting matter; and was intending to go on with more, had I not suddenly been stopped by the lower edge of the paper. this circumstance, (happily for you, for I should have put you to sleep else,) has 'called back my wand'ring thoughts,'[5] & I will now give you what I at first intended this letter should be wholly composed of, Philosophical Information & Ideas.

[The correspondence between Faraday and Abbott was, as the above letter makes clear, originally intended for the purposes of self-improvement, both in literary style and scientific information. Accordingly, many of Faraday's letters to Abbott contained a

---

5   Cp. James Macpherson (trans.), *The Poems of Ossian*, 3 vols. (London: Miller, 1812), III, p. 282 (footnote): 'Young virgins of Lutha arise, call back the wandering thoughts of Malvina.' Miller's bookshop was at 50 Albemarle Street; Miller was thus a neighbour of the Royal Institution, which is at 21 Albemarle Street, though in the year Miller published his *Ossian*, his business was bought by John Murray II, who went on to make 50 Albemarle Street the centre of his publishing empire.

good deal of news about scientific experiments Faraday had performed or read about. But increasingly Faraday wrote about other topics, including details of his personal and professional life. In these two excerpts from letters of 1813, when Faraday was on his continental tour with Sir Humphry Davy, and 1816, when he had returned to London, Faraday addresses his views on literary style. The first gives evidence of Faraday's criteria for literary judgment, highlighting especially his preference for the integration or matching of form and content. In the second extract he identifies faults in his own writing, which falls short of the highly organic style he prefers. In this style the structure is clear but not dominant or obtrusive. Both extracts reveal the importance of the pleasure and ease of the reader in Faraday's stylistic desiderata, as well as the serious and detailed consideration he gave, over a period of years, to the ways in which the aesthetic and informative aspects of writing should support one another.]

From a letter to Abbott, 8 March 1813, commenting on some unidentified verses sent to him by Abbott:[6]

I think them indeed beautifull & impressive and not only that but the subject itself or rather the reasoning that the verses contain is excellent & good—too often we find beauty & deformity linked together sublime language & an insignificant subject full & affirmative words & no matter but here each part will support that credit it appears to have in the whole and one part will bear as strict an examination as another[.][7]

From a letter to Abbott, 31 December 1816:[8]

The observation contained in yours of the 25th respecting the various causes and influences which have retarded our mutual communication together with my own experience which on this point you are aware has been great make it desirable that our plans should be such as to facilitate the object we have in view in the writing of letters[.] That object is I believe the communication of information between us and the habit of arranging in a proper and orderly manner our ideas on any given or casual subject so that they may be placed with credit and service to ourselves on paper[.] This object strikes me would in part be attained by giving in addition to the general tone of a liberal & friendly letter something of the essayical to our communications.[9] I do not mean that every letter should

---

6   *Correspondence*, I, p. 44.

7   In all quotations from *Correspondence*, full stops in square brackets are James' editorial additions.

8   *Correspondence*, I, pp. 148–49.

9   'Essayical': the OED wrongly gives 1860 as the first use of this word.

be an essay but that when a thought or a series of thoughts on any subject particular for the moment enters the mind that the liberty be allowed of throwing them into form on paper though perhaps unconnected with what has gone before or may succeed it. This indeed I believe is the plan we have actually followed but I am not sure that I had so conceived the thing before at least I had not marked out in my own mind that in pursuance of our object I might set down and scribble to you without preface what I aim at and what are my intentions and though as I before observed we have both virtually followed this plan yet I have at this time given it something like form or ground or expression or whatever else you please that I might be more con[s]cious of it and make use to a greater extent of the liberty it allows me[.]

I must confess that I have always found myself unable to arrange a subject as I go on as I perceive many others apparently do thus I could not begin a letter to you on the best methods of renovating our correspondence and proceeding regularly with my subject consider each part in order and finish by a proper conclusion my paper and matter together[.] I always find myself obliged if my argument is of the least importance to draw up a plan of it on paper and fill in the parts by recalling them to mind either by association or otherwise and this done I have a series of major & minor heads in order & from which I work out my matter—Now this method unfortunately though it will do very well for the mere purpose of arrangement & so forth yet it introduces a dryness and stiffness into the style of the piece composed by it for the parts come together like bricks one flat on the other and though they may fit yet have the appearance of too much regularity and it is my wish if possible to become acquainted with a method by which I may write my exercise in a more natural and easy progression [.] I would if possible imitate a tree in its progression from roots to a trunk to branches twigs & leaves where every alteration is made with so much ease & yet effect that though the manner is constantly varied the effect is precise and determined [.] Now in this situation I apply to you for assistance[.] I want to know what method or what particular practice or exercise in composition you would recommend to prevent the orderly arrangement of A1 A2 A3. B1. B2 C1. C2 C3. C4 &c or rather to prevent this orderly arrangement from appearing too artificial—I am in want of all those conjunctions of style those corollaries &c by which parts of a subject are put together with so much ease and which produce so advantageous an effect and as you have frequently in your contributions to our portfolios given me cause to admire your success & my own deficiency on this point I beg that you will communicate to me your method of composing or if it is done spontaneously & without effort on your part that you will analyse your mental proceedings whilst writing a letter and give me an account of that part which you conceive conducive to so good an end—

Faraday, from *Observations on the Means of Obtaining Knowledge* (1817)[10]

[The City Philosophical Society played an important part in Faraday's self-education. As well as conversation evenings and scientific lectures by its founder, John Tatum, the CPS provided a weekly lecture, delivered in rotation by its members. Faraday became a member in 1810 and gave his first lecture that year, on the topic of electricity. The lecture printed here was given in 1817, around a year and a half before Faraday founded his essay-circle. It includes of a description of the five methods of improving one's knowledge outlined by Isaac Watts (for Watts's own account of these methods, see below, pp. 216–17), and an exhortation—comparatively mild by Faraday's standards—to the members of the CPS to dedicate themselves more energetically and effectively to self-improvement. The structure of the essay may be felt to confirm Faraday's own view (expressed in the letter to Abbott above, p. 178) that his compositional methods at this time prioritized clarity over smooth flow.

The stated aims of this lecture are practical rather than philosophical; Faraday urges giving attention to techniques for acquiring knowledge instead of wasting time on questions of epistemology. But despite this emphasis on practical techniques, Faraday shows considerable interest in issues of philosophy of mind throughout his speculative and literary writings of the late 1810s, including his contributions to the essay-circle. He addresses the workings of the imagination, the reason and the memory several times and in some depth, though, as he writes here with characteristic self-deprecation, he has 'but a slight acquaintance with authors who have considered the matter.' Among the fruits of this interest was a recurrent concern with the formation of habits, and in this lecture Faraday introduces the idea of 'inertia of the mind', the habit of mental laziness, which he goes on to explore in much greater detail in the following extract.

Several CPS lectures of the 1810s were printed, but it is not clear how they were selected, or how widely they were distributed. This lecture by Faraday has not received a great deal of attention from biographers; Joseph Agassi describes this and the 'Mental Inertia' lecture as 'rather silly in their Wattsian naïveté,' ignoring the correlation between Faraday's optimism about the possibilities for self-improvement and the

---

10   Michael Faraday, *Some Observations on the Means of Obtaining Knowledge, and on the Facilities Afforded by the Constitution of the City Philosophical Society* (London: Effingham Wilson, 1817).

emerging national impetus towards promoting auto-didacticism.[11] Though his focus is on individual effort rather than on the need for state and philanthropic support for self-education, Faraday's writings on the topic are not far out of line with those of leading activists and promoters of education such as Henry Brougham.]

'Read to the body of members, at 53 Dorset-street, Salisbury-square, Feb. 19, 1817.

[...]

It cannot be necessary for me to enlarge on the advantages of knowledge, to men professedly assembled in the pursuit of it. Whatever the primeval state of things may have been, the experience of every day, and every hour, carries with it a conviction of the important truth, that in the present state, it is the most essential requisite to the mind of man. It is possible that the unreflecting, being acquainted only with the small circle immediately around him; and, from the force of custom, seeing that circle, not in its true form, but distorted; may not perceive this truth to the full extent; but a little experience in the affairs of life, or a very short acquaintance with the proceedings of those around us, will correct the hasty immature judgment, and convince that of all earthly things knowledge is the first.

We see men of genius and learning continually rising above the horizon of common life, and claiming by their attainments the attention and submission of their fellow creatures. Each one of them, in his sphere, is able to sway a multitude: the wise consider and obey, because they perceive him able to lead; the ignorant gaze in wonder, and submit, they know not why; the cunning fawn, flatter, and crouch to him, in hopes to profit undeservedly by the deserved merits of another.

When knowledge is considered in a more extensive view, and as it affects an age, or a kingdom; it is able to confer lustre and dignity, of an everlasting nature, and to form epochs, which the historian glories to dwell upon, and to transmit with his warmest breath of praise to future ages. It confers upon kingdoms their noblest marks of distinction and superiority; and, at the same time that it raises to, enables them to retain, their elevated situation. What is it that has preserved the names of Bacon, Newton, Locke, and Boyle, to us? 'tis the knowledge they possessed. What was it that made them the glory of the age and nation in which they lived? 'twas still their knowledge. 'Tis the same distinction which makes

---

11   Joseph Agassi, *Faraday as a Natural Philosopher* (Chicago: University of Chicago Press, 1971), p. 28.

Asia superior to Africa, and Europe to Asia; and it always will ultimately place that nation, age, or individual, which possesses it most eminently, at the head of the rest.

Arguments have been urged against knowledge, as being pernicious in its effects; as degrading man from that simplicity and innocence given to him by nature, and introducing into his life a multiplicity of low dishonourable excitements, which are only to be gratified by artificial means. With these arguments I am but little acquainted, nor do I feel envious of the knowledge of those who can advance them. I disclaim the character which may attach to such a declaration, of judging only from one statement of things, by saying, that a very slight attention was sufficient to convince me that a judgment had been made, from the abuse rather than the use of knowledge. There must be but few, however, who seriously imagine a question can arise respecting the value of that, which above all other things is capable of raising the character of a man, an age, or a nation, in the eyes of the rest of the world, and which has obtained the applause and approbation of all men, both virtuous and vicious, from the commencement until now.

But, leaving you to the exertion of your judgment in awarding, and your imagination in exalting, the praises of knowledge; I shall proceed to those observations, which a consideration of it has given rise to in my own mind, and which are intended for your hearing this evening.

Knowledge, I think, may be defined to be an acquaintance with causes, effects, laws, and principles. As it respects the important division of human nature into two parts, mind and matter, it may be divided into two kinds, moral and natural. The first will relate to the passions, affections, and influences, of the mind; to her virtues and vices; to her relation with beings similar to herself, and to her Creator. The latter comprises all the varieties and forms of matter; its various juxta-positions, with the effects produced by them; and the laws which are observed to be prevalent over it.

In our knowledge *of* knowledge I will venture to say, that it is important to know, rather how to acquire it, than what it is. We cannot, indeed, appreciate it properly before we are in possession; and, though we may be strongly impressed by the consideration of a person in whom it shines supereminent, and may praise and commend his attainments; yet we are more usefully employed in devising means of ascending to the height at which he stands, than in estimating his exact position on it. The latter, indeed, we cannot do; 'tis he alone who can survey the horizon around him, and form a correct judgment of his situation; and, though standing at the bottom we may perceive the path even up to the very summit, yet we cannot tell the views that will gradually open upon us from it as we ascend.

Our pursuits, gentlemen, in life, are partial: each, under the exhilerating influence of hope, looks forward to some object before him, and labours for its attainment; the objects are various and many, and, even though several may aim at the possession of an individual one, yet, their situations being different, different paths to it must be followed. The object of the author is renown; he writes for it, and to obtain it makes his knowledge consist in that of men and manners. Renown is also the soldier's aim; but, to procure it, he pursues a different course of studies, and acts in a different way; and the orator, wishing to be renowned, consults the propriety of his language and the force of sounds. The merchant's aim is riches; his appropriate knowledge is of goods, markets, and trade. The alchymist's aim was the same, but he applied himself to the study of the secret and mystical properties of substances.

It results from this variety in the pursuits of men, that an infinity of sub-divisions have been made among the objects of human understanding; and that every one finds occasion to strike out original means of satisfying his desires and inquiries: so that, however perfect the means of obtaining knowledge may be, as applied by one person, they are not entirely applicable when transferred to another; on this account, it is desirable that some general directions be laid down, to which every person may refer in the improvement of the understanding, leaving the application of them to particular circumstances, in his own power.

I have ventured to bring this subject forward under the disadvantage of having but a slight acquaintance with authors who have considered the matter, and under the still greater inconvenience of having but slightly considered it myself. My store of learning respecting knowledge abstractedly considered, has been gathered some time since from the writings of Lord Bacon, and from a work by Dr. Watts, on the Improvement of the Mind, and which I consider so good in its kind, that no person ought to be without it.

Dr Watts says, I believe, that there are five methods of obtaining knowledge; these are, conversation, lectures, reading, observation, and study.

I shall consider each of these separately, but not abstractly; for, in bringing forward this subject to the view of the Society, I wish also to place in sight the facilities which are afforded by the constitution adopted in this place, and to excite a desire in the members to take advantage of them; and here I must be allowed to say, that it is my firm belief, that were all the benefits which may be derived from a vigorous exercise and enjoyment of the powers and privileges of the *City Philosophical Society* well known and duly appreciated, each member would feel eager to share in the general good they present, and regret that such estimable advantages had been until now suffered to remain unemployed: for myself, I have perceived and used them: and it is but natural, that one who has gained much by the Society should feel grateful for it, and endeavour to express it in terms of praise and respect. It has increased my stores of mental enjoyment, and as it has taught me liberality, I recommend it liberally to others: nor can I refrain from saying, that I know no institution, with means so small, and professions so humble, calculated to produce so much effect, or results so highly valuable.

I trust I shall be excused for the warmth of my feelings on this occasion: I do not express myself thus, because I imagine you are not conscious of the true value of the Society; but having experienced, to a great extent, its beneficial effects, I am willing to testify my consciousness of them. I shall now consider the means of obtaining knowledge, and, as I before said, with reference to those afforded by our constitution.

CONVERSATION is a very pleasing and effective mean [sic] of acquiring information. When a subject is once started, the thoughts gradually enliven and pursue it with more ardour, the chase is exhilerated by the new observations that are made on both sides, and an idea is frequently evolved, by the collision of opinion, that would never have arisen, either from lectures, reading, observation, or study. If a principle be laid down, the objection to it may be made and answered immediately; if a statement be obscure, it may be cleared up without delay; if doubts arise, they may be solved; while the whole train of reasoning, connected with the subject, is still in mind: so that, there does not appear to be a more amusing and effectual method of obtaining knowledge than this.

Is it not then singular that a means so pleasing, so effective, and so important, should be neglected so sadly, when it is so easily obtained? *Our private evenings* are calculated for conversation improved. They admit, not of that desultory kind of chit-chat, which is characteristic of a vacuity of mind, and where indeed method would be ill applied; but of a regular, orderly interchange of thoughts and opinions; of an easy colloquial transference of information; of question and answer; or of observation; without end. Our subjects are not confined, our laws are not curbing, and our incitements are numerous; yet it is with regret I observe, that so low are those evenings appreciated, that not one half of our members generally attend.

I cannot help thinking that it is the mere inertia of the mind that deprives us of the company of many of our members; they have not come one night, and they do not come another; they have staid away, and do stay away without a thought: for my own part, so highly do I value the opportunities of our conversations, that I would rather be absent on any lecture night, than on a private evening. But to proceed to the second means of obtaining knowledge:

LECTURING has its advantages; some of them are as follows. A person who comes forward to lecture is supposed to be very well acquainted with his subject, and to give correct and undoubted information: whereas, in conversation we often form groups where all are searchers after knowledge, no one being in the possession. Again, as the subject is predetermined, it receives, we are to suppose, previous consideration and arrangement; it is therefore more methodical and regular; its parts are better adapted to each other, and we remember them with more ease. In experimental lectures also, there is the advantage of apparatus and other demonstrative means, all which tend to facilitate the acquirement of knowledge. With these aids, therefore, lecturing, though inferior to conversation in some things, surpasses it in others.

But lecturing, as practised in this Society, possesses advantages over those just enumerated. It is capable of improving not only those who are lectured, but also the lecturer. He makes it, or ought to make it, an opportunity for the exertion of his mental powers, that so by using he may strengthen them; and if he is truly in earnest, he will do as much good to himself as to his audience. He, in imparting that to others, which shall inform, instruct, and amuse, is himself obtaining the power of doing so with the greatest effect: and what pleasure is there greater than that of having the power of persuasion,—of having the learned for listener,—of communicating knowledge?

The constitution of our Society looks rather to those who are behind, than those who are forward. Its intentions are to gather up such as remain, or proceed more slowly, and place them with the rest: equality is indeed its principle, though, at the same time that it labours to preserve a state of uniformity, it permits every one to follow the incitements of his inclination and peculiar genius. Now, were this intention to be realized;

were all to come forward and assist in improving others; in fine, were the Society what it ought to be; how varied would be its lectures, how extensive the subjects it would embrace, and how enhanced the value of it to the members!

I regret much, that in noticing READING as a mean of learning, I am unable to say we are in possession of it to any extent. Reading has peculiarities which well entitle it to notice, and make it indispensable to the seeker after knowledge. The care with which books are written far surpasses that with which lectures are delivered, or conversation passed; we therefore get the author's meaning in them in its purest form; we are able to consider and reconsider it; if a passage is doubtful, we can refer to it and give it mature deliberation; and after having read a subject, and given it all the attention required, we can again revert to the book, and see that we have not lost our author's meaning among the multitude of thoughts, but possess it aright. I am sorry, therefore, that possessing all these advantages, we are so deficient in this mean, though I cannot be surprised that the case is as it is. With our parsimonious and economical subscriptions, it can scarcely be imagined, that to apparatus, lectures, and conversations, a library should be added; or that what Societies of great extent cannot accomplish, our small number, with lesser means, can; and yet, in the face of every disadvantage, a number of very useful books have been collected, and will prove, I trust, the nucleus of an excellent future library.

OBSERVATION is a method of learning open to every man; and in common life, each most extensively makes use of it. Opportunities for its exertion occur as well in society as elsewhere; but there is one peculiar branch of it, for which we possess facilities as a body, which many of us do not as individuals: I allude to the making of experiment. Experimental investigations are merely investigations carried on by observation: a fact is observed, on which a judgment is formed; and then, a deduction being drawn, another fact is observed, which, as it accords with or opposes the foregoing judgment, strengthens or weakens it. I refer you to the questions in Natural Philosophy, which have at different times been brought before the Society, and which have been illustrated by experiment, as instances of the facilities afforded us in that path to knowledge, called observation.

STUDY is the last method of obtaining information, I have to notice. It is indubitably the most important; as opening to us new stores of knowledge, with which we were formerly unacquainted. It is the only mean of extending the bounds of learning. The man who studies has always an original mind; for to study, is to vary ascertained matters, and to elicit new. To judge, to deduce, is the noble and exalted employment of the student; and the last and best means of acquiring knowledge, and that which corrects all others, is to study. Without it, conversation, lectures, reading, and observation, would, like dreams, merely present images and figures to amuse the fancy for a while, but which would quickly vanish, and be lost for ever. Connected with it, they are sources of profit, pleasure, and happiness, and become the springs of universal good to mankind.

Our Society is not at all deficient in those means which encourage a disposition to study. I shall refer more particularly to the port-folio which has been established for the reception of such papers, analysis, or essays, either on lectures, questions, or independent subjects, as may be contributed by the members. This port-folio supplies the place of a report, and each one who comes forward is asked to place in it either his question or lecture; or, if he please, any original paper: so that, it *should really* be the archives of the Society. It circulates among the members with the books of the library.

I feel much pleasure in the contemplation of what this plan will produce for us; and expect, when I next see it, to be gratified by the perusal of some original papers; and I am proud that the circumstances of lecturing, &c. have given me a right to contribute my mite to the general stock.

Referring to the effect which it has in inducing study, in such as contribute to it, I can as yet only speak from my own experience; there, however, it is satisfactory, and I declare, with great pleasure, that a consciousness that my papers should be deposited in such a situation has urged me to pay more attention to the analysis of my lectures, and to consider with greater care the subject of a question before I brought it forward. Even on this very paper I have been induced to bestow greater care from that circumstance, and have endeavoured to express my thoughts clearly, and order them correctly, because they are to remain in the annals of the Society.

I will not detain you longer, gentlemen, from the expression of your opinions on this subject, than to point out to you two modes in which you may treat it. The question may be formally put: whether the means of acquiring knowledge, which I have pointed out, are sufficient to the extent that I have described? or, as I should rather wish it, the conversation may turn on the means afforded by the organisation of the Society, and on such improvements of those means as may suggest themselves to the members as being practicable?

Faraday, from 'Observations on the Inertia of the Mind' (1818)[12]

[Faraday gave this lecture at the CPS in the month that the essay-circle began work. Several themes in the lecture have a bearing on the work of the group and Faraday's contributions to it in particular. One is Faraday's belief in human improveability, and his view that it is to be achieved through the individual conscience and will. Only once in the lecture does he acknowledge the possible effects of wider society on an individual's progress. Even more than in the previous year's *Observations on the Means of Obtaining Knowledge*, Faraday's purpose here is to shame his audience into further and greater efforts towards self-improvement, and though he comments several times on the potential of the City Philosophical Society to help in such efforts, his chief emphasis is on the duty of the individual to fulfil his nature by drawing himself out of idleness and dissipation and into an industrious, moral and energetic life.

A related theme which runs through this lecture as well as some of Faraday's contributions to the Mental Exercises is that of habit: Faraday seems to be fascinated at this period by its power to confirm the individual in virtue or vice. He introduced the idea of 'inertia of the mind' in his 1817 CPS lecture; here he develops it very considerably to create an analogy between mechanical systems and mental processes: a kind of mechanics of psychology. He describes the analogy as founded in 'playfulness', but the tone of the lecture is very earnest. Geoffrey Cantor, in his very important study of Faraday in the context of his religious life, points out that the call to 'perfection' made in the second paragraph of this lecture should be understood as an affirmation of the injunction '*Be perfect*: keep the commandments, and thou shalt live,' made by the founder of the Sandemanian sect.[13] This comparison reminds us that Faraday's passionate impulse towards self-improvement for himself and others, though it frequently adopted aspects of the 'polite', secular and even worldly goals of early nineteenth-century education, was primarily driven by ideas about divine judgement and the salvation of the individual. Faraday's impossibly high standards (for example, in seeking—Democritus-like—a person 'who has never relaxed but when fatigue required it') reflect the urgency of the attempt to meet divine demands. But we should not forget that he couches those standards, here and elsewhere, partly in terms of success in the temporal world, particularly as underpinning security in business. This is, presumably, a nod to the interests of his audience and certainly to the rules of the CPS, which barred religious discussion. But in explicitly distinguishing morality from religion—a distinction Faraday also made in other arenas where theological points would not have been inappropriate—he opens a space in which he can move easily from spiritual to temporal descriptions of human behaviour, translating (some) religious requirements into secular terms and thus equipping himself to operate effectively in the worldly realm and to avoid quixotic or hermetic otherness.

---

12   CPB, I, pp. 337–63.
13   Cantor, p. 112.

The idea of inertia entered physics via Newton, though he used the Latin form of the term. Inertia is, as a textbook on mechanics published in the same year as this lecture defines it, the quality by which matter resists a change to its state of rest or uniform rectilinear motion.[14] Thus, it is crucial to the Newtonian understanding of the universe, helping to guarantee the predictability of all mechanical systems. Faraday points out that insofar as minds, like objects in mechanics, tend to stay in the same state unless an outside force intervenes, such 'mental inertia' may be virtuous or vicious depending on the initial state of the mind. In 1871, the year after this lecture was published in Bence Jones' *Life and Letters of Michael Faraday*, the great physicist James Clerk Maxwell adapted Faraday's idea of 'mental inertia' in his 'Introductory Lecture' as Professor of experimental physics at Cambridge University. In this lecture Clerk Maxwell used 'mental inertia' to describe a philosophic (or even psychological) problem afflicting the scientific investigator when he brings theory to bear on reality: 'not only the difficulty of recognising, among the concrete objects before us, the abstract relation which we have learned from books, but also the distracting pain of wrenching the mind away from the symbols to the objects, and from the objects back to the symbols.'[15] This seems a significant refinement of Faraday's views as expressed in this essay—perhaps more an *homage* to Faraday's place in physics than a reconstruction of his original 'inertia of the mind'.]

Read at the City Philosophical Society, 1 July 1818.

Man is an improving animal: Unlike the animated world around him which remains in the same constant state he is continually varying; and it is one of the noblest prerogatives of his nature that in the highest of earthly distinctions he has the power of raising and exalting himself continually.—The transitory state of man has been held up to him, as a memento of his weakness; to man *degraded* it may with justice; to man as he ought to be it is no reproach; and in knowledge, that man only is to be contemned and despised, who is *not* in a state of transition.

We are by our nature progressive: We are placed by the creator in a certain state of things resulting from the pre-existence of Society combined with the laws of nature. Here we commence our existence our earthly career. The extent before us is long and he who reaches farthest in his time has best done his duty and has most honor. The goal before us is perfection always within sight but too far distant to be reached: Like a point in the utmost verge of perspective it seems to recede before us and

---

14   James Wood, *The Principles of Mechanics*, sixth edn (Cambridge: Deighton, 1818), p. 8.

15   James Clerk Maxwell, 'Introductory Lecture on Experimental Physics' (1871), in W. D. Niven (ed.), *The Scientific Papers of James Clerk Maxwell*, 2 vols. (Mineola: Dover, 2003), II, pp. 241–55 (p. 248).

we find as we advance that the distance far surpasses our conception of it
Still however we are not deceived; each step we move repays abundantly
the exertion made and the more eager our race the more novelties and
pleasures we obtain

Some there are who on this plain of human life content themselves with
that which their predecessors put into their possession and they remain
idle and inactive on the spot where nature has dropped them—Others
exist who can well enjoy the advantages in advance but are too idle to
exert themselves for their possession: and these are well punished by the
envy which their very sensibility and sentient powers engender within
them at sight of the success of others—A third set are able and willing to
advance in knowledge but they must be lead; and but few attain to the
distinguished honor of being first on the plain; and of taking the of their
generation of the age and of the world.[16]

It can scarcely be possible that my opinion should be mistaken in what
I have said; but least [sic] any one misconceive me I shall take the liberty
of discriminating some few points before I proceed farther in asserting
the improveability of man.

First then all theological considerations are banished from the Society
and of course from my remarks; and whatever I may say has no reference
to a future state or to the means which are to be adopted in this world
in anticipation of it. Next I have no intention of substituting any thing
for religion; but I wish to take that part of human nature which is
independant of it. Morality Philosophy, Commerce, the various institutions and habits of society are independent of religion and may exist
either with or without it. They are always the same and can dwell alike in
the breasts of those who from opinion are entirely opposed in the set of
principles the include[17] in the term Religion; or in those who have none.

To discriminate more closely if possible I will observe that we have *no*
right to judge religious opinions: but the human nature of this evening
is that part of man which we *have* a right to judge; and I think it will be
found on examination that this humanity as it may perhaps be called will
accord with what I have before described as being in our own hands so
improveable and perfectible.

Lastly by advancement on the plain of Life I mean advancement in
those things which distinguish man from beasts—Sentient advancement

---

16 'The of their generation': word missing in MS.
17 'The include': word missing in MS.

It is not him who has soared above his fellow creatures in power; it is not him who can command most readily the pampering couch the costly luxury; but it is he[18] who has done most good to his fellows; he who has directed them in the doubtful moment, strengthened them in the weak moment aided them in the moment of necessity and enlightened them in their ignorance that leads the ranks of mankind.

Such then is our state and such our duty. We are placed on a certain point in the immensity of time with the long the interminable chains of moral good and of human knowledge lying about our path. We are able to place them strait before us to take them as our guides and even to develop them to others far beyond the spot where we found them, and it is our duty to *do* so—Some there are perverse enough to entangle them even wilfully to delight in destroying the arrangements which nature points out and to retard their very neighbours in their efforts. But by far the greater part are content to let things remain as the are. They make no efforts themselves but on the contrary hang as weights upon the exertions of others who labour for the public good.—Now it is with the spirit which animates or rather benumbs these that I would have to do. I trust there are not many who retrograde, and for the sake of human nature I will not believe that the observations which apply to them should be general

There is a power in Natural Philosophy of an influence, universal; and yet withall so obscure in its nature, so unobtrusive, that for many ages no idea of it existed It is called *Inertia*.—It tends to retain every body in its present state, and seems like the spirit of constancy impressed upon matter. Whatever is in motion is by it retained in motion; and whatever is at rest, remains at rest under its sway. It opposes every *new* influence, strengthens every *old* one

Is there nothing in the human mind which seems analogous to this power? Is there no spiritual effect comparable to this corporeal one?—What are habits?—Old Prejudices?—They seem something like a retention in a certain state due to somewhat more than the active impulses of the moment.—As far as regards them, the mind seems inclined to remain in the state in which it is; and the words which enunciate part of our natural law well describe exactly the effect[19]—The agreement is strange but it nevertheless is evident and exact thus far; and it is possible

18   'It' inserted in MS.
19   'Describe' inserted in MS.

we shall find it to exist even in its more active states We have only to ascertain whether the mind which has once received an impulse, which has become active and made progressive continues in that state; and we can decide at once on the analogy.

I do not know whther you will require of me to prove that such is the case before you will admit it; the impression on my own mind is that it is eminently so; and I doubt not but that your own observation will confirm my conclusions.—The man who has once turned his mind to an art goes on more and more improving in it; the man who once begins to observe rapidly improves in the faculty;—and to illustrate at once the force of mental inertia to retain the mind either at rest or in motion how difficult our endeavours to set about a mere affair how facil [sic] our progress when once engaged.—Every little delay illustrates more or less the Inertia of the passive mind; every new observation every fresh discovery that of the active mind.

Perhaps in playfulness we may endeavour to trace the analogy still further.—Inertia is an essential property of matter—is it a never failing attendant on the mind?—I hope it is: for as it seems to be in full force whenever the mind is passive I trust it is also in power when she is actively engaged.—Was the idle mind ever yet easy to be placed in activity? Was the dolt ever willing to resign inanity for perception? or are they not always found contented to remain as they were, satisfied with their situation? They are like the Shepherd Magnus; altho' on a barren rock, their efforts to remove are irksome and unpleasant; and they seem chained to the spot by a power over which they have no controul, of which they have no perception.

Again in activity what intellectual being would resign his employment? who would be content to forego the pleasures hourly crowding upon him; each new thought, perception, or judgement is sufficient reward in itself for his past labours and all the future is pure enjoyment. There is a labour in thought but none who have once engaged in it would willingly resign it. Intermissions I speak not of; 'tis the general habit and tenor of the mind that concerns us and that which has once been made to taste the pleasures of its own voluntary exertions will not by a slight cause be made to forego them

There is still another point of analogy between the Inertia of Matter and that of the Mind and though not essential in either case yet the circumstances exist in both. I refer to what may be called disturbing forces.—If the inertia of matter were to be exerted alone it would tend according to the original state of rest or of motion to preserve the universe eternally the same or to make it ever changing. At present it is doubtful whether both these effects do not take place; but they certainly do not happen in the same manner. The centripetal force, the centrifugal force, the force resulting from chemical action and that which originates in muscular exertion are at all times active in changing and varying the states induced by inertia, sometimes aiding, sometimes counteracting its effect.—These are represented among intellectual beings by the sensations perceptions, passions, and other mental influences which interfere (frequently so much to our inconvenience) in the dictates of our reason.—The philosopher who has perceived and enjoyed the advantages resulting from the actual performance of his own experiments and the use of his own senses has all his industry (I would say Inertia) destroyed by the lassitude of a hot day and gravitates into inactivity Another has his reasoning crossed by his inclination some thoughts are driven one way some another and his mind becomes a mere chaos—Others there are again whose inertia is assisted by the repeated action of other causes and they go on with accellerated [sic] energy So vanity, ambition, pride, interest, and a thousand other influences tend to make men redouble their efforts; and the effect is such, that what appeared at first an impassable barrier easily gives way before the increasing power opposed to it.

Inertia as it regards matter is a term sufficiently well understood both in a state of rest and of motion,—As it is not my intention to attempt a description of functions of the mind according to strict mathematical terms I shall resign the exclusive use of the word at present and adopt two others which according to the sense they have acquired from usage will I believe supply its place with accuracy—*Apathy* will represent the Inertia of a passive mind *Industry* that of an active mind.

It is curious to consider how we qualify ideas, essentially the same, according to the words made use of to represent them. I might talk of mental inertia for a long time without attaching either blame or praise to it; without the chance even of doing so; but mention Apathy and Industry and the mind simultaneously censures the one and commends the other. Yet the things are the same; both Idleness and Industry are habits and habits result from Inertia.

Let us first consider the Inertia of the sluggish mind. This is Apathy—Idleness.—Perhaps there never yet was a person who could be offered as a complete instance of this state: One who made not the slightest advancement in the paths of knowledge. It is not possible there should be such where perception and reason exists though but in the slightest degree. Society must of necessity entrain such a being even though against his will; and he will be moved like the rocky fragment in a mountain torrent a fit display of the energetic powers about him and of his own mean inanimated state.

But for want of this complete illustration we may select instances where the general character is heavy and dull; or where that idleness which has been dignified unjustly with the name of contentment exists. Or, we may take a particular individual and select such parts of his character as are most subject to the benumbing influence of apathy. We cannot fail of finding (each in his own circle) plenty like to the first of these and perhaps I should not assert too much if I were to say we are all included among the latter

I have promised to apply my observations to the society; and I regret that the task as it regards apathetic inertia is so easy. You must be conscious of the illustration afforded me in our meetings of a languid state of mind. Of indeed an indifference which seems to palsy every effort made to give activity to the system Or if you are not a slight consideration will soon make you aware of it—Perhaps however *I* view the society from a peculiar point of view; perhaps the appearance to others is very different to that presented to me. It is possible I may have mistaken the nature of it and yet from the repeated statements I have made of what I have considered its nature and spirit; and from the acquiescence with which they have been received that is hardly possible.—What then is the Society? Is it not an association of persons who willing to communicate and receive information, have agreed to form certain periodical opportunities when intercourse shall be facilitated, and subscribed to certain rules by which that intercourse shall be regulated? Has not each one tacitly agreed to bring his attention if not his opinion to bear on the subject introduced? Are not the subjects left open and various as nature itself that all may be satisfied each selecting according to his taste? Is there any demand for perfection; for elaborate reasoning and sound judgement; or is any impediment thrown in the way of the simplest observation? Is there any attempt to put down those who are incompetent? or is incompetency in the slightest manner included in the idea of the Society? On the contrary is not all free? Is not the simplest effort received with thanks? Is any other qualification desired by the Society in its members than the plain simple wish to improve

What then (in the name of Improvement I ask it) what is the reason that with all these facilities without a single apparent difficulty we are destitute in subject meagre in interest. Alas it must be Apathy. That Minister of ignorance has spread his wing over us and we shrink into indolence. Our effort are [sic] approved by his power; and indeed by our mean sensations of ease he triumphs over our better judgement and thrusts us down to contempt.—And is it possible that a being endowed with such high capabilities as man and destined to such eminent purposes should see his powers withered, his objects unattained through the influence of that mean thing habit, and *still* remain content? Can it be that the *degradation* and a *consciousness* of it exist at one and the same time in the same being? Or has Apathy so powerful an agent in self complacency that conviction is put to flight and allowed no place in the breast?—Whatever the reason the melancholy truth is evident that we are fit for the noblest purposes but that we fulfill them not.

Nor is it over that appropriation of the reasoning powers alone which constitute literary and scientific knowledge that this demon sways his withering sceptre: he triumphs also over the busy walks of commerce, and, alas in the humble paths of morality.

You shall sometimes see a tradesman set out in life with excellent prospects: stimulated by hope, ambition, interest, emulation, the incitement of his friends and his own gratifications he will exert every nerve to secure success and he will succeed. You shall see this man gain on the world, 'till he stands a fair example to others of the prosperity attendant on Industry He is raised above want; even the want of a luxury.—But later in life you shall see this man "fall from his high estate" and accompanied by refinement regret and contempt sink into poverty and misery.[20]—The cause—is idleness—apathy.—Early in life he had been stimulated to personal exertions and his due reward was prosperity. With it however came enjoyment, and as his wealth increased so did the love of its pleasures. That full draught might be taken of the sweetened cup of life he resigned his cares into the hands of subordinate managers and gave himself up to habits of enjoyment and ease—The strong interest which made his affairs prosper no longer governs them; but a secondary feeling actuates those to whom they are entrusted and the energy of the measures taken for their preservation sinks in proportion There is now no individuality between the results and the manager Neglect creeps in; the shadows of confusion come over. At some thwarted moment the

---

20   'Fall from his high estate': unidentified.

master *sees* this; he would fain rise to activity but habit has imperceptibly taken possession of him; he struggles into exertion but his exertions are momentary and he falls again into supineness. Delays retard the aid he should bring whilst they accelerate the fate attending him until at last, when too late, the bright prospects and the solid realities recede together into obscurity and chaos.

You will tell me perhaps that this is imaginary or that at most it occurs but now and then in very insulated instances: but I will give it as my own opinion that every tradesman realizes it more or less. Where is the man that has used his utmost exertions in the prosecution of his affairs? Where is the person who has never relaxed but when fatigue required it? Has pleasure never taken place of business at an inconvenient moment? Has an appointment never been missed through careless delay? Has any one reason to congratulate himself that he has lost nothing through inattention and neglect?—If you assent to what these questions imply you assent to my proposition and allow that Apathy is stronger at times even than Interest.

In morality I fear I should not have so difficult a task in establishing my assertion as in interest. When we continually see the former giving way under the influence of the latter there is but little hope that it should withstand this influence or that that which has conquered the stronger power shall not overcome the weaker. Morality seems the natural impression of the deity within us It ministers only to the serene and healthy but quiet pleasures of the heart and has little to do with the passions and gratifications of the human being of this age—It is continually buffeted about in the tempest of temporal excitement and rarely fails to suffer. Perhaps if the human being were placed out of the sphere of earthly influence, were not dependant upon it for support and found no tempting pleasures in its productions he might become concious [sic] even spontaneously of the gratifications arising from the fulfilment of duties and become more and more virtuous for virtue's sake, But crossed as his good resolutions are by temptations and excitements some effect must be produced which tends to warp the result of his conviction and prevent that progression which ought to have place.—Some take the system of morality as they find it for their standard; and at no farther than it directs; forgetting that the institutions and the abuses of Society frequently sanction vice of the most gross or the most contemptible kind. Ask the Glutton whether moderation is a virtue and excess a vice? he will tell you yes but his moderation is eating drinking and feasting and

his excess only that which produces dropsy apoplexy and death. Ask the
gentleman what is the greatest disgrace to him he tells you a *lie*: but all the
falsities of civilised and polite life are excluded from that term when *he*
uses it.—The Morality of these persons therefore is the convenient system
they have made up for themselves; gratification generally prevents them
from perceiving any other and if it fails apathy secures them from any
improvement.—Others can perceive the right and the wrong and have
no objection to inculcate the purest principles. They do not like however
to resign the pleasures they can secure by a slight practical trespass of
their own rules and that which in reality is the result of degraded taste
and idleness they call expediency, and excuse their little derelictions from
pure virtue by naming them necessary submissions to the present state of
things

But leaving this melancholy picture of the effects of apathy on the
human mind in your hands for consideration I shall hasten to put an end
to these observations by a few on the effects of Industry or the Inertia of
an active mind.

Industry is the natural state of man and the perfection of his nature
is dependant on it. The progression which distinguishes him from every
thing else in the material world is maintained by it alone. The Sun rises
and sets and rises and sets again. Spring summer autumn and winter
succeed each other only to be succeeded by the same round A plant rises
from out the earth puts forth leaves and buds, it strengthens arrives at
maturity, and then dies giving place to other individuals who traverse the
same changes. An animal is born, grows up, and at last gives signs even
of intelligence; but he dies without having improved his species: and it is
man alone who leaves a memento behind him by his deeds of his having
existed; who surpasses his predecessors, exalts his present generation, and
supports those that follow him.

These effects however which distinguish him from every other animated
being are only to be produced by industry. It is *that* which enables him
to add to the sum of knowledge already in possession of the world; to
increase the stock of good which enobles [sic] his nature. If he be not
active and not in a state of improvement what better is he than the brutes?
in his own nature none and it is only what Society has superinduced upon
him of *its* manner and customs that distinguishes him from them.

Dryden I think wrote an Epitaph upon such an one and it is very
expressive of the vacuity of character and paucity of interest which such a
being possesses or excites.

Here lies Sir John Guise
No one laughs no one crys
Where he's gone or how he fares
No one knows no one cares.

―――――――

I have already endeavoured to establish the analogy between a habit of Industry and the Inertia of a moving body; and as I fear I have too much trespassed upon your time and your good judgement in the foregoing attempts I shall not farther pursue it.—I am sure that it is not needful for me to point out the good effects which would result to the Society from the *active* exertions of its members. They must either have felt concious [sic] of it already or otherwise have found reasons against me which it would be politic in one first to hear.—I shall in conclusion merely make an observation which I trust will extenuate me from the charge of harshness and put a question (rather for form's sake than the question itself) with which I shall leave it in your hands

I have said that the Inertia of matter is continually blended with other forces which complex its results and render them apparently contrary to their cause: and also that in this respect it resembles the inertia of the mind.—This of course is equivalent to an avowal that there are *natural* disturbing forces of the inertia of the mind & that an irregular, a retarded, or even an inverted progression must at times take place in knowledge and morality without any gross charge being incurred by mankind. I do not deny it It was not however my particular object to discuss these forces but the more general and fundamental one If any therefore feels offended with what may appear like animadversions he is at perfect liberty to take shelter behind these extenuations and secure himself from censure.

In pursuing the analogy in my own mind of this general influence to which both matter and mind are subject I was led to a conclusion respecting mental inertia which though I have no reason to doubt I should be fearful of venturing on my own authority alone. I will therefore put it in the form of a Query supposing however that still you will direct your conversation if you feel incited as much to the current remarks as to the question which will terminate them.—Inertia has a sway as absolute in Natural Philosophy over moving bodies as over those at rest. It therefore does not retard motion or change but is as frequently active in continuing that state as in opposing it—Now is this the case with mental inertia?

That I may ask the question more distinctly I will preface it by two others, which, if disallowed will give rise to conversation; if allowed, will prepare for the third. Are there not *more passive* than active minds in the world? Is mental inertia as puissant in active as in idle cases? Then what is the cause of the state implied by the first question? or what is the reason that unlike the material world there is so much more of inanimation than of activity in the intellectual world?

Faraday's indexes to eighteenth-century periodicals

[Faraday recorded these lists of papers from *The Spectator, The Idler* and *The Rambler* in CPB. They are reprinted here for the sake of what they suggest about Faraday's literary interests.]

Faraday's index to *The Spectator*
[For the first two entries, Faraday gave a brief title; in the second, he noted only the numbers of the papers, so I have added an indication of the topics.][21]

595 On false taste
626 Novelty

385 [On friendship][22]
471 [On hope][23]
593 [On dreams]
626 [Novelty as a spur to intellectual endeavour]

Faraday's index to *The Idler*[24]
[Faraday left the rest of the page in CPB blank, evidently intending to add to this brief list. The note on the subject of each paper is Faraday's.]

22. Improvement
23. Friendship
36. On Composition or Style
38. Imprisonment
43. Procrastination

---

21   CPB, I, p. 395.
22   This paper is quoted with a citation, CPB, I, p. 8, 'Friendship'.
23   This paper is quoted with a citation, CPB, I, p. 8. under the heading 'Hope'.
24   CPB, I, p. 382.

Faraday's index to *The Rambler*[25]
[The numbers and brief titles are Faraday's records; the longer titles in square brackets are taken from the edition in *The Works of Samuel Johnson*, ed. Arthur Murphy, 12 vols. (London: Nichols *et al.*, 1816), vols. 4–6.]

17   Uncertainty of life [The frequent contemplation of death necessary to moderate the passions]

13   Secrecy [The duty of secrecy. The invalidity of all excuses for betraying secrets]

28   Fancied virtue [The various arts of self-delusion]

29   Prescience [The folly of anticipating misfortunes]

31   Pertinacity of opinion [The defence of a known mistake highly culpable]

185 Forgiveness of injuries[26] [The prohibition of revenge justifiable by reason. The meanness of regulating our conduct by the opinions of men]

64   Friendship [The requisites to true friendship]

70   Moral Virtue [Different men virtuous in different degrees. The vicious not always abandoned]

72   Good nature [The necessity of good humour]

74   Peevishness [Peevishness equally wretched and offensive. The character of Tetrica]

114 On sanguinary laws [The necessity of proportioning punishments to crimes]

137 On literary courage[27] [The necessity of literary courage]

111 Impropriety of haste in life [Youth made unfortunate by its haste and eagerness]

---

25   CPB, I, p. 176
26   This paper is quoted with a citation, CPB, I, p. 85. Faraday's heading: 'Resentment'.
27   This paper is quoted with a citation, CPB, I, p. 74. Faraday's heading: 'Wonder'.

Faraday, from 'Observations on Mental Education' (1854)

[This lecture greatly postdates all of the other materials in this edition: it was written when Faraday was 62, but demands inclusion here because it illustrates his lifelong concern with the themes of self-education, mental discipline and the duty of the individual to improve himself to the utmost possible extent. It represents, in fact, his fullest public statement on these themes, and was so important to him that he included it in his 1859 collection of *Experimental Researches in Chemistry and Physics*, where it sits somewhat oddly among the scientific papers. Faraday insisted that the lecture belonged in that volume because it was 'so immediately connected' in 'nature and origin with my own experimental life, considered either as cause or consequence,' and in the context of this edition it provides a satisfying bookend to this selection of Faraday's educational writings.[28]

Some of the ways in which Faraday frames his subject in this lecture are similar to his writings on self-education from the 1810s: most importantly, perhaps, his entire shelving of the religious aspect of self-education. Here he explains, more explicitly than in his earlier lectures, that no human mind, no matter how finely disciplined, can break through to the divine, so that there is no possibility that 'man by reasoning could find out God.' As Geoffrey Cantor points out, this represented a major difference between Faraday's understanding of the power of science and that of the natural theologians who had dominated the public ideology of British science in the first half of the nineteenth century.[29] However, despite this explicit separation of religious from mundane, Faraday's language on this occasion is frequently at least quasi-religious, and indeed he describes the lecture as an 'open declaration, almost a confession.' Faraday had been accustomed to preaching to the Sandemanian congregation in London since his appointment as an elder in 1840: this experience may have affected the way in which he allowed a degree of religious feeling into his secular rhetoric. The language of confession is especially apparent as he presents himself as merely one self-improver among many, equally liable to failures of judgment as others: 'I have learned to know that I fall infinitely short of that efficacious exercise of the judgment which may be attained.'

Reading this lecture in conjunction with Faraday's writings of the 1810s on similar themes, striking differences emerge. Naturally Faraday's own place in his account of the progress of knowledge is very different here: by 1854, he is able and indeed obliged to speak with the authority of his immense professional and hardly less great personal stature.[30] Another interesting change from his earlier lectures is the degree to

---

28 *Experimental Researches in Chemistry and Physics* (London: Taylor and Francis, 1859), pp. 463–91; p. 491.

29 Cantor, p. 198.

30 On aspects of Faraday's iconic personal status, see Graham Gooday, 'Faraday Reinvented: Moral Imagery and Institutional Icons in Victorian Electrical Engineering', *History of Technology*, 15 (1993), 190–205 and Geoffrey Cantor, 'The

which he acknowledges the effects of wider society on the individual self-improver. 'Society, as a body, may act powerfully in the cause,' he writes here; but on the whole in this piece he sees society as having a generally deleterious effect on self-education, because the standards of judgment and accuracy of the general public are so low. This lecture was given during Faraday's highly public controversy against the proponents of table-turning, which had begun in June 1853 when he published a letter in *The Times* describing his experimental investigation into the phenomenon and concluding roundly that 'the system of education that could leave the mental condition of the public body in the state in which this subject has found it must have been greatly deficient in some very important principle.'[31] The resistance of believers in table-turning and other paranormal activities to scientific method and fact disturbed him greatly; and in this lecture he proposes not a new programme of national education to correct the ignorance on which belief in the paranormal must be founded but, characteristically, a renewed commitment to individual self-education.

This address was one of a highly prestigious series of lectures on education given at the Royal Institution in 1855, and was delivered in the presence of Prince Albert.][32]

If the term education may be understood in so large a sense as to include all that belongs to the improvement of the mind, either by the acquisition of the knowledge of others, or by increase of it through its own exertions, then I may hope to be justified for bringing forward a few desultory observations respecting the exercise of the mental powers in a particular direction, which otherwise might seem out of place. The points I have in view are general, but they are manifest in a striking manner, among the physical matters which have occupied my life; and as the latter afford a field for exercise in which cogitations and conclusions can be subjected to the rigid tests of fact and experiment—as all classes employ themselves more or less in the consideration of physical matters, and may do so with great advantage, if inclined in the least degree to profit by educational

Scientist as Hero: Public Images of Michael Faraday', in Michael Shortland and Richard Yeo (eds.), *Telling Lives in Science: Essays in Scientific Biography* (Cambridge: Cambridge University Press, 1996), pp. 171–94.

31 *The Times* (30 June 1853), p. 8, col D. Faraday followed this letter to *The Times* with another on the same subject to the *Athenaeum* on 2 July. For discussion of this episode see Elspeth Crawford, 'Learning from Experience', in David Gooding and Frank A. J. L. James (eds.), *Faraday Rediscovered: Essays on the Life and Work of Michael Faraday, 1791–1867* (Basingstoke: Macmillan, 1985), pp. 211–27.

32 The lecture was first published in a collection of the addresses given in this RI series: *Lectures on Education: Delivered at the Royal Institution of Great Britain* (London: Parker, 1854), pp. 39–90.

practices—so I hope that what I may say will find its application in every condition of life.

Before entering upon the subject, I must take one distinction which, however it may appear to others, is to me of the utmost importance. High as man is placed above the creatures around him, there is a higher and far more exalted position within his view; and the ways are infinite in which he occupies his thoughts about the fears, or hopes, or expectations of a future life. I believe that the truth of that future cannot be brought to his knowledge by any exertion of his mental powers, however exalted they may be; that it is made known to him by other teaching than his own, and is received through simple belief of the testimony given. Let no one suppose for a moment that the self-education I am about to commend in respect of the things of this life, extends to any considerations of the hope set before us, as if man by reasoning could find out God. It would be improper here to enter upon this subject further than to claim an absolute distinction between religious and ordinary belief. I shall be reproached with the weakness of refusing to apply those mental operations which I think good in respect of high things to the very highest. I am content to bear the reproach. Yet, even in earthly matters, I believe that the invisible things of HIM from the creation of the world are clearly seen, being understood by the things that are made, even His eternal power and Godhead; and I have never seen anything incompatible between those things of man which can be known by the spirit of man which is within him, and those higher things concerning his future, which he cannot know by that spirit.

Claiming, then, the use of the ordinary faculties of the mind in ordinary things, let me next endeavour to point out what appears to me to be a great deficiency in the exercise of the mental powers in every direction; three words will express this great want, *deficiency of judgment*. I do not wish to make any startling assertion, but I know that in physical matters multitudes are ready to draw conclusions who have little or no power of judgment in the cases; that the same is true of other departments of knowledge; and that, generally, mankind is willing to leave the faculties which relate to judgment almost entirely uneducated, and their decisions at the mercy of ignorance, prepossessions, the passions, or even accident.

Do not suppose, because I stand here and speak thus, making no exceptions, that I except myself. I have learned to know that I fall infinitely short of that efficacious exercise of the judgment which may be attained.

There are exceptions to my general conclusion, numerous and high; but if we desire to know how far education is required, we do not consider the few who need it not, but the many who have it not; and in respect of judgment, the number of the latter is almost infinite. I am moreover persuaded, that the clear and powerful minds which have realized in some degree the intellectual preparation I am about to refer to, will admit its importance, and indeed its necessity; and that they will not except themselves, nor think that I have made my statement too extensive.

[...]

Having endeavoured to point out this great deficiency in the exercise of the intellect, I will offer a few remarks upon the means of subjecting it to the improving processes of instruction. Perhaps many who watch over the interests of the community, and are anxious for its welfare, will conclude that the development of the judgment cannot properly be included in the general idea of education; that as the education proposed must, to a very large degree, be of *self*, it is so far incommunicable; that the master and the scholar merge into one, and both disappear; that the instructor is no wiser than the one to be instructed, and thus the usual relations of the two lose their power. Still, I believe that the judgment may be educated to a very large extent, and might refer to the fine arts, as giving proof in the affirmative; and though, as respects the community and its improvement in relation to common things, any useful education must be of *self*, I think that society, as a body, may act powerfully in the cause. Or it may still be objected that my experience is imperfect, is chiefly derived from exercise of the mind within the precincts of natural philosophy, and has not that generality of application which can make it of any value to society at large. I can only repeat my conviction, that society occupies itself now-a-days about physical matters and judges them as common things. Failing in relation to them, it is equally liable to carry such failures into other matters of life. The proof of deficient judgment in one department shows the habit of mind, and the general want, in relation to others. I am persuaded that all persons may find in natural things an admirable school for self-instruction, and a field for the necessary mental exercise; that they may easily apply their habits of thought, thus formed, to a social use; and that they ought to do this, as a duty to themselves and their generation.

Let me try to illustrate the former part of the case, and at the same time state what I think a man may and ought to do for himself.

The *self*-education to which he should be stimulated by the desire to improve his judgment, requires no blind dependence upon the dogmas of others, but is commended to him by the suggestions and dictates of his own common sense. The first part of it is founded in mental discipline: happily it requires no unpleasant avowals; appearances are preserved, and vanity remains unhurt; but it is necessary that a man *examine himself,* and *that* not carelessly. On the contrary, as he advances, he should become more and more strict, till he ultimately prove a sharper critic to himself than any one else can be; and he ought to intend this, for, so far as he consciously falls short of it, he acknowledges that others may have reason on their side when they criticise him. A first result of this habit of mind will be an internal conviction of *ignorance on many things respecting which his neighbours are taught,* and that his opinions and conclusions on such matters ought to be advanced with reservation. A mind so disciplined will be *open to correction upon good grounds in all things,* even in those it is best acquainted with, and should familiarize itself with the idea of such being the case; for though it sees no reason to suppose itself in error, yet the possibility exists. The mind is not enfeebled by this internal admission, but strengthened; for if it cannot distinguish proportionately between the probable right and wrong of things known imperfectly, it will tend either to be rash or to hesitate; whilst that which admits the due amount of probability is likely to be justified in the end. It is right that we should stand by and act on our principles; but not right to hold them in obstinate blindness, or retain them when proved to be erroneous. I remember the time when I believed a spark was produced between voltaic metals as they approached to contact (and the reasons why it might be possible yet remain); but others doubted the fact and denied the proofs, and on re-examination I found reason to admit their corrections were well-founded. Years ago I believed that electrolytes could conduct electricity by a conduction proper; that has also been denied by many through long time: though I believed myself right, yet circumstances have induced me to pay that respect to criticism as to reinvestigate the subject, and I have the pleasure of thinking that nature confirms my original conclusions. So though evidence may appear to preponderate extremely in favour of a certain decision, it is wise and proper to hear a counter-statement. You can have no idea how often and how much, under such an impression, I have desired that the marvellous descriptions which have reached me might prove, in some points, correct; and how frequently I have submitted myself to hot fires, to friction with magnets, to the passes of hands, &c., lest I should be shutting out discovery;—encouraging the strong desire that something might be true, and that I might aid in the development of a new force of nature.

Among those points of self-education which take up the form of *mental discipline*, there is one of great importance, and, moreover, difficult to deal with, because it involves an internal conflict, and equally touches our vanity and our ease. It consists in the *tendency to deceive ourselves* regarding all we wish for, and the necessity of *resistance to those desires*. It is impossible for any one who has not been constrained, by the course of his occupation and thoughts, to a habit of continual self-correction, to be aware of the amount of error in relation to judgment arising from this tendency. The force of the temptation which urges us to seek for such evidence and appearances as are in favour of our desires, and to disregard those which oppose them, is wonderfully great. In this respect we are all, more or less, active promoters of error. In place of practising wholesome self-abnegation, we ever make the wish the father to the thought: we receive as friendly that which agrees with, we resist with dislike that which opposes us; whereas the very reverse is required by every dictate of common sense. [...] I could give you many illustrations personal to myself, about atmospheric magnetism, lines of force, attraction, repulsion, unity of power, nature of matter, &c.; or in things more general to our common nature, about likes and dislikes, wishes, hopes, and fears; but it would be unsuitable and also unnecessary, for each must be conscious of a large field sadly uncultivated in this respect. *I will simply express my strong belief, that that point of self-education which consists in teaching the mind to resist its desires and inclinations, until they are proved to be right, is the most important of all, not only in things of natural philosophy, but in every department of daily life.*

There are numerous precepts resulting more or less from the principles of mental discipline already insisted on as essential, which are very useful in forming a judgment about matters of fact, whether among natural things or between man and man. Such a precept, and one that should recur to the mind early in every new case, is, to *know the conditions* of the matter respecting which we are called upon to make a judgement. To suppose that any would judge before they professed to know the conditions would seem to be absurd; on the other hand, to assume that the community *does wait* to know the conditions before it judges, is an assumption so large that I cannot accept it. Very few search out the conditions; most are anxious to sink those which oppose their preconceptions; yet none can be left out if a right judgment is to be formed. It is true, that many conditions must ever remain unknown to us, even in regard to the simplest things in nature: thus as to the wonderful action of gravity, whose law never fails us, we cannot say whether the bodies are acting truly at a distance, or by a physical line of force as a connecting link between them. The great majority think the former is the case; Newton's judgment is for the latter. But of the conditions which are within our reach, we should search out all; for in relation to those which remain unknown or unsuspected, we are in that very ignorance (regarding judgment) which it is our present object, first to make manifest, and then to remove.

One exercise of the mind, which largely influences the power and character of the judgment, is the habit of forming *clear and precise ideas*. If, after considering a subject in our ordinary manner, we return upon it with the special purpose of noticing the condition of our thoughts, we shall be astonished to find how little precise they remain. On recalling the phenomena relating to a matter of fact, the circumstances modifying them, the kind and amount of action presented, the real or probable result, we shall find that the first impressions are scarcely fit for the foundation of a judgment, and that the second thoughts will be best. For the acquirement of a good condition of mind in this respect, the thoughts should be trained to a habit of clear and precise formation, so that vivid and distinct impressions of the matter in hand, its circumstances and consequences, may remain.

Before we proceed to consider any question involving physical principles, we should set out with *clear ideas* of the naturally possible and impossible. There are many subjects uniting more or less of the most sure and valuable investigations of science with the most imaginary and unprofitable speculation, that are continually passing through their various phases of intellectual, experimental, or commercial development: some to be established, some to disappear, and some to recur again and again, like ill weeds that cannot be extirpated, yet can be cultivated to no result as wholesome food for the mind. Such, for instance, in different degrees, are the caloric engine, the electric light, the Pasilalinic sympathetic compass, mesmerism, homoeopathy, odylism, the magneto-electric engine, the perpetual motion, &c.: all hear and talk of these things; all use their judgment more or less upon them, and all might do that effectively, if they were to instruct themselves to the extent which is within their reach. I am persuaded that natural things offer an admirable school for self-instruction, a most varied field for the necessary mental practice, and that those who exercise themselves therein may easily apply the habits of thought thus formed to a social use: but as a first step in such practice, clear ideas should be obtained of what is possible and what impossible. Thus, it is impossible to *create* force. We may employ it; we may evoke it in one form by its consumption in another; we may hide it for a period; but we can neither *create* nor *destroy* it. We may cast it away; but where we dismiss it, there it will do its work. If, therefore, we desire to consider a proposition respecting the employment or evolution of power, let us carry our judgment, educated on this point, with us. If the proposal include the double use of a force with only one excitement, it implies a creation of power, and that *cannot be*. If we could by the fingers draw a heavy piece of wood or stone upward without effort, and then, letting it sink, could produce by its gravity an effort equal to its weight, that would be a creation of power, and *cannot be*.

[...]

In like manner we should accustom ourselves to clear and definite language, especially in physical matters; giving to a word its true and full, but measured meaning, that we may be able to convey our ideas clearly to the minds of others. Two persons cannot mutually impart their knowledge, or compare and rectify their conclusions, unless both attend to the true intent and force of language. If by such words as attraction, electricity, polarity, atom, they imply different things, they may discuss facts, deny results, and doubt consequences for an indefinite time without any advantageous progress. I hold it as a great point in self-education that the student should be continually engaged in forming exact ideas, and in expressing them clearly by language. Such practice insensibly opposes any tendency to exaggeration or mistake, and increases the sense and love of truth in every part of life.

I should be sorry, however, if what I have said were understood as meaning that education for the improvement and strengthening of the judgment is to be altogether repressive of the imagination, or confine the exercise of the mind to processes of a mathematical or mechanical character. I believe that, in the pursuit of physical science, the imagination should be taught to present the subject investigated in all possible, and even in impossible views; to search for analogies of likeness and (if I may say so) of opposition—inverse or contrasted analogies; to present the fundamental idea in every form, proportion, and condition; to clothe it with suppositions and probabilities,—that all cases may pass in review, and be touched, if needful, by the Ithuriel spear of experiment. But all this must be *under government*, and the result must not be given to society until the judgment, educated by the process itself, has been exercised upon it. Let us construct our hypotheses for an hour, or a day, or for years; they are of the utmost value in the elimination of truth, 'which is evolved more freely from error than from confusion;'[33] but, above all things, let us not cease to be aware of the temptation they offer; or, because they gradually become familiar to us, accept them as established. We could not reason about electricity without thinking of it as a fluid, or a vibration, or some other existent state or form. We should give up half our advantage in the consideration of heat if we refused to consider it as a principle, or a state of motion. We could scarcely touch such objects by experiment, and we should make no progress in their practical application without hypothesis; still it is absolutely necessary that we should learn to doubt the conditions we assume, and acknowledge we are uncertain, whether heat and electricity are vibrations or substances, or either.

[...]

The mind naturally desires to settle upon one thing or another; to rest upon an affirmative or a negative; and that with a degree of absolutism which is irrational and improper. In drawing a conclusion, it is very difficult, but not the less necessary, to make it *proportionate* to the evidence: except where certainty exists (a case of rare occurrence), we should consider our decisions as probable only. The probability may appear very great, so that in affairs of the world we often accept such as certainty, and trust our welfare or our lives upon it. Still, only an uneducated mind will confound probability with certainty, especially when it encounters a contrary conclusion drawn by another from like data. This suspension in degree of judgment will not make a man less active in life, or his conclusions less certain as truths; on the contrary, I believe him to be the more ready for the right amount and direction of action on any emergency; and am sure his conclusions and statements will carry more weight in the world than those of the incautious man.

[...]

The education which I advocate will require *patience* and *labour of thought* in every exercise tending to improve the judgment. It matters not

33 Francis Bacon, *The New Organon*, trans. Michael Siverthorne, ed. Lisa Jardine and Michael Silverthorne (Cambridge: Cambridge University Press, 2000), p. 130: 'truth emerges more quickly from error than from confusion.' I am grateful to Frank James for pointing out that Faraday also uses this quotation in a letter of 7 November 1848 to William Whewell, noting that the saying 'has been to me practically useful and a source of continual pleasure' (*Correspondence*, III, p. 723).

on what subject a person's mind is occupied, he should engage in it with the conviction that it will require mental labour. A powerful mind will be able to draw a conclusion more readily and more correctly than one of moderate character; but both will surpass themselves if they make an earnest, careful investigation, instead of a careless or prejudiced one; and education for this purpose is the more necessary for the latter, because the man of less ability may, through it, raise his rank and amend his position. I earnestly urge this point of self-education, for I believe it to be more or less in the power of every man greatly to improve his judgment. I do not think that one has the complete capacity for judgment which another is naturally without. I am of opinion that all may judge, and that we only need to declare on every side the conviction that mental education is wanting, and lead men to see that through it they hold, in a large degree, their welfare and their character in their own hands, to cause in future years an abundant development of right judgment in every class.

This education has for its first and its last step *humility*. It can commence only because of a conviction of deficiency; and if we are not disheartened under the growing revelations which it will make, that conviction will become stronger unto the end. But the humility will be founded, not on comparison of ourselves with the imperfect standards around us, but on the increase of that internal knowledge which alone can make us aware of our internal wants. The first step in correction is to learn our deficiencies, and having learned them, the next step is almost complete: for no man who has discovered that his judgment is hasty, or illogical, or imperfect, would go on with the same degree of haste, or irrationality, or presumption as before. I do not mean that all would at once be cured of bad mental habits, but I think better of human nature than to believe, that a man in any rank of life, who has arrived at the consciousness of such a condition, would deny his common sense, and still judge and act as before. And though such self-schooling must continue to the end of life to supply an experience of deficiency rather than of attainment, still there is abundant stimulus to excite any man to perseverance. What he has lost are things imaginary, not real; what he gains are riches before unknown to him, yet invaluable; and though he may think more humbly of his own character, he will find himself at every step of his progress more sought for than before, more trusted with responsibility and held in pre-eminence by his equals, and more highly valued by those whom he himself will esteem worthy of approbation.

[...]

When men, more or less marked by their advance, are led by circum-stances to give an opinion adverse to any popular notion, or to the assertions of any sanguine inventor, nothing is more usual than the attempt to neutralize the force of such an opinion by reference to the mistakes which like educated men have made; and their occasional misjudgments and erroneous conclusions are quoted, as if they were less competent than others to give an opinion, being even disabled from judging like matters to those which are included in their pursuits by the very exercise of their minds upon them. How frequently has the reported judgment of Davy, upon the impossibility of gas-lighting on a large scale, been quoted by speculators engaged in tempting moneyed men into companies, or in the pages of journals occupied with the popular fancies of the day; as if an argument were derivable from that in favour of some special object to be commended! Why should not men taught in the matter of judgment far beyond their neighbours, be expected to err sometimes, since the very education in which they are advanced can only terminate with their lives? What is there about them, derived from *this education*, which sets up the shadow of a pretence to perfection? Such men cannot learn all things, and may often be ignorant. The very progress which science makes amongst them as a body is a continual correction of ignorance, *i.e.* of a state which is ignorance in relation to the future, though wisdom and knowledge in relation to the past. [...]

If we are to estimate the utility of an educated judgment, do not let us hear merely of the errors of scientific men, which have been corrected by others taught in the same careful school; but let us see what, as a body, they have produced, compared with that supplied by their reproachers. Where are the established truths and triumphs of ring-swingers, table-turners, table-speakers? What one result in the numerous divisions of science or its applications can be traced to their exertions? Where is the investigation completed, so that, as in gas-lighting, all may admit that the principles are established and a good end obtained, without the shadow of a doubt?

If we look to electricity, it, in the hands of the careful investigator, has advanced to the most extraordinary results: it approaches at the motion of his hand; bursts from the metal; descends from the atmosphere; surrounds the globe: it talks, it writes, it records, it appears to him (cautious as he has learned to become) as a universal spirit in nature. If we look to photography, whose origin is of our own day, and see what it has become in the hands of its discoverers and their successors, how wonderful are the results! [...]

What has clairvoyance, or mesmerism, or table-rapping done in comparison with results like these? What have the snails at Paris told us from the snails at New York? [...]

In conclusion, I will freely acknowledge that all I have said regarding the great want of judgment manifested by society as a body, and the high value of any means which would tend to supply the deficiency, have been developed and declared on numerous occasions, by authority far above any I possess. The deficiency is known hypothetically, but I doubt if in reality; the individual acknowledges the state in respect of others, but is unconscious of it in regard to himself. As to the world at large, the condition is accepted as a necessary fact; and so it is left untouched, almost ignored. I think that education in a large sense should be applied to this state of the subject, and that society, though it can do little in the way of communicated experience, can do much, by a declaration of the evil that exists and of its remediable character, by keeping alive a sense of the deficiency to be supplied, and by directing the minds of men to the practice and enlargement of that self-education which every one pursues more or less, but which under conviction and method would produce a tenfold amount of good. I know that the multitude will always be behindhand in this education, and to a far greater extent than in respect of the education which is founded on book learning. Whatever advance books make, they retain; but each new being comes on to the stage of life, with the same average amount of conceit, desires, and passions, as his predecessors, and in respect of self-education has all to learn. Does the circumstance that we can do little more than proclaim the necessity of instruction, justify the ignorance, or our silence, or make the plea for this education less strong? Should it not, on the contrary, gain its strength from the fact that all are wanting more or less? I desire we should admit that, as a body, we are universally deficient in judgment. I do not mean that we are utterly ignorant, but that we have advanced only a little way in the requisite education, compared with what is within our power.

If the necessity of the education of the judgment were a familiar and habitual idea with the public, it would often afford a sufficient answer to the statement of an ill-informed or incompetent person; if quoted to recall to his remembrance the necessity of a mind instructed in a matter, and accustomed to balance evidence, it might frequently be an answer to the individual himself. Adverse influence might, and would, arise from the careless, the confident, the presumptuous, the hasty, and the dilatory man, perhaps extreme opposition; but I believe that the mere acknowledgment and proclamation of the ignorance, by society at large, would, through its moral influence, destroy the opposition, and be a great means to the attainment of the good end desired: for if no more be done than to lead such to turn their thoughts inwards, a step in education is gained: if they are *convinced* in any degree, an important advance is made; if they learn only to *suspend* their judgment, the improvement will be one above price.

It is an extraordinary thing, that man, with a mind so wonderful that there is nothing to compare with it elsewhere in the known creation, should leave it to run wild in respect of its highest elements and qualities. He has powers of comparison and judgment, by which his final resolves, and all those acts of his material system which distinguish him from the brutes, are guided:—shall he omit to educate and improve them when education can do much? Is it towards the very principles and privileges that distinguish him above other creatures, he should feel indifference? Because the education is internal, it is not the less needful; nor is it more the duty of a man that he should cause his child to be taught than that he should teach himself. Indolence may tempt him to neglect the self-examination and experience which form his school, and weariness may induce the evasion of the necessary practices; but surely a thought of the prize should suffice to stimulate him to the requisite exertion: and to those who reflect upon the many hours and days, devoted by a lover of sweet sounds, to gain a moderate facility upon a mere mechanical instrument, it ought to bring a correcting blush of shame, if they feel convicted of neglecting the beautiful living instrument, wherein play all the powers of the mind.

I will conclude this subject:—believe me when I say I have been speaking from self-conviction. I did not think this an occasion on which I ought to seek for flattering words regarding our common nature; if so, I should have felt unfaithful to the trust I had taken up; so I have spoken from experience. In thought I hear the voice, which judges me by the precepts I have uttered. I know that I fail frequently in that very exercise of judgment to which I call others; and have abundant reason to believe that much more frequently I stand manifest to those around me, as one who errs, without being corrected by knowing it. I would willingly have evaded appearing before you on this subject, for I shall probably do but little good, and may well think it was an error of judgment to consent: having consented, my thoughts would flow back among the events and reflections of my past life, until I found nothing present itself but an open declaration, almost a confession, as the means of performing the duty due to the subject and to you.

The Improvement of the Mind

Isaac Watts, from *The Improvement of the Mind* (1741)[1]

[Faraday frequently acknowledged the importance of Isaac Watts's mid-eighteenth-century handbook for self-improvers for his own views on mental discipline and the development of the faculties. In the year before the essay-circle was launched, indeed, he described *The Improvement of the Mind* as a book 'no person ought to be without.'[2] Watts provided his readers with the outline of a system by which fairly modest materials could be made to yield lasting results; he emphasized the vital importance of method in all aspects of self-education, particularly in reading. Like most eighteenth- and even nineteenth-century commentators on the matter, he saw indiscriminate or superficial reading as a waste of time and likely to weaken the mental faculties. Faraday, who was always anxious to make his time as productive as possible, practised a number of Watts's precepts during the 1810s and 1820s, including keeping a commonplace book; and the Faraday biographer, L. Pearce Williams, suggests that the formation of the essay-circle itself was in response to Watts's favouring discussion groups.][3]

---

1   Isaac Watts, *The Improvement of the Mind: Or, A Supplement to the Art of Logic* (London: Edwards and Knibb, 1821).

2   In a lecture to the CPS in 1817, Faraday announced of Watts's book, 'I consider [it] so good in its kind, that no person ought to be without it' (Faraday, *Some Observations on the Means of Obtaining Knowledge, and on the Facilities Afforded by the Constitution of the City Philosophical Society* (London: Effingham Wilson, 1817), p. 9. George Riebau, the bookbinder to whom Faraday was apprenticed during his teens, recorded in 1813 that 'Dr. Watts's improvement of the mind, was then read and frequent took in [Faraday's] Pocket, when he went an Early walk in the Morning' (*Correspondence*, I, p. 67).

3   Williams, p. 13; and see pp. 12–13 for a more substantial discussion of Faraday's debts to Watts.

Part I: 'Introduction'

No man is obliged to learn and know every thing; this can neither be sought nor required, for it is utterly impossible: yet all persons are under some obligation to improve their own understanding; otherwise it will be a barren desert, or a forest overgrown with weeds and brambles. Universal ignorance or infinite errors will overspread the mind, which is utterly neglected, and lies without any cultivation.

Skill in the sciences is indeed the business and profession but of a small part of mankind; but there are many others placed in such an exalted rank in the world, as allows them much leisure and large opportunities to cultivate their reason, and to beautify and enrich their minds with various knowledge. Even the lower orders of men have particular callings in life, wherein they ought to acquire a just degree of skill; and this is not to be done well without thinking and reasoning about them.

The common duties and benefits of society, which belong to every man living, as we are social creatures, and even our native and necessary relations to a family, a neighbourhood, or government, oblige all persons whatsoever to use their reasoning powers upon a thousand occasions; every hour of life calls for some regular exercise of our judgment, as to time and things, persons and nations; without a prudent and discreet determination in matters before us, we shall be plunged into perpetual errors in our conduct. Now that which should always be practised must at some time be learnt.

Besides, every son and daughter of Adam has a most important concern in the affairs of a life to come, and therefore it is a matter of the highest moment for every one to understand, to judge, and to reason right about the things of religion. [...]

Thus it appears to be the necessary duty, and the interest of every person living, to improve his understanding, to inform his judgment, to treasure up useful knowledge, and to acquire the skill of good reasoning, as far as his station, capacity, and circumstances, furnish him with proper means for it. Our mistakes in judgment may plunge us into much folly and guilt in practice. By acting without thought or reason, we dishonour the God that made us reasonable creatures, we often become injurious to our neighbours, kindred, or friends, and we bring sin and misery upon ourselves: for we are accountable to God our judge for every part of our irregular and mistaken conduct. where he hath given us sufficient advantages to guard against those mistakes.

Chapter I

It is also another considerable advantage of conversation, that it furnishes the student with the knowledge of men and the affairs of life, as reading furnishes him with book learning. A man who dwells all his days among books, may have amassed a vast heap of notions; but he may be a mere scholar, which is a contemptible sort of character in the world. A hermit, who has been shut up in his cell in a college, has contracted a sort of mould and rust upon his soul, and all his airs of behaviour have a certain awkwardness in them; but these awkward airs are worn away by degrees in company: the rust and the mould are filed and brushed off by polite conversation. The scholar now becomes a citizen or a gentleman, a neighbour and a friend; he learns how to dress his sentiments in the fairest colours, as well as to set them in the strongest light. Thus he brings out his notions with honour; he makes some use of them in the world, and improves the theory by the practice.

Part II, chapter II: 'Of an Instructive Style'

The most necessary and most useful character of a style fit for instruction is that to be plain, perspicuous, and easy. [...]

1. Accustom yourself to read those authors who think and write with great clearness and evidence; such as convey their ideas into your understanding as fast as your eye or tongue can run over their sentences: this will imprint upon the mind an habit of imitation; we shall learn the style with which we are very conversant, and practise it with ease and success.
2. Get a distinct and comprehensive knowledge of the subject which you treat of, survey it on all sides, and make yourself perfect master of it; then you will have all the sentiments that relate to it in your view and under your command: and your tongue will very easily clothe those ideas with words which your mind has first made so familiar and easy to itself. [...]
3. Be well skilled in the language which you speak; acquaint yourself with all the idioms and special phrases of it, which are necessary to convey the needful ideas on the subject of which you treat in the most various and most easy manner to the understanding of the

hearer: the variation of a phrase in several forms is of admirable use to instruct: it is like turning all sides of the subject to view; and if the learner happen not to take in the ideas in one form of speech, probably another may be successful for that end. [...]

4. Acquire a variety of words, a *copia verborum*. Let your memory be rich in synonimous terms, or words expressing the same thing: this will not only attain the same happy effect with the variation of phrases in the foregoing direction, but it will add a beauty also to your style, by securing you from an appearance of tautology, or repeating the same words too often, which sometimes may disgust the ear of the learner.

5. Learn the art of shortening your sentences, by dividing a long complicated period into two or three small ones. When others connect and join two or three sentences in one by relative pronouns, as which, whereof, wherein, whereto, &c., and by parenthesis frequently inserted. do you rather divide them into distinct periods; or at least if they must be united, let it be done rather by conjunctions and copulatives, that they may appear like distinct sentences, and give less confusion to the hearer or reader.

> I know no method so effectually to learn what I mean, as to take now and then some page of an author, who is guilty of such long involved parenthetical style, and translate it into plainer English, by dividing the ideas or the sentences asunder, and multiplying the periods, till the language become smooth and easy, and intelligible at first reading.

6. Talk frequently to young and ignorant persons upon subjects which are new and unknown to them, and be diligent to inquire whether they understand you or no; this will put you upon changing your phrases and forms of speech in a variety, till you can hit their capacity, and convey your ideas into their understanding.

Samuel Johnson, from *The Rambler* (1751)[4]

[Faraday was an enthusiastic reader of Johnson, as the index he compiled of numbers of *The Rambler* indicates. In CPB he frequently noted epigrams from Johnson; these include sentences from Boswell's *Life of Johnson* as well as from *The Rambler*.[5] Johnson is a key authority in the Mental Exercises, as Table 4 (p. 33) shows; he is cited seven times, exceeded only by the Bible. Johnson stood with Addison at the pinnacle of the tradition of English essay-writing which the essay-circle members admired and attempted to emulate. Faraday's personal relish for Johnson—and for Addison and Pope—grounds his literary taste in classicism, though he was also very fond of contemporary writers, including Byron and Thomas Moore, lines from whose highly fashionable poem *Lalla Rookh* (1817) Faraday copied into CPB.[6] Faraday, in fact, is an example of the early nineteenth-century common reader's ability to move comfortably between Augustan and Romantic literature without, perhaps, being aware of crossing any significant boundary between the two.

The essay excerpted here was one of Faraday's favourites: it is listed in his *Rambler* index and quoted in a note in CPB; further, the Locke allusion with which this extract opens was recorded twice by Faraday in CPB.][7]

The chief art of learning, as *Locke* has observed, is to attempt but little at a time. The widest excursions of the mind are made by short flights frequently repeated; the most lofty fabricks of science are formed by the continued accumulation of single propositions.

It often happens, whatever be the cause, that impatience of labour, or dread of miscarriage, seizes those who are most distinguished for quickness of apprehension; and that they who might with greatest reason promise themselves victory, are least willing to hazard the encounter. This diffidence, where the attention is not laid asleep by laziness, or dissipated by pleasures, can arise only from confused and general views, such as negligence snatches in haste, or from the disappointment of the first hopes formed by arrogance without reflection. To expect that the intricacies of science will be pierced by a careless glance, or the eminences of fame ascended without labour, is to expect a particular privilege, a power denied to the rest of mankind; but to suppose that the maze is

---

4   From *The Rambler*, no. 137 (9 July 1751), in Johnson, *The Works of Samuel Johnson*, ed. Arthur Murphy, 12 vols. (London: Nichols *et al.*, 1810), V, pp. 418–22.
5   E.g. CPB, I, pp. 8, 162, 170.
6   CPB, I, pp. 171–74.
7   *The Rambler* index: CPB, I, p. 176; 'Wonder': CPB, I, p. 74; Locke quotations: CPB, I, pp. 77 and 169.

inscrutable to diligence, or the heights inaccessible to perseverance, is to submit tamely to the tyranny of fancy, and enchain the mind in voluntary shackles.

It is the proper ambition of the heroes in literature to enlarge the boundaries of knowledge by discovering and conquering new regions of the intellectual world. To the success of such undertakings, perhaps, some degree of fortuitous happiness is necessary, which no man can promise or procure to himself; and therefore doubt and irresolution may be forgiven in him that ventures into the unexplored abysses of truth, and attempts to find his way through the fluctuations of uncertainty, and the conflicts of contradiction. But when nothing more is required, than to pursue a path already beaten, and to trample obstacles which others have demolished, why should any man so much distrust his own intellect as to imagine himself unequal to the attempt?

It were to be wished that they who devote their lives to study would at once believe nothing too great for their attainment, and consider nothing as too little for their regard; that they would extend their notice alike to science and to life, and unite some knowledge of the present world to their acquaintance with past ages and remote events.

Nothing has so much exposed men of learning to contempt and ridicule, as their ignorance of things which are known to all but themselves. Those who have been taught to consider the institutions of the schools, as giving the last perfection to human abilities, are surprised to see men wrinkled with study, yet wanting to be instructed in the minute circumstances of propriety, or the necessary forms of daily transaction; and quickly shake off their reverence for modes of education, which they find to produce no ability above the rest of mankind.

Books, says Bacon, *can never teach the use of books*. The student must learn by commerce with mankind to reduce his speculations to practice, and accommodate his knowledge to the purposes of life.

It is too common for those who have been bred to scholastick professions, and passed much of their time in academies where nothing but learning confers honours, to disregard every other qualification, and to imagine that they shall find mankind ready to pay homage to their knowledge, and to crowd about them for instruction. They therefore step out from their cells into the open world with all the confidence of authority and dignity of importance; they look round about them at once with ignorance and scorn on a race of beings to whom they are equally unknown and equally contemptible, but whose manners they must imitate, and with whose opinions they must comply, if they desire to pass their time happily among them.

To lessen that disdain with which scholars are inclined to look on the common business of the world, and the unwillingness with which they condescend to learn what is not to be found in any system of philosophy, it may be necessary to consider that, though admiration is excited by abstruse researches and remote discoveries, yet pleasure is not given, nor affection conciliated, but by softer accomplishments, and qualities more easily communicable to those about us. He that can only converse upon questions, about which only a small part of mankind has knowledge sufficient to make them curious, must lose his days in unsocial silence, and live in the crowd of life without a companion. He that can only be useful on great occasions, may die without exerting his abilities, and stand a helpless spectator of a thousand vexations which fret away happiness, and which nothing is required to remove but a little dexterity of conduct and readiness of expedients.

No degree of knowledge attainable by man is able to set him above the want of hourly assistance, or to extinguish the desire of fond endearments, and tender officiousness; and therefore, no one should think it unnecessary to learn those arts by which friendship may be gained. Kindness is preserved by a constant reciprocation of benefits or interchange of pleasures; but such benefits only can be bestowed, as others are capable to receive, and such pleasures only imparted as others are qualified to enjoy.

By this descent from the pinnacles of art no honour will be lost; for the condescensions of learning are always overpaid by gratitude. An elevated genius employed in little things, appears, to use the simile of *Longinus*, like the sun in his evening declination, he remits his splendour but retains his magnitude, and pleases more though he dazzles less.

Thomas Williams, from *The Moral Tendencies of Knowledge* (1815)[8]

[Thomas Williams attended and spoke at the City Philosophical Society during the years when Faraday and his friend, Benjamin Abbott, were members, though they were not contemporaries: Williams must have been at least 20 years older than Abbott and Faraday. He was a Dissenting minister and, in the 1790s, a fairly prolific writer on theology, the author of—among others—*A Vindication of the Calvinist Doctrines of Human Depravity* and a two-part rebuttal of Thomas Paine's *Age of Reason*, titled *The Age of Infidelity*.[9] In the nineteenth century he diversified into commenting on national politics, writing both on the amelioration of the condition of the poor and the folly of radicalism.[10]

As a fellow member of metropolitan self-improvement societies, Williams gives an interesting comparison with Faraday, particularly in terms of their views on auto-didacticism and artisan self-improvement. Williams' religious tenets, while Dissenting, differed significantly from Sandemanian beliefs; but it is his class politics more than his Calvinism that drives his argument in this lecture. Firmly on the side of popular education and against conservative reaction, Williams is careful to draw a very sharp distinction between his listeners and the poor whose claim to education is in doubt; he reassures his audience that far from stirring up popular revolt, the spread of knowledge through British society will result in a more peaceful nation: 'the more enlightened are the lower classes, the less have we to apprehend from popular excesses.' Thus Williams makes a direct connection between the maintenance of the social order in Britain and the spread of popular education—a far more topical and political comment than the members of the essay-circle were prepared to make.

Abbott noted in a memoir that Williams habitually broke or bent the CPS's ban on religious discussion.[11] But Williams claimed in the preface to this lecture that he had respected the CPS's rules in drafting his talk and that the religious material included in the published version had been omitted from the lecture delivered at Dorset Street; accordingly, I have omitted it from the brief extract reprinted here.][12]

---

8   Thomas Williams, *The Moral Tendencies of Knowledge: A Lecture, Delivered before the City Philosophical Society, Dorset Street; and the Christian Philological Society, Spital-fields* (London: printed for the author, n.d. [1815]), p. 1, pp. 30–31..

9   Thomas Williams, *A Vindication of the Calvinist Doctrines of Human Depravity [...]* (London, 1799); *The Age of Infidelity: In Answer to Thomas Paine's Age of Reason* (London: Button, 1795–96).

10   Thomas Williams, *Means of Improving the Condition of the Poor: A Lecture, Delivered at the Minor Institute, August 22 1816* (London: n. publ., [1816]); *Constitutional Politics: Or, the British Constitution Vindicated [...]* (London: Parsons, 1817).

11   Frank A. J. L. James, 'The Tales of Benjamin Abbott: A Source for the Early Life of Michael Faraday', *British Journal for the History of Science*, 25 (1992), 229-40 (p. 236).

12   Williams, *The Moral Tendencies of Knowledge*, p. iv.

The Necessity of KNOWLEDGE is like that of light,—without it we can do nothing: but as different occupations require various degrees of light, so various degrees of knowledge are requisite to the different classes of society. But to the middle classes I consider knowledge as most important; and in these, generally, it is most successfully cultivated:—for though an *Arkwright* may arise from the lowest class, and a *Stanhope* be found among the highest, these are instances which attract our admiration for their singularity.[13]

[...]

I rejoice in reflecting on the unprecedented extent to which knowledge is spreading among the lower classes, by means of schools of every description, and especially those of general instruction. I see with pleasure the emulation, not to say *strife*, among all sects and parties in this benevolent work; and that, not only in London, but in every part of the kingdom, 'young men and maidens, old men and children,'[14] are all employed in communicating or acquiring the elements of education. I am happy farther in the increase of literary and philosophical Societies, like this; and, instead of feeling jealousy, I should be glad to see one in every quarter of the metropolis, and all as well attended as our own. Public Lectures are a happy medium of diffusing knowledge, because they convey instruction in the form of recreation;—and it is certainly more rational to spend an hour or two in investigating, or in disseminating, the principles of taste and literature, of philosophy and religion, than to fly to those vain amusements which never improve, but generally dissipate the mind, debase the understanding, and vitiate the morals. Relaxation is in all ranks of life necessary; but those who give up their leisure to popular amusements, are seldom fit for business.

We have long been ranked as a learned nation;—we are now aspiring to deserve the character: for though in every art,—in every science,—in every branch of literature,—we have names which rank among the first in Europe, it is the general complexion of society which forms the national character. We must be wise and virtuous as individuals, to form a wise and virtuous nation. Mr. Burke compares political society to a pyramid, of which the lower orders form the base, and the privileged orders the gilded ornaments at top. The strength of the pyramid depends

13 The inventor and manufacturer, Sir Richard Arkwright (1732–92), was the son of a tailor; Charles Stanhope, third Earl Stanhope (1753–1816), was a Fellow of the Royal Society, a mathematician and classicist.

14 Psalm 148.12.

upon its base, and the peace and happiness of society upon the people:—but a large population, wholly unenlightened, can be relied upon for nothing but riot and commotion. Public peace depends on principle, and principle on knowledge; and the more enlightened are the lower classes, the less have we to apprehend from popular excesses.

Isaac Taylor, from *Self-Cultivation Recommended: Or, Hints to a Youth Leaving School* (1817)[15]

[Isaac Taylor, like Thomas Williams, was a Dissenting minister, based from 1811 until his death in 1829 at Ongar, about 30 miles north-east of London. Taylor and his wife, Ann, both wrote books of advice and guidance: his titles included *Advice to the Teens: Practical Helps Towards the Formation of One's Own Character* (1818) and *Character Essential to Success in Life: Addressed to Those who are Approaching Manhood* (1820), though his most commercially successful publications were his illustrated travel books for children. *Self-Cultivation* was the best-selling of his advice books: it went into four editions in Britain and was also published in America.

Compared with Williams' CPS lecture above, Taylor's focus is on self-improvement achieved through individual, private diligence rather than national improvement achieved through popular education. His emphasis on studying people as well as nature and technology is perhaps useful in reading the Mental Exercises, so many contributions to which deal with social and personal behaviour rather than abstract or scientific subjects. And the high value that Taylor places on training and exercising individual judgement, and on disciplining but not rejecting the legitimate pleasures of the imagination, resonates strongly with the views Faraday expresses in 'On Imagination and Judgement'.]

The grand object of self-education is the mind; to cultivate the intellectual powers. This is the man's self; this is capable of much improvement; this imperiously demands our care; and this will, beyond all calculation, repay us.

On principle, then, aim to give these faculties their due. Many, as drawn by one delightful prospect or another, cultivate those powers of mind which are allied thereto.

This is only partial; it is liable to become desultory, or it may fail entirely. Principle will feel the bounden duty of enriching, training, and rendering effective, all the mighty, but dormant energies of intellect. To

---

15   Isaac Taylor, *Self-Cultivation Recommended: Or, Hints to a Youth Leaving School* (London: Rest Fenner, 1817), pp. 95–99.

starve the mind, will be considered as a species of self-destruction. To suffer torpor to benumb, or perversion to debase any one faculty, will be ranked among errors of deep malignity.

Store, then, the perceptive powers with well-digested notions, upon every subject within reach. Be covetous of knowledge; and do not slightingly contemn any one species, as unworthy notice, if a fair opportunity offer of gaining an insight into its principles. A cursory glance of mere curiosity, guided by intelligence, has sometimes given a hint, which at some distant day has proved of great importance. Some knack or acquirement, regarded at the time as a mere amusement, has, in seasons of adversity, become the means of obtaining a comfortable livelihood:—thus many of the French nobility, while emigrants, maintained themselves. Search through nature; her exhaustless stores will be ever new: become well acquainted with art; the ingenuity of man has operated, almost with creative effect, upon the raw materials which nature afforded. Look at men; study what the world really is. Many mistake widely, and ensure future disappointments, by expecting more from the world than it can possibly give, and much more than it actually yields. Study men, and be aware of their intrinsic value; lest, esteeming fair professions too highly, confidence should be betrayed to loss, perhaps to ruin; or lest, from a few base transactions, a misanthropic cast should be given to the feelings, and man should be undervalued; to the great privation of solace, and the injuriously benumbing of kindly affections in the mind so distrusting. Refuse on principle to give place to false ideas, on subjects so nearly connected with all your conduct, and with all your feelings. Especially, omit not that most important of all studies, the study of thyself. False ideas here are commonly formed, and always are they productive of evil. Know your true value, and do not cast yourself away on trifles: know your true value, and do not arrogantly assume rights, or regards, or honours, which are not due: which will not be yielded; not, however, without a contest; and that, possibly, of more injury than than the acquisition can be gain.

Such knowledge will tend to give the powers of judgment beneficial exercise. To see, is sometimes to be deceived, if we do not accustom ourselves to examine, to compare, to weigh. Whatever we contemplate judiciously, becomes in its turn the means of rectifying our notions on some following case. The liability to imposition is small while the mind is thus exercised. He who wishes not to be deceived, should set himself purposely to examine and form his judgments; not hastily, at a glance, but with care and due consideration. Do not suffer yourself, therefore, to be hurried by temper, or volatility, or carelessness, into erroneous estimates. Cultivate the power of judging accurately; it requires great attention, but it is of absolute necessity, and well repays the man for all the labour which the youth endured to attain it. Cultivate, too, the powers of memory: that is, on principle store it with ideas of value; on principle refuse to glut it with error, trash, and ribaldry. What is observed worthy of notice should be well imprinted, and frequently recollected. The habit will grow; and every fresh attainment in knowledge, whether by reading or by observation, will give occasion to the intelligent to correct former misapprehensions; to recollect what of a similar nature was known before; perhaps by the comparison of these together, to elicit some new idea.

Nor neglect what may delight and rectify. Prompt, and yet restrain, the excursive, wild, or if rightly governed, almost creative powers of the imagination. On principle resist those day-dreams in which the young are delighted to indulge: dreams of honour, wealth, and happiness, which never can be realized; the relish of which, however, sometimes renders insipid the best enjoyments of actual life. The appetite for novels, if indulged, leads much to this deception, and is one of its principal evils. Yet do not refuse the polish, the refinement, given to the taste and feelings by the best poetry, and those works of literature in which the human mind ranges beyond plain matter of fact. Not to have the imagination a little warmed and elevated, is to run the danger of being a mere plodder.

From *The Black Dwarf* (1819)[16]

[In contrast with the moderate voices of Williams and Taylor above, and the reformist Brougham below, Thomas Wooler's *The Black Dwarf* sees popular education as inevitably leading to radical social change. Running from 1817 to 1824, *The Black Dwarf* was one of several important radical periodicals of the time; as Kevin Gilmartin notes, it was 'filled with the rhetoric of improvement,' which it used to powerfully 'oppositional' ends.[17] Wooler, like the CPS member and radical publisher William Hone, was a victim of repressive legislation against the press; in 1817 he was prosecuted twice for seditious libel. He won one trial and successfully appealed against the guilty verdict in the other, but was tried again in 1819 on political grounds, and was this

---

16   *The Black Dwarf*, vol. 3, no. 22 (2 June 1819), p. 343.
17   Kevin Gilmartin, *Print Politics: The Press and Radical Opposition in Early Nineteenth-Century England* (Cambridge: Cambridge University Press, 1996), p. 45.

time convicted and jailed.[18] The passage below, which was published during the final months of the essay-circle's existence, pictures popular education as part of a conflict with the armed forces of the state; both the rhetoric and the premises of Wooler's claims would probably have horrified Faraday and his friends, since they reflect the antagonistic model of the class politics of education and popular enlightenment which the essay-circle does its best to ignore.]

The progress of public opinion is now unimpeded. The heartless enemies of reform content themselves with holding their entrenchments, in the forlorn hope of defending the citadel of corruption from our assaults. Defeated in the field, notwithstanding the glitter of the bayonets in their centre, and embarrassed in their finances, they dare not venture to cope with us openly any longer. By all the petty artifices congenial to little and malignant minds, they still endeavour to irritate, and to injure: and in some instances they still succeed. [...] Their agents are actively on the watch for a sortie upon any supposed defenceless friend of freedom; but for open, honest warfare with us they have no further stomach. They scowl at us with the angry glare of a toothless tiger—'willing to wound, but yet afraid to strike'.[19] In the meanwhile, KNOWLEDGE, the TRUE FORCE, is rapidly embodying the energies of reason. Thousands of enquirers throng to the means and opportunity of instruction; and the thirst for information is too strong to receive any serious check. Thanks to the Sunday Schools, they have enabled thousands to read and judge for themselves, to learn that they are men, and expected by their Creator to maintain the rank in the creation, to which his benevolence has destined them. Every where political schools are springing up, in which the dogmas of no leader are taught, but where the sources of free enquiry and comparison are thrown open to all.

18 For an account of Wooler's trials, see James A. Epstein, *Radical Expression: Political Language, Ritual, and Symbol in England, 1790–1850* (Oxford: Oxford University Press, 1994), pp. 29–69.

19 Alexander Pope, 'Epistle to Arbuthnot' (1734), l. 203.

Mary Shelley, from *Frankenstein* (1818)[20]

[One of the intriguing but insoluble questions of Faraday studies is whether he ever read *Frankenstein*, which was of course published in the year the essay-circle was formed. Faraday's taste for novels is well attested, but it is very difficult to be certain about which he read, beyond a few dating mainly from his later years, during which time Faraday told a friend that he liked 'stirring' novels, 'with plenty of life, plenty of action, and very little philosophy. Why, I can do the philosophy for myself.'[21] His religious beliefs seem not to have greatly affected his choice of novels (he read and enjoyed at least one sensation novel with a highly coloured plot centring on murder— *Paul Ferroll*, written by 'V' and published in 1855), though his passionately anti-paranormal views could affect his pleasure in reading fiction, as when he objected to the fantastic elements in the final chapters of *Jane Eyre*.[22] There can be little doubt, at any rate, that Faraday would have been acquainted with the story of Shelley's novel, given its debt to Faraday's early mentor, Humphry Davy, and its high profile in popular culture more generally.[23]

Regardless of how direct Faraday's knowledge of the novel was, there are interesting comparisons to be made between ideas about self-education, class and enfranchisement in *Frankenstein* and the Mental Exercises. These two otherwise vastly different contemporary texts share a concern with the effects of outsider status on intelligent and inquiring people, as well as with what it is that distinguishes a cultivated from an uncultivated person. Most importantly, both the essay-circle and Mary Shelley explore the possibilities of constructing identity from surrounding materials—in the case of *Frankenstein*, biological materials and, in that of Faraday and his friends, cultural ones.

The extracts from the novel reprinted below contrast the formal, scientific, public education which Frankenstein receives at Ingolstadt with the informal, literary, private education which the creature picks up while he is living in the De Laceys' shed. There are, however, similarities as well as contrasts to be drawn between the educational

---

20   [Mary Shelley], *Frankenstein: Or, The Modern Prometheus*, 3 vols. (London: Lackington *et al.*, 1818).

21   Frederick Pollock, *Personal Remembrances [...]*, 2 vols. (London: Macmillan, 1887), I, p. 245.

22   Hamilton, pp. 349–50. And see brief discussion of Faraday's novel reading in Cantor, p. 113.

23   David M. Knight notes that Davy's 1802 inaugural lecture at the Royal Institution was a source for the lecture Professor Waldman gives in *Frankenstein*, and comments: 'it seems that Davy's most famous pupil was Frankenstein' (*Humphry Davy: Science and Power* (Cambridge: Cambridge University Press, 1996), p. 121). For detailed discussion of the connections between Davy's and Shelley's work, see Laura E. Crouch, 'Davy's *A Discourse, Introductory to a Course of Lectures on Chemistry*: A Possible Scientific Source for Frankenstein', *Keats-Shelley Journal*, 27 (1978), 35–44.

experiences of the two characters. Both begin as extremely naïve readers, lacking experience and so falling into credulous relationships with their reading material (in Frankenstein's case, this is grossly outdated alchemy; in the creature's, the altogether nobler content of Plutarch, Goethe and Milton): thus both have crucial lessons to learn about the proper balance of imagination and critical judgment in reading. Of the two kinds of education examined in the novel, Shelley seems to be far more interested in the autodidactic model in which deep compassion compensates for lack of materials and system. More than her attempts to engage with electrical science, perhaps, it is her thought experiment about the effect of self-education on selfhood that links Shelley's novel to the work of the essay-circle.]

From vol. I, pp. 72–81:

Partly from curiosity, and partly from idleness, I went into the lecturing room, which M. Waldman entered shortly after. This professor was very unlike his colleague. He appeared about fifty years of age, but with an aspect expressive of the greatest benevolence; a few grey hairs covered his temples, but those at the back of his head were nearly black. His person was short, but remarkably erect; and his voice the sweetest I had ever heard. He began his lecture by a recapitulation of the history of chemistry and the various improvements made by different men of learning, pronouncing with fervour the names of the most distinguished discoverers. He then took a cursory view of the present state of the science, and explained many of its elementary terms. After having made a few preparatory experiments, he concluded with a panegyric upon modern chemistry, the terms of which I shall never forget:—

"The ancient teachers of this science," said he, "promised impossibilities, and performed nothing. The modern masters promise very little; they know that metals cannot be transmuted, and that the elixir of life is a chimera. But these philosophers, whose hands seem only made to dabble in dirt, and their eyes to pour over the microscope or crucible, have indeed performed miracles. They penetrate into the recesses of nature, and shew how she works in her hiding-places. They ascend into the heavens; they have discovered how the blood circulates, and the nature of the air we breathe. They have acquired new and almost unlimited powers; they can command the thunders of heaven, mimic the earthquake, and even mock the invisible world with its own shadows."

I departed highly pleased with the professor and his lecture, and paid him a visit the same evening. His manners in private were even more mild and attractive than in public; for there was a certain dignity in his mien during his lecture, which in his own house was replaced by the greatest affability and kindness. He heard with attention my little narration concerning my studies, and smiled at the names of Cornelius Agrippa, and Paracelsus, but without the contempt that M. Krempe had exhibited. He said, that "these were men to whose indefatigable zeal modern philosophers were indebted for most of the foundations of their knowledge. They had left to us, as an easier task, to give new names, and arrange in connected classifications, the facts which they in a great degree had been the instruments of bringing to light. The labours of men of genius, however erroneously directed, scarcely ever fail in ultimately turning to the solid advantage of mankind." I listened to his statement, which was delivered without any presumption or affectation; and then added, that his lecture had removed my prejudices against modern chemists; and I, at the same time, requested his advice concerning the books I ought to procure.

"I am happy," said M. Waldman, "to have gained a disciple; and if your application equals your ability, I have no doubt of your success. Chemistry is that branch of natural philosophy in which the greatest improvements have been and may be made; it is on that account that I have made it my peculiar study; but at the same time, I have not neglected the other branches of science. A man would make but a very sorry chemist, if he attended to that department of human knowledge alone. If your wish is to become really a man of science, and not merely a petty experimentalist, I should advise you to apply to every branch of natural philosophy, including mathematics."

He then took me into his laboratory, and explained to me the uses of his various machines; instructing me as to who I ought to procure, and promising me the use of his own, when I should have advanced far enough in the science not to derange their mechanism. He also gave me the list of books which I had requested; and I took my leave.

Thus ended a day memorable to me; it decided my future destiny.

Chapter III

From this day natural philosophy, and particularly chemistry, in the most comprehensive sense of the term, became nearly my sole occupation. I read with ardour those works, so full of genius and discrimination, which modern inquirers have written on these subjects. I attended the lectures, and cultivated the acquaintance, of the men of science of the university,; and I found even in M. Krempe a great deal of sound sense and real information, combined, it is true, with a repulsive physiognomy and manners, but not on that account the less valuable. In M. Waldman I found a true friend. His gentleness was never tinged by dogmatism; and his instructions were given with an air of frankness and good nature, that banished every idea of pedantry. It was, perhaps, the amiable character of this man that inclined me more to that branch of natural philosophy which he professed, than an intrinsic love for the science itself. But this state of mind had place only in the first steps towards knowledge: the more fully I entered into the science, the more exclusively I pursued it for its own sake. That application, which at first had been a matter of duty and resolution, now became so ardent and eager, that the stars often disappeared in the light of morning whilst I was yet engaged in my laboratory.

As I applied so closely, it may be easily conceived that my progress was rapid. My ardour was indeed the astonishment of the students; and my proficiency, that of the masters. Professor Krempe often asked me, with a sly smile, how Cornelius Agrippa went on? whilst M. Waldman expressed the most heartfelt exultation in my progress. Two years passed in this manner, during which I paid no visit to Geneva, but was engaged, heart and soul, in the pursuit of some discoveries, which I hoped to make. None but those who have experienced them can conceive of the enticements of science. In other studies you go as far as others have gone before you, and there is nothing more to know; but in a scientific pursuit there is continual food for discovery and wonder. A mind of moderate capacity, which closely pursues one study, must infallibly arrive at great proficiency in that study; and I, who continually sought the attainment of one object of pursuit, and was solely wrapt up in this, improved so rapidly, that, at the end of two years, I made some discoveries in the improvement of some chemical instruments, which procured me great esteem and admiration at the university. When I had arrived at this point, and had become as well acquainted with the theory and practice of natural philosophy as depended on the lessons of any of the professors at Ingolstadt, my residence there being no longer conducive to my improvements, I thought of returning to my friends and my native town, when an incident happened that protracted my stay.

From vol. II, ch. 4, pp. 58–59, 62–63, 67:

"By degrees I made a discovery of still greater moment. I found that these people possessed a method of communicating their experience and feelings to one another by articulate sounds. I perceived that the words they spoke sometimes produced pleasure or pain, smiles or sadness, in the minds and countenances of the hearers. This was indeed a godlike science, and I ardently desired to become acquainted with it. But I was baffled in every attempt I made for this purpose. Their pronunciation was quick; and the words they uttered, not having any apparent connection with visible objects, I was unable to discover any clue by which I could unravel the mystery of their reference. By great application, however, and after having remained during the space of several revolutions of the moon in my hovel, I discovered the names that were given to some of the most familiar objects of discourse: I learned and applied the words *fire*, *milk*, *bread*, and *wood*. I learned also the names of the cottagers themselves. The youth and his companion had each of them several names, but the old man had only one, which was *father*. The girl was called *sister*, or *Agatha*; and the youth *Felix*, *brother*, or *son*. I cannot describe the delight I felt when I learned the ideas appropriated to each of these sounds, and was able to pronounce them. I distinguished several other words, without being able as yet to understand or apply them; such as *good*, *dearest*, *unhappy*.

"I spent the winter in this manner.

[...]

"This reading had puzzled me extremely at first; but, by degrees, I discovered that he uttered many of the same sounds when he read as when he talked. I conjectured, therefore, that he found on the paper signs for speech which he understood, and I ardently longed to comprehend these also; but how was that possible, when I did not even understand the sounds for which they stood as signs? I improved, however, sensibly in this science, but not sufficiently to follow up any kind of conversation, although I applied my whole mind to the endeavour: for I easily perceived that, although I eagerly longed to discover myself to the cottagers, I ought not to make the attempt until I had first become master of their language; which knowledge might enable me to make them overlook the deformity of my figure; for with this also the contrast perpetually presented to my eyes had made me acquainted.

[...]

"These thoughts exhilarated me, and led me to apply with fresh ardour to the acquiring the art of language. My organs were indeed harsh, but supple; and although my voice was very unlike the soft music of their tones, yet I pronounced such words as I understood with tolerable ease. It was as the ass and the lap-dog; yet surely the gentle ass, whose intentions were affectionate, although his manners were rude, deserved better treatment than blows and execration.

From vol. II, ch. 7, pp. 99–104:

"One night, during my accustomed visit to the neighbouring wood, where I collected my own food, and brought home firing for my protectors, I found on the ground a leathern portmanteau, containing several articles of dress and some books. I eagerly seized the prize, and returned with it to my hovel. Fortunately the books were written in the language the elements of which I had acquired at the cottage; they, consisted of *Paradise Lost*, a volume of *Plutarch's Lives*, and the *Sorrows of Werter*. The possession of these treasures gave me extreme delight; I now continually studied and exercised my mind upon these histories, whilst my friends were employed in their ordinary occupations.

"I can hardly describe to you the effect of these books. They produced in me an infinity of new images and feelings, that sometimes raised me to ecstasy, but more frequently sunk me into the lowest dejection. In the *Sorrows of Werter*, besides the interest of its simple and affecting story, so many opinions are canvassed, and so many lights thrown upon what had hitherto been to me obscure subjects, that I found in it a never-ending source of speculation and astonishment. The gentle and domestic manners it described, combined with lofty sentiments and feelings, which had for their object something out of self, accorded well with my experience among my protectors, and with the wants which were forever alive in my own bosom. But I thought Werter himself a more divine being than I had ever beheld or imagined; his character contained no pretension, but it sunk deep. The disquisitions upon death and suicide were calculated to fill me with wonder. I did not pretend to enter into the merits of the case, yet I inclined towards the opinions of the hero, whose extinction I wept, without precisely understanding it.

"As I read, however, I applied much personally to my own feelings and condition. I found myself similar, yet at the same time strangely unlike to the beings concerning whom I read and to whose conversation I was a listener. I sympathized with, and partly understood them, but I was unformed in mind; I was dependent on none and related to none. 'The path of my departure was free;' and there was none to lament my annihilation. My person was hideous, and my stature gigantic: what did this mean? Who was I? What was I? Whence did I come? What was my destination? These questions continually recurred, but I was unable to solve them.

"The volume of *Plutarch's Lives* which I possessed, contained the histories of the first founders of the ancient republics. This book had a far different effect upon me from the *Sorrows of Werter*. I learned from Werter's imaginations despondency and gloom: but Plutarch taught me high thoughts; he elevated me above the wretched sphere of my own reflections, to admire and love the heroes of past ages. Many things I read surpassed my understanding and experience. I had a very confused knowledge of kingdoms, wide extents of country, mighty rivers, and boundless seas. But I was perfectly unacquainted with towns, and large assemblages of men. The cottage of my protectors had been the only school in which I had studied human nature; but this book developed new and mightier scenes of action. I read of men concerned in public affairs governing or massacring their species. I felt the greatest ardour for virtue rise within me, and abhorrence for vice, as far as I understood the signification of those terms, relative as they were, as I applied them, to pleasure and pain alone. Induced by these feelings, I was of course led to admire peaceable law-givers, Numa, Solon, and Lycurgus, in preference to Romulus and Theseus. The patriarchal lives of my protectors caused these impressions to take a firm hold on my mind; perhaps, if my first introduction to humanity had been made by a young soldier, burning for glory and slaughter, I should have been imbued with different sensations.

"But *Paradise Lost* excited different and far deeper emotions. I read it, as I had read the other volumes which had fallen into my hands, as a true history. It moved every feeling of wonder and awe, that the picture of an omnipotent God warring with his creatures was capable of exciting. I often referred the several situations, as their similarity struck me, to my own.

Henry Brougham, from *Practical Observations upon the Education of the People* (1825)²⁴

[Henry Brougham's pamphlet *Practical Observations upon the Education of the People* was not the first, but was certainly one of the most influential, of his salvos in support of popular education. Brougham's work in this field can be broadly divided into two arenas: as a Whig MP with considerable national popularity following his successful defence of Queen Caroline in the House of Lords, Brougham used some of his political capital to persuade the government to investigate charity schooling in England and Wales, though he did not succeed in his larger aim of instituting state education in the 1820s and 1830s. And outside Parliament, Brougham was a powerful and effective activist for both children's and adults' education; perhaps his most important contributions to artisan education were his leading role in the establishment of Mechanics' Institutes in many industrial and manufacturing towns, and his work in founding and running the Society for the Diffusion of Useful Knowledge from 1826, together with its associated publishing ventures for popular readers.

Practical Observations was published in 1825 (parts of it having appeared in the *Edinburgh Review* the previous year) and went into over 20 editions within two years. It aroused serious and sustained controversy, most of all for its possible effects on harmonious class relations. One critic described it as 'one tissue of theoretical absurdities' and proposed that the title should really be 'Chimerical Notions upon the Education of the People, calculated to overturn the Government, for the good Order of Society and the Peace of the Country!!!'²⁵ Among more credible responses, a hostile review in *Blackwood's* attacked Brougham's proposals for focusing on comparatively privileged mechanics rather than on the much needier labouring classes, for ignoring moral education and concentrating on scientific and political learning, and for tending to promote industrial and civic discord.²⁶ The *Edinburgh Review*, on the other hand, and not surprisingly given Brougham's very close connection with it, praised both Brougham and his scheme lavishly: 'since the time when the Scriptures were first printed and circulated in the common tongue, there has been no such benefit conferred on the great body of the people, as seems now to be held out to them in the institutions which it is the business of this little work to recommend and explain.'²⁷

---

24 Henry Brougham, *Practical Observations upon the Education of the People, Addressed to the Working Classes and their Employers*, thirteenth edn (London: Longman *et al.*, 1825).

25 'A Country Gentleman', *The Consequences of a Scientific Education to the Working Classes of this Country Pointed Out; and the Theories of Mr Brougham on that Subject Confuted* (London: Cadell, 1826), p. 19, p. 46.

26 [David Robinson], 'Brougham on the Education of the People', *Blackwood's Edinburgh Magazine*, 17 (May 1825), 534–51.

27 [Francis Jeffrey], 'Education of the People', *Edinburgh Review*, 41 (January 1825), 508–10 (508).

The pamphlet postdates the essay-circle by six years: but even if the network it proposes of institutions and industrial practices designed to support artisan education had existed in the 1810s, it is not certain that Faraday and his friends would have benefitted directly from it. They seem to have thought of themselves rather as Thomas Williams addressed them in his lecture to the CPS—i.e. as fortunate enough to be able to educate themselves and to acquire appropriate polish independently, without help or direction from organizations designed to guide the education of the less fortunate. Faraday, for one, was an active and sometimes critical member of the CPS, but while this afforded him opportunities (for instance, to practice lecturing), the CPS did not see its role as guiding the direction of its members' reading or thinking. The essay-circle members would certainly not have envisaged their self-improvement activities as having much in common with Brougham's vision of workmen establishing reading clubs in their shops, for example. Nonetheless, the basic structures of Brougham's proposed mechanisms for working-class education were comparable to those which Faraday and his friends adopted. Both emphasized the self-determination of the self-educator (though Brougham, who had in mind a less comfortable segment of society, saw help from the upper classes as essential); both put a high value on small-scale collective organizations such as conversation societies and lecture groups; and in Franklin and Bacon both shared emblems of the value of education to practical men.]

[I]t is no doubt manifest, that the people themselves must be the great agents in accomplishing the work of their own instruction. Unless they deeply feel the usefulness of knowledge, and resolve to make some sacrifices for the acquisition of it, there can be no reasonable prospect of this grand object being attained. But it is equally clear, that to wait until the whole people with one accord take the determination to labour in this good work, would be endless. A portion of the community may be sensible of its advantages, and willing at any fair price to seek them, long before the same laudable feeling becomes universal; and their successful efforts to better their intellectual condition cannot fail to spread more widely the love of learning, and the disrelish for sensual and vulgar gratifications.

But although the people must be the source and the instruments of their own improvement, they may be essentially aided in their efforts to instruct themselves. Impediments which might be sufficient to retard or wholly to obstruct their progress, may be removed; and efforts which, unassisted, might prove fruitless, arising perhaps from a transient, or only a partial enthusiasm for the attainment of knowledge, may, through judicious encouragement, become effectual, and settle into a lasting and an universal habit. A little attention to the difficulties that principally beset the working classes in their search after information, will lead us to the knowledge both of the direction in which their more affluent neighbours can lend them most valuable assistance, and of the part which must be borne by themselves.

Their difficulties may all be classed under one or other of two heads—want of money, and want of time.

[...]

The day, indeed, seems now to break, when we may hope to see no marked line of separation between the two classes [i.e. workmen and scientific investigators]. I trust another distinction will also soon be known no more. The circulation of cheap works of a merely amusing kind, as well as those connected with the arts, is at present very great in England; those of an aspect somewhat more forbidding, though at once moral, interesting, and most useful, is very limited; while in Scotland there is a considerable demand for them. Habits of reading longer formed in that country, have taught the inhabitants, that nothing in reality can be more attractive than the profound wisdom of every day's application, sustained by unbounded learning, and embellished with the most brilliant fancy, which so richly furnishes every page of the Essays of Bacon.

[...]

I can hardly imagine, for example, a greater service being rendered to the [working] men, than expounding to them the true principles and mutual relations of population and wages; and both they and their masters will assuredly experience the effects of the prevailing ignorance upon such questions, as soon as any interruption shall happen in the commercial prosperity of the country, if indeed the present course of things, daily tending to lower wages as well as profits, and set the two classes in opposition to each other, shall not of itself bring on a crisis. To allow, or rather to induce the people to take part in those discussions, is therefore not merely safe, but most wholesome for the community, and yet some points connected with them are matter of pretty warm contention in the present times; [...]. Why then may not every topic of politics, party as well as general, be treated of in cheap publications? [...] The peace of the country, and the stability of the government, could not be more effectually secured than by the universal diffusion of this kind of knowledge.

[...]

[S]ocieties for the express purpose of promoting conversation are a most useful adjunct to any private or other education received by the working classes. Those who do not work together in numbers, or whose occupation is of a noisy kind, may thus, one or two evenings in the week, meet and obtain all the advantages of mutual instruction and discussion. An association of this kind will naturally combine with its plan the advantages of a book club. The members will most probably be such as are engaged in similar pursuits, and whose train of reading and thinking may be nearly the same. The only considerable evils which they will have to avoid, are, being too numerous, and falling too much into debate. From twenty to thirty seems a convenient number; and nearer the former than the latter. The tone ought to be given from the beginning, in ridicule of speech-making, both as to length and wordiness. A subject of discussion may be given out at one meeting for the next; or the chairman may read a portion of some work, allowing each member to stop him at any moment, for the purpose of controverting, supporting, or illustrating by his remarks the passage just read. To societies of this kind master workmen have the power of affording great facilities.

[...]

But if extending the bounds of science itself be the grand aim of all philosophers in all ages, they indirectly, but surely, accomplish this object, who enable thousands to speculate and experiment for one to whom the path of investigation is now open. It is not necessary that all who are taught, or even any large proportion, should go beyond the rudiments; but whoever feels within himself a desire and an aptitude to proceed further, will press forward; and the chances of discovery, both in the arts and in science itself, will be thus indefinitely multiplied. Indeed, those discoveries immediately connected with experiment and observation, are most likely to be made by men, whose lives being spent in the midst of mechanical operations, are at the same time instructed in the general principles upon which these depend, and trained betimes to habits of speculation. He who shall prepare a treatise simply and concisely unfolding the doctrines of Algebra, Geometry, and Mechanics, and adding examples calculated to strike the imagination, of their connexion with other branches of knowledge, and with the arts of common life, may fairly claim a large share in that rich harvest of discovery and invention which must be reaped by the thousands of ingenious and active men, thus enabled to bend their faculties towards objects at once useful and sublime.

[...]

I rejoice to think that it is not necessary to close these observations by combating objections to the diffusion of science among the working classes, arising from considerations of a political nature. Happily the time is past and gone when bigots could persuade mankind that the lights of philosophy were to be extinguished as dangerous to religion; and when tyrants could proscribe the instructors of the people as enemies to their own power. It is preposterous to imagine that the enlargement of our acquaintance with the laws which regulate the universe, can dispose to unbelief. It may be a cure for superstition—for intolerance it will be the most certain cure; but a pure and true religion has nothing to fear from the greatest expansion which the understanding can receive by the study either of matter or of mind. The more widely science is diffused, the better will the Author of all things be known, and the less will the people be 'tossed to and fro by the sleight of men, and cunning craftiness, whereby they lie in wait to deceive.'[28] To tyrants, indeed, and bad rulers, the progress of knowledge among the mass of mankind is a just object of terror: it is fatal to them and their designs; they know this by unerring instinct, and unceasingly they dread the light. But they will find it more easy to curse than to extinguish. It is spreading in spite of them, even in those countries where arbitrary power deems itself most secure; and in England, any attempt to check its progress would only bring about the sudden destruction of him who should be insane enough to make it.

To the Upper Classes of society, then, I would say, that the question is no longer whether or not the people shall be instructed—for that has been determined long ago, and the decision is irreversible—but whether they shall be well or ill taught—half informed or as thoroughly as their circumstances permit and their wants require. Let no one be afraid of the bulk of the community becoming too accomplished for their superiors. Well educated, and even well versed in the most elevated sciences, they assuredly may become; and the worst consequence that can follow to their superiors will be, that to deserve being called their *betters*, they too must devote themselves more to the pursuit of solid and refined learning; the present public seminaries must be enlarged; and some of the greater cities of the kingdom, especially the metropolis, must not be left destitute of the regular means within themselves of scientific education.

To the Working Classes I would say, that this is the time when by a great effort they may secure for ever the inestimable blessing of knowledge. Never was the disposition more universal among the rich to lend the requisite assistance for setting in motion the great engines of

---

28 Ephesians 4.14.

instruction; but the people must come forward to profit by the opportunity thus afforded, and they must themselves continue the movement once begun. Those who have already started in the pursuit of science, and tasted its sweets, require no exhortation to persevere; but if these pages should fall into the hands of any one at an hour for the first time stolen from his needful rest after his day's work is done, I ask of him to reward me (who have written them for his benefit at the like hours) by saving threepence during the next fortnight, buying with it Franklin's Life, and reading the first page. I am quite sure he will read the rest; I am almost quite sure he will resolve to spend his spare time and money, in gaining those kinds of knowledge which from a printer's boy made that great man the first philosopher, and one of the first statesmen of his age. Few are fitted by nature to go as far as he did, and it is not necessary to lead so perfectly abstemious a life, and to be so rigidly saving of every instant of time. But all may go a good way after him, both in temperance, industry and knowledge, and no one can tell before he tries how near he may be able to approach him.

The Pleasures of the Imagination

Joseph Addison, from *The Spectator* (1712)[1]

[Addison's importance to Faraday is not reflected in the number of times he is cited in the Mental Exercises. As Table 3 in the Introduction indicates, Addison and *The Spectator* rank far below Johnson and *The Rambler* in numbers of direct references in the contributions. However, Addison's influence on one essay in particular—Faraday's 'On the Pleasures and Uses of the Imagination'—is profound. Faraday's unfinished index to *The Spectator* in CPB does not include no. 411; nevertheless, a comparison of its arguments shows unmistakeably the debt that Faraday's essay owed to this paper, as I outline in the footnotes to that essay.]

> Avia Pieridum peragro loca, nullius ante
> Trita solo; juvat integros accedere fontes;
> *Atque haurire:*—
> LUCR. I, 925.

> In wild unclear'd, to muses a retreat,
> O'er ground untrod before I devious roam;
> And, deep-enamour'd, into latent springs
> Presume to peep at coy virgin Naiads.

Our sight is the most perfect and most delightful of all our senses. It fills the mind with the largest variety of ideas, converses with its objects at the greatest distance, and continues the longest in action without being tired or satiated with its proper enjoyments. The sense of feeling can indeed give us a notion of extension, shape, and all other ideas that enter at the eye, except colours; but at the same time it is very much straitened and confined in its operations to the number, bulk, and distance of its

---

1   Joseph Addison, *The Spectator*, no. 411, first paper on 'The Pleasures of the Imagination' (21 June 1712), from *The Papers of Joseph Addison, Esq. [...]*, 4 vols. (Edinburgh, 1790), III, pp. 242–45.

particular objects. Our sight seems designed to supply all these defects, and may be considered as a more delicate and diffusive kind of touch, that spreads itself over an infinite multitude of bodies, comprehends the largest figures, and brings into our reach some of the most remote parts of the universe.

It is this sense which furnishes the imagination with its ideas; so that by the pleasures of the imagination, or fancy (which I shall use promiscuously) I here mean such as arise from visible objects, either when we have them actually in our view, or when we call up their ideas into our minds by paintings, statues, descriptions, or any the like occasion. We cannot indeed have a single image in the fancy that did not make its first entrance through the sight; but we have the power of retaining, altering and compounding those images which we have once received into all the varieties of picture and vision that are most agreeable to the imagination: for by this faculty a man in a dungeon is capable of entertaining himself with scenes and landscapes more beautiful than any that can be found in the whole compass of nature.

There are few words in the English language which are employed in a more loose and uncircumscribed sense than those of the *fancy* and the *imagination*. I therefore thought it necessary to fix and determine the notion of these two words, as I intend to make use of them in the thread of my following speculations, that the reader may conceive rightly what is the subject which I proceed upon. I must therefore desire him to remember, that by the pleasures of the imagination I mean only such pleasures as arise originally from sight, and that I divide these pleasures into two kinds: my design being first of all to discourse of those primary pleasures of the imagination which entirely proceed from such objects as are before our eyes; and in the next place, to speak of those secondary pleasures of the imagination which flow from the ideas of visible objects, when the objects are not actually before the eye, but are called up into our memories, or formed into agreeable visions of things that are either absent or fictitious.

The pleasures of the imagination, taken in their full extent, are not so gross as those of sense, nor so refined as those of the understanding. The last are indeed more preferable, because they are founded on some new knowledge or improvement in the mind of man; yet it must be confessed, that those of the imagination are as great and as transporting as the other. A beautiful prospect delights the soul as much as a demonstration; and a description in Homer has charmed more readers than a chapter in

Aristotle. Besides, the pleasures of the imagination have this advantage above those of the understanding, that they are more obvious and more easy to be acquired. It is but opening the eye and the scene enters. The colours paint themselves on the fancy, with very little attention of thought or application of mind in the beholder. We are struck, we know not how, with the symmetry of anything we see, and immediately assent to the beauty of an object, without inquiring into the particular causes and occasions of it.

A man of polite imagination is let into a great many pleasures that the vulgar are not capable of receiving. He can converse with a picture, and find an agreeable companion in a statue. He meets with a secret refreshment in a description, and often feels a greater satisfaction in the prospect of fields and meadows than another does in the possession. It gives him indeed a kind of property in everything he sees, and makes the most rude uncultivated parts of nature administer to his pleasures; so that he looks upon the world, as it were, in another light, and discovers in it a multitude of charms that conceal themselves from the generality of mankind.

There are indeed but very few who know how to be idle and innocent, or have a relish of any pleasures that are not criminal; every diversion they take is at the expense of some one virtue or another, and their very first step out of business is into vice or folly. A man should endeavour, therefore, to make the sphere of his innocent pleasures as wide as possible, that he may retire into them with safety, and find in them such a satisfaction as a wise man would not blush to take. Of this nature are those of the imagination, which do not require such a bent of thought as is necessary to our more serious employments, nor, at the same time, suffer the mind to sink into that negligence and remissness, which are apt to accompany our more sensual delights; but, like a gentle exercise to the faculties, awaken them from sloth and idleness, without putting them upon any labour or difficulty.

We might here add, that the pleasures of the fancy are more conducive to health than those of the understanding, which are worked out by dint of thinking, and attended with too violent a labour of the brain. Delightful scenes, whether in nature, painting, or poetry, have a kindly influence on the body as well as the mind, and not only serve to clear and brighten the imagination, but are able to disperse grief and melancholy, and to set the animal spirits in pleasing and agreeable motions. For this reason Sir *Francis Bacon*, in his Essay upon Health, has not thought it improper to prescribe to his reader a poem or a prospect, where he particularly dissuades him from knotty and subtle disquisitions, and advises him to pursue studies that fill the mind with splendid and illustrious objects, as histories, fables, and contemplations of nature.

I have in this paper, by way of introduction, settled the notions of those pleasures of the imagination which are the subject of my present undertaking, and endeavoured by several considerations to recommend to my reader the pursuit of those pleasures. I shall in my next Paper examine the several sources from whence these pleasures are derived.

Mark Akenside, from *The Pleasures of the Imagination* (1744)[2]

[Mark Akenside's considerable popularity in the late eighteenth and early nineteenth centuries has not been matched by centrality in the critical canon in the twentieth, though Robin Dix's recent scholarly editions and critical work have done a great deal to restore his standing among eighteenth-century poets.[3] Akenside's work was included in several of the standard collections of British poets in the first decades of the 1800s, as well as appearing in free-standing editions with biographies of the author by Samuel Johnson and Alexander Dyce. St Clair points out that in 1817 Akenside could still be held up by no less a critic than Hazlitt as a benchmark against which Wordsworth appeared only a 'little inferior.'[4] Faraday was thus very much of his era in admiring Akenside's poetry. He copied 10 lines from his Ode VI, 'Hymn to Cheerfulness' into CPB:[5]

> "Thou *cheerfulness* by Heaven design'd
> To rule the pulse that moves the mind,
> Whatever fretful passion springs,
> Whatever chance or nature brings
> To strain the tuneful poise within,
> And disarrange the sweet machine;

---

2   Mark Akenside, from *The Pleasures of the Imagination*, Book IV, in *The Works of the British Poets*, ed. Thomas Park, 42 vols. (London, 1805–08), XXV, pp. 165–171 (pp. 169–71).

3   See especially Robin Dix (ed.), *The Poetical Works of Mark Akenside* (Madison: Fairleigh Dickinson University Press, 1996) and *Mark Akenside: A Reassessment* (Madison: Fairleigh Dickinson University Press, 2000); and Dix, *The Literary Career of Mark Akenside: Including an Edition of his Non-Medical Prose* (Madison: Fairleigh Dickinson University Press, 2006).

4   St Clair, p. 285.

5   CPB, I, p. 160.

Thou, Goddess, with a master hand
Dost each attemper'd key command,
Refine the soft and swell the strong,
Till all is concord, all is song."[6]

The extract below is from Akenside's most important poem, written when he was in his very early 20s, *The Pleasures of Imagination* (later very substantially revised and published as *The Pleasures of the Imagination*). The poem appeared in 1744 on the recommendation of Samuel Johnson. The 1794 and later editions were accompanied by a preface by Anna Barbauld, who explained that the 'ground-work' of the poem was laid in Addison's *Spectator* essays collected under the same title.[7] She stressed that the likely audience for Akenside's poem was educated, inquiring and intellectual: 'those who have studied the metaphysics of mind, and who are accustomed to investigate abstract ideas, will read [the poem] with a lively pleasure.'[8] The extract comes from the fragmentary fourth book and describes the forms which creativity takes in response to beauty, dwelling especially—and in Miltonic language—on the power of the poet, whose capacity for creation Akenside extols as all but divine. The passage builds on Addison's assertion that 'a man of polite imagination is let into a great many pleasures that the vulgar are not capable of receiving' and as such may have had particular resonance for readers conscious of their own efforts towards self-improvement and cultural citizenship. Faraday's essay on 'The Pleasures and Uses of the Imagination', like this passage from Akenside, gives the poet priority among imaginative artists, but instead of focusing on the maker of art, Faraday identifies most closely with the observer: instead of shaping new and better worlds (as in Akenside), the imagination for Faraday 'wanders in the infinite divisibility of matter, or in the immensity of space' (above, p. 65).

Samuel Smiles' *Self-Help* (1859) discussed Faraday and Akenside in the same paragraph as examples of men who became successful despite humble backgrounds; following Smiles, the same connection was pointed out by numerous Victorian and Edwardian writers on self-improvement.[9] Smiles did not, however, draw the further connection that both were men of science (Akenside was a physician and Fellow of the Royal Society). Akenside's description of the cultured and creative man's capacity to understand, not merely experience, natural beauties, to 'scan the secret laws / Which bind them to each other' might well have appealed to Faraday as a scientist.]

---

6   Faraday has characteristically omitted much of the punctuation, and altered the comma ending the final line quoted here to a full stop. Compare, for example, with the text in *The Poetical Works of Mark Akenside*, I, p. 22.

7   Mark Akenside, *The Pleasures of Imagination [...]* (London: Cadell and Davies, 1794), p. 7.

8   Ibid., p. 6.

9   Samuel Smiles, *Self-Help; with Illustrations of Character, Conduct, and Perseverance*, ed. Peter W. Sinnema (Oxford: Oxford World's Classics, 2002), pp. 23–24.

Yet indistinct,
In vulgar bosoms, and unnotic'd lie
These pleasing stores, unless the casual force
Of things external prompt the heedless mind
To recognize her wealth. But some there are
Conscious of Nature, and the rule which man
O'er nature holds: some who, within themselves
Retiring from the trivial scenes of chance
And momentary passion, can at will
Call up these fair exemplars of the mind;
Review their features; scan the secret laws
Which bind them to each other: and display
By forms, or sounds, or colours, to the sense
Of all the world their latent charms display:
Even as in Nature's frame (if such a word,
If such a word, so bold, may from the lips
Of man proceed) as in this outward frame
Of things, the great Artificer portrays
His own immense idea. Various names
These among mortals bear, as various signs
They use, and by peculiar organs speak
To human sense. There are who by the flight
Of air through tubes with moving stops distinct,
Or by extended chords in measure taught
To vibrate, can assemble powerful sounds
Expressing every temper of the mind
From every cause, and charming all the soul
With passion void of care. Others meantime
The rugged mass of metal, wood, or stone,
Patiently taming; or with easier hand
Describing lines, and with more ample scope
Uniting colours, can to general sight
Produce those permanent and perfect forms,
Those characters of heroes and of gods,
Which from the crude materials of the world
Their own high minds created. But the chief
Are poets; eloquent men, who dwell on earth
To clothe whate'er the soul admires or loves
With language and with numbers. Hence to these

A field is open'd wide as Nature's sphere;
Nay, wider: various as the sudden acts
Of human wit, and vast as the demands
Of human will. The bard nor length, nor depth,
Nor place, nor form controuls. To eyes, to ears,
To every organ of the copious mind,
He offereth all its treasures. Him the hours,
The seasons him obey: and changeful time
Sees him at will keep measure with his flight,
At will outstrip it. To enhance his toil,
He summoneth from the uttermost extent
Of things which GOD hath taught him every form
Auxiliar, every power; and all beside
Excludes imperious. His prevailing hand
Gives, to corporeal essence, life and sense
And every stately function of the soul.
The soul itself to him obsequious lies,
Like matter's passive heap; and as he wills,
To reason and affection he assigns
Their just alliances, their just degrees:
Whence his peculiar honours: whence the race
Of men who people his delightful world,
Men genuine and according to themselves,
Transcend as far th'uncertain sons of earth,
As earth itself to his delightful world
The palm of spotless beauty doth resign.

Index